TRURO

TRURO

The Story of a Cape Cod Town

Richard F. Whalen

Library of Congress Number: 2002091039
ISBN :   Hardcover   1-4010-5146-4
                Softcover   1-4010-5145-6

This book was printed in the United States of America.

The author gratefully acknowledges permission to reprint previously copyrighted material.

Chapter 2, "Before the Pilgrims: European Adventurers," and the introduction to Appendix A are based on the author's article, "Where Did Martin Pring Anchor in New England"in the summer 1998 issue of *The Historical Journal of Massachusetts.*

Every effort has been made to trace the owners of copyrighted materials in this book, but in some instances this has proven impossible. The author and publisher will be glad to receive information leading to more complete acknowledgments in subsequent printings of this book and meanwhile extend their apologies for any omissions.

          Library of Congress Cataloguing-in-Publication Data
     Whalen, Richard F.
          Truro: The Story of a Cape Cod Town
          Includes Annotated Bibliography
          Includes index
          1. Truro (Mass.)–History. I. Title.

14803
To order additional copies of this book, contact:
Xlibris Corporation
1-888-795-4274
www.Xlibris.com
Orders@Xlibris.com

CONTENTS

ILLUSTRATIONS

INTRODUCTION:
A SKETCH OF
HISTORIC TRURO TODAY

It's the smallest and most pristine town on Cape Cod and not what off-Cape people think of when they think of Cape Cod. Mostly undeveloped, mostly non-commercial, it has no Main Street, no stop lights, no sidewalks, no supermarket, no fast food restaurant, no cinema, no doctor's office, no drugstore, no mail delivery. Many of its roads are unpaved sand tracks, and most of its intersections have no stop signs. More than two-thirds of town is in the Cape Cod National Seashore. Not many people have ever heard of Truro. It's not famous, like Hyannis, but that's all right with townsfolk who would like to see it continue as a seaside community that is more rural than suburban. At the same time, this tiny town can look back on a remarkable history that rivals that of more famous towns and cities.

Truro's history has been influenced for four centuries by the saltwater that bounds it on its two long sides. Its shape is a curving triangle at Cape Cod's wrist, with the base resting on the town's boundary with Wellfleet. The Atlantic Ocean bounds it on the east. On the west is Cape Cod Bay, then Provincetown Harbor to

the north and finally a short boundary line with Provincetown
across sand dunes to the triangle's apex at the Atlantic. From north
to south is about eleven miles. At its widest point, the Wellfleet
boundary, it is only three miles across; and near the north end of
the triangle, at East Harbor, less than half a mile from bay to
ocean.

Truro's greatest assets are long stretches of ocean and bay
beaches and scenic saltwater vistas. Its most prominent landmark
is Highland Light on the site of Cape Cod's first lighthouse. Its
most enduring controversy has been whether and how to dredge
its tidal harbor where the Pamet River meets Cape Cod Bay. Its
most recent preoccupation has been how to preserve the rural aspects of this seaside town that make it attractive and eminently
livable in the face of pressure for more residential and even some
commercial development. Waterfront and waterview properties are
prime real estate and values have soared despite the erosion of the
coast by storms and a rising sea level. Alarmed, the town's environmentalists have mobilized to promote conservation of the town's
natural resources and preserve open space to the extent possible.

The pine woods that cover most of Truro may look like a long-
standing feature of the town, but they are not. For most of its
history and until a half-century ago, Truro's landscape was mostly
barren and treeless, the result of centuries of farming, grazing and
lumbering. With the end of farming and grazing, pitch pine and
black pine took over. The pines are already giving way to oaks and
other hardwoods, and within a century the hardwoods will predominate, as they did when the Pilgrims arrived.

White-tail deer abound in the woods, although they are quite
shy except around gardens. Some years a pair of coyotes digs a den
in the woods, but the legendary Pamet puma has not reappeared.
Fox have their good years and bad. Raccoons, skunks, opossums
and otters are year-rounders. Wild turkeys have made a comeback
after naturalists launched a few on the Outer Cape. Freshwater
fish are stocked in a half-dozen kettle ponds in the southeast corner of town.

Truro is so narrow that it's not hard to find a spot of high ground where you can see saltwater to the east and to the west. The prospect made Henry David Thoreau feel as though he were standing on the deck of a ship at sea. Winter northeast storms pound the ocean beaches, cutting away the coastal bank and shrinking Truro's real estate. Storms from the west hit the bay beaches, which are vulnerable to the occasional hurricane. Inland, however, are tranquil woods and meadows, hollows and ponds, and the marshes of the Pamet River valley.

Seen from the air, Truro and the Outer Cape looks like a fragile sliver of a sand spit just barely projecting above the surface of the Atlantic Ocean. In fact, ocean storms have washed over coastal dunes and temporarily cut Truro in half at two low spots—at the head of the Pamet Valley, which cuts across Truro to Cape Cod Bay, and in the nineteenth century at the upper reaches of what is now Pilgrim Lake, which spans Truro at its narrowest point. Ocean waves erode both long sides of the Truro triangle, and very soon in geologic time, storms and the rising sea level will submerge the Outer Cape, and Truro will be gone forever.

· · ·

Only one highway runs the length of Truro from Wellfleet to Provincetown. Motorists arriving from the south on Route 6, the mid-Cape highway, see only pine/oak forests, with an occasional glimpse of a pond. Most of the land on each side is in the Cape Cod National Seashore. The only sign of commerce before Truro Center at the Pamet River was Jack's Gas until gasoline leaks shut down gasoline sales in 1998; the station has continued to sell firewood from big piles of imported logs. The ancient frame shack is thought to be one of the models for a famous painting by Edward Hopper entitled "Gas."

Truro Center, one of the two villages in the town, can easily be missed. It's located off to the side of the Route 6 on the Pamet River. Once in a while a motorist stops at the Truro post office and asks someone: "Where can I find the center of Truro?" The answer: "Mister (or Ma'am), you're in it." Unlike most communities, Truro has no downtown, except facetiously; no line-up of stores along a street; no streets lined with houses on quarter-acre plots..

For the nine months of the off-season, "downtown Truro" consists solely of the post office, a good place to meet neighbors and catch up on town gossip, especially late Saturday morning before it closes for the day. No stores are open. Dorothy's Gift Shop, which rented videotapes and sold newspapers and sundries, closed when the proprietors, Bert and Joan Stranger, retired in 2000. An antique shop and a restaurant are down the road one way, and up the other way are three real estate offices, a seamstress, an interior decorator, a gift shop and a nursery selling heaths and heathers.

In the summertime, Truro Center comes alive. A fisherman sells seafood and the town issues beach stickers in a building that has usually lacked for tenants. The harbinger of the summer season, however, is the re-opening of a deli-grocery store in a ramshackle building next to the post office. No country store, upscale JAMS stocks gourmet groceries, wine and exotic coffees to satisfy the craving of summer people (and some retirees) for urban delicacies. Its name has nothing to do with jam; it's the initials of the family of the owners, who have somewhat controversial plans to re-build downtown Truro for their own store, space for several others and a new post office.

The Pamet River, classified as a "scenic river," is one of only three rivers in Massachusetts given top priority for protection. The tidal river is a looping estuary flanked by saltwater marshes that extends from Pamet Harbor on Cape Cod Bay to a dike next to the post office in Truro Center. Despite periodic dredging, continual silting of the channel and the anchorages at Pamet Harbor has caused problems for centuries for townsfolk who want to make a deeper harbor for bigger boats. In the early 1800s, the harbor was a booming fishing port; today, it has a launching ramp and moorings for shallow-draft power boats, some small sailboats and a few fishing boats. North of the harbor is Corn Hill, where the Pilgrims found Indian corn caches. From the dike at Truro Center to the ocean the Pamet River is a meandering body of fresh water, almost stagnant, that reaches to within a hundred yards of the Atlantic Ocean at Ballston Beach.

Edward A. Wilson, noted Truro illustrator and painter, drew this map for the Truro chamber of commerce in mid-twentieth century. (Courtesy Perry Wilson Anthony.)

The village of North Truro is a scattering of houses at the cross-roads of Route 6A and Highland Road. Anchoring it is Dutra's Market, the only place in town to buy groceries in the off-season. Next to Dutra's are a service station and two summer-season restaurants. Yellow school buses used to be parked across the way, but they left and the lot became somewhat more rural when a landscaper bought it for his piles of sand, loam, gravel and firewood, right in the center of the village. North Truro's minuscule post office is at the south end of the hamlet. East out Highland Road stands Highland Light, a beacon for mariners since 1798. The lighthouse, recently moved back from the eroding cliff edge, and the nearby historical museum, recently expanded, attract thousands of tourists each year. Laid out around them is a nine-hole golf course, one of the oldest in the United States.

The north end of town, less than a mile across from ocean to bay, is a study in contrasts. On the ocean side are the broad, "walking sand dunes" that reminded early visitors of Sahara Desert. Pilgrim Lake separates the barren dunes from a row of motels and cottage colonies strung along Beach Point, which is no longer a point but a low, narrow strip of sand between the lake and Provincetown Harbor. On Beach Point are squeezed the four-lane Route 6, two-lane 6A, and more than two hundred motels and cottages plus some beach houses on small lots. They stand side-by-side along two and half miles of shoreline that looks more like an extension of Provincetown than part of the more bucolic Truro.

Beach Point was once truly a point. At its northwest end, an inlet connected Provincetown Harbor with what was then East Harbor, sometimes called "Eastern Harbor." After much acrimonious debate, the inlet was dammed in 1869. Motels now stand where nine-foot tides used to pour through the inlet to East Harbor. The blowing sand and silting that caused problems throughout Truro's history continue, and Pilgrim Lake will be filled with sand by mid-century.

. . .

All Truro is divided into three population groups: locals, washashores and summer people. The locals, or natives, are the first class citizens. They rightly consider Truro *their* town. Although their numbers are falling, their real estate values are rising. Only a few are from old Truro families, and the line between the locals and washashores is beginning to blur. Locals from other Outer Cape towns and washashore children who were born elsewhere but grew up in town are sometimes granted *de facto* local status, especially if they work in town.

The great majority of washashores arrived as adults, often as senior citizens. They left their careers in the big cities or launched second careers or brought their careers with them and continued working in home offices with personal computers, fax machines and the Internet. A surprisingly large number have been authors, artists, journalists and university professors. Although it's difficult to define and count those who consider themselves retired, they constitute about a quarter of the town's year-round population and their numbers are increasing. (The 1989 census showed that 34 percent of Truro households received social security payments and 22 percent retirement income–categories that overlap.) About a hundred year-rounders–five percent of the population–serve on nearly thirty boards, committees and commissions that help run the town. Most of the work is done in the nine months of the off-season when Truro is a much quieter town.

Although the town has no industry, it does have four working farms, a plant nursery and a vineyard. Rock Spray Nursery grows half a million heaths and heathers every year on three acres off Depot Road. Truro Vineyards, the only commercial vineyard on Cape Cod, produces more than fourteen thousand bottles of red, white and blush wines from European grapes grown on its four acres. A dozen stores and businesses scattered along a short stretch of Route 6 include a spice store in an old boat storage building, an automobile repair shop, self-storage buildings and a new operations center for Seamen's Bank that has the town's only automated teller machine. The biggest year-round employer by far is town government with more than a hundred people on the payroll. About half are full-time positions, notably schoolteachers, town hall employees and the police.

Truro is primarily a town of summer vacation homes. Fully two-thirds of its 2,500 houses are owned by summer people. These second homes, some of them million-dollar properties, are empty most of the year. In general, the bigger the house in Truro, the more likely it is to be unoccupied except in summer. Summer people pay their real estate taxes, take income tax deductions for second-home taxes and mortgages, and await the day they can retire to Truro. Many of today's washashores were once summer people, either as owners or renters.

In July and August, Truro's population explodes to an estimated twelve thousand–six times the off-season population. The town's half-dozen restaurants, most of them closed the rest of the year, are busy every night. The quiet hamlets of Truro Center and North Truro swarm with summer strangers. On sunny days, the beach parking lots are full, although there's plenty of room for sunbathing on the long expanses of beaches between parking lots.

For such a small town, Truro has experienced a remarkable history. Four centuries ago, English adventurers spent the summer in Truro before the Pilgrims arrived. The Pilgrims almost settled in Truro instead of Plymouth. Truro was a whaling town without the big, deep-sea ships, a thriving fishing port without a deepwater harbor, and a writers' and artists' retreat without the gaudy reputation of neighboring Provincetown. Throughout its history, Truro was vulnerable to enemy raiders, bombardments, suspected espionage agents and potential missile attacks. During the Revolutionary War, British cannonballs landed in Truro, and a handful of Truro men took more than 450 British prisoners after a shipwreck. More than a hundred ships grounded and sank off Truro, wrecks that took the lives of scores of mariners, many of them from Truro. Pilgrim Lake was East Harbor before its inlet was closed by a dike that caused a storm of controversy. Few towns its size have had to grapple so long with environmental problems–from eroding shore-lines and silting harbors to over-development. Few towns of any size have such a colorful and controversial heritage, beginning with the Pamet Indians, the first to grow crops in its fields, hunt deer in its woods, fish off its shores and harvest shellfish from its sand flats.

PART I:

Pamet Indians, European Adventurers and the Pilgrims

CHAPTER 1:
INDIAN GRAVES, SKELETONS
AND WIGWAMS

On a cold and snowy day in December 1620, a Pilgrim scouting party of sixteen men from the *Mayflower* was crossing Corn Hill in what is now Truro when they came upon a mound that looked like an Indian grave but was much bigger and was covered with boards. They had seen other Indian grave sites in Truro and had dug up caches of corn, so they were curious to see what might be in the mound. One of the Pilgrims, William Bradford, who wrote a narrative of their arrival and settlement in America, described what they found.

Under the boards was a woven mat of rushes and under that a bow but no arrows. Then came another mat and under it an assortment of bowls, trays and dishes and a board a few feet long "finely carved and painted, with three tines or branches, on the top like a crown." Under these artifacts was a new mat in good condition and under this mat they found two bundles, one larger and one smaller.

In the bundles were the bodies of an adult and a child, both covered with "a great quantity of perfect red powder." The adult's hair was yellow, not black like an Indian's, and the corpse was dressed in a sailor's canvas jacket and cloth breeches. Along with the body were a knife, a large sewing needle "and two or three old iron things." The child's body was decorated with "bracelets of fine white beads." Beside it was a small bow "and some other odd knacks."

The Pilgrims were puzzled: "Some thought it was an Indian lord and king. Others said the Indians all have black hair, and never was any seen with brown or yellow hair. Some thought it was a Christian of some special note, which had died amongst them, and they thus buried him to honor him. Others thought they [the Indians] had killed him and did it in triumph over him."

The Pilgrim's exhumation of the Indian grave in Truro was the first recorded archaeological dig in North America. Although they were amateurs, Bradford recorded their observations in considerable detail, if not with the rigor that modern-day archaeologists require. Much later, archaeologists would identify more than thirty-five prehistoric Indian sites in Truro, making the town one of the richest sources for Indian studies in New England.

The corpses were undoubtedly Indian in the view of Warner F. Gookin, who interpreted the evidence in 1950 in *The Bulletin of the Massachusetts Archaeological Society*. He showed that red ochre turned white hair yellow and suggested that the European clothing came from the ill-fated survivors of a French ship wrecked at the tip of Cape Cod a few years earlier. Indians liked to array themselves with oddments of European clothing. The boards would have come from a shipwreck. The red ochre, an earthen oxide, is familiar to archaeologists. Indians considered it a valuable pigment for the afterlife. Gookin concluded that the bodies were that of an elderly Indian with white hair turned yellow by the oxide and a grandchild who died at the same time, about two years before the Pilgrims opened their grave. The red ochre and other artifacts were common mortuary offerings found in Indian graves.

• • •

In the beginning, Truro was all Indian territory. For thousands of years, the Indians had the land to themselves. They arrived on Cape Cod about ten thousand years ago, after the Ice Age ended and the glaciers, which were up to a mile thick, began their retreat north, leaving behind the sand and gravel deposits that formed Cape Cod. About 2,500 years ago, when the land and climate were growing more hospitable, Indians on Cape Cod became more numerous. Archaeologists have found a concentration of artifacts dating to that period, when the Indians were hunters, gatherers and fishers. The earliest evidence for agriculture dates to around a thousand years ago when the Indians were planting corn, beans, squash and tobacco, according to Cape Cod archaeologist Fred Dunford in *Secrets in the Sand*.

Early explorers from Europe reported seeing many Indians on Cape Cod. The first was Bartholomew Gosnold, who may have anchored briefly in Provincetown Harbor in 1602 and who named Cape Cod. He saw only a single Indian during his one day on shore, but he stopped later in the Chatham area at the Cape's elbow and his chronicler reported, "This coast is very full of people." Martin Pring described his encounters with scores of Indians during his visit to Truro the following year; and three years later, Samuel de Champlain would see as many as six hundred Indians at Chatham.

Captain John Smith identified Indians he saw near the tip of Cape Cod as "the people of Pawmet." (He was the same John Smith who said that Pocahontas had rescued him from execution by her father, the tribal chief, near Jamestown, Virginia.) Smith was exploring and mapping the coastline from Maine to Cape Cod Bay in 1614, and the name Pawmet appears for the first time in his *Description of New England*. Pamet, in various spellings, would become the name of the first settlement, and it has survived as the name of Truro's tidal river. Smith's "people of Pawmet" were one of a half-dozen tribes of the Wampanoags in southeastern New En-

gland. Later spellings included Payomet, Paomett, Paomet and finally Pamet. The word is believed to have meant "the wading place"
or "at the shallow cove" in the Wampanoag Indian dialect–references to the tidal river that bisected the land where the Pamet
Indians were living when the Pilgrims arrived.

. . .

After digging up the grave, the Pilgrims came across two Indian dwellings, and their observations turned anthropological. The framework
of the wigwams was made "with long, young sapling trees, bended
and both ends stuck in the ground." The wigwams were rounded,
like an arbor, and high enough that the English could stand upright
inside. The Indians were accomplished weavers of mats and baskets.
The dwelling's framework was covered with thick mats of rushes and
other plants. A mat was also used for a door, which was about a three
feet high. A mat covered the hole in the roof that served as a chimney.
The inside was lined "with newer and fairer mats," and around the
perimeter were more mats for beds. Outside were "bundles of flags,
and sedge, bulrushes and other stuff to make mats."

On the inside walls, the Pilgrims saw deer feet, deer antlers
and eagle claws. They found "wooden bowls, trays and dishes,
earthen pots, handbaskets made of crabshells wrought together,
also an English pail or bucket; it wanted a bail but it had two iron
ears." Baskets were of various sizes, some finer and some more rugged. "Some were curiously wrought with black and white in pretty
works." Two or three were filled with "parched acorns, pieces of
fish and a piece of broiled herring." The Pilgrims also found "a
little silk grass, a little tobacco seed and some other seeds which
we knew not." The Pamet Indian family had left their dwelling
recently, perhaps upon sighting the Pilgrims, for the visitors also
found "two or three deer's heads, one whereof had been newly
killed, for it was still fresh."

Archaeologists consider that the Indian settlements in Truro
were semi-permanent. They have found no signs of well-estab-

lished villages lasting continuously over several generations, although families lived months at a time in Truro and perhaps several years. Their communities, scattered over an acre or two, were loose clusters of domed dwellings made of mats. The dwellings were simple, practical and portable. Family groups could dismantle their dwellings and move to a new location, perhaps several days travel distant, whenever the natural resources began to be overtaxed.

The next report of Indian artifacts was made two centuries later by Henry David Thoreau, the traveler and essayist. He roamed Truro on several visits in the 1850s and reported seeing "many traces [of Indians] . . . near Great Hollow and at High Head, near East Harbor River—oysters, clams, cockles and other shells mingled with ashes and the bones of deer and other quadrupeds. I picked up half a dozen arrowheads and in an hour or two could have filled my pockets with them."

Thirty years later, Shebnah Rich, who wrote the first book-length history of Truro, examined an extensive pile of shells near a swamp at Corn Hill: "It is, perhaps, a half-acre in extent, several feet deep, covered by a solid, rich, emerald sward nearly the whole year. The shells are great and soft clams, quahaug, scallop, oyster, razor, cockle, and fragments of deer bones. Arrowheads are often found. Oysters must have been abundant, as they predominate. The slow waste of the lime, mixing with the decomposition of bones, has produced a soil rich and hot as guano that might be, it would seem, used to advantage as a fertilizer."So plentiful were the lime-rich shells left by the Indians after their feasting that the early colonists hauled away cartloads to use in mortar for construction. In 1705, the first colonists to claim control of the land in Pamet would vote to fine anyone who took away shells without permission. They wanted to keep the shell piles for their own use. Rich also says that Tom's Hill between the Pamet River and the Little Pamet branch was a favorite abode of the Indians; the early settlers called it Indian Neck. In his day, shell piles and arrowheads were found there in abundance.

For twentieth century archaeologists, the most important sites in Truro were at High Head at the northern end of town and at Corn Hill on Cape Cod Bay. Archaeologists worked dozens of digs in a mile-square area at High Head. They found large piles of shells, one of them three feet deep; and they collected arrowheads, double-pointed spearheads, pottery shards, stone tools and artifacts of bone and antler. In the same area, some Truro boys in 1946 found a medium-size shallow bowl and what appeared to be a cup and pestle used to make paint pigments.

. . .

Corn Hill and its slopes extending into the Little Pamet Valley were also a favorite site for Indian communities and Indian burials. Archaeologists found arrowheads, tomahawks, spear points, broken pottery, bones and evidence of cooking fires on Corn Hill, particularly at the north end where it meets Great Hollow.

Seven skeletons of Indians have been unearthed in Truro, most of them in the nineteenth and twentieth centuries. The Pilgrims found the first two. In 1864, two Truro boys—William P. Rich and his cousin—found a human skeleton emerging from the surface of the cliff face above the bay beach on Corn Hill. With it, they found a stone hatchet and a small copper cup. The gradual erosion of the cliff face had exposed the Indian's grave. In 1915, an archaeologist found another grave on Corn Hill, which contained the bones of a young girl and an infant. In 1947, the skeleton of an adult Indian was removed from a shallow burial mound at High Head; and in 1952, construction excavations unearthed a skeleton at the north end of Corn Hill.

The Indian skeletons, bones and artifacts from Truro are preserved in a number of private collections and public museums. The Robert S. Peabody Museum of Archaeology at Andover, Massachusetts, has a large collection of skeletal remains, and the Truro Historical Society has scores of arrowheads. Most of the readily available artifacts have been gleaned from the site surfaces. By the end of the twentieth century, descendants of the prehistoric Indians had secured a more respectful attitude towards the remains of their ancestors, who believed strongly in the importance of undisturbed burial.

Until the 1600s, Truro's Indians had only sporadic contacts with Europeans. In the previous century, fishing and trading vessels from Europe ranged the northeast coast of America, and a few may have gone aground on the Atlantic shore of the Outer Cape. Some probably anchored in Provincetown Harbor. No records, however, provide evidence of these visits, although historians consider them to have been quite likely. The first recorded contact of Indians with Europeans in Truro occurred at the start of the 1600s, but the first Europeans were not—as is commonly believed—the Pilgrims.

CHAPTER 2:
BEFORE THE PILGRIMS:
EUROPEAN ADVENTURERS

U ntil recently, most historians have assumed that the first Europeans on record to explore the Outer Cape were the Pilgrims, who arrived in 1620. Famous in American history, the Pilgrims' arrival at Provincetown Harbor and settlement at Plymouth have overshadowed the voyage of Captain Martin Pring. Preceding the Pilgrims by seventeen years, Pring anchored at Pamet Harbor in Truro in the summer of 1603. He and his men spent almost two months in Truro. They built a small stockade and planted an experimental garden. They harvested sassafras trees, roots and all, to take back to England and market as a cure for syphilis. Bands of Indians visited their camp out of curiosity and for entertainment, occasionally staying for a meal of peas and beans. If anyone can be designated the "discoverer" of Truro, it would be Martin Pring, who arrived at Pamet Harbor in the year Queen Elizabeth I died..

The narrative of Pring's summer sojourn at Pamet Harbor has not received the attention it deserves. It is the second oldest record of the English presence in North America, the first being the accounts of Bartholomew Gosnold's voyage to Cape Cod just one year earlier. Pring's narrative, while rich with colorful description of the Indians and appearance and artifacts, is vague about where he anchored.

Historians at first put Pring's anchorage at Edgartown on Martha's Vineyard, then at Plymouth. Finally, locating Pring's anchorage at Pamet Harbor was suggested separately but simultaneously by two men, the British historian David B.Quinn and the Reverend Warner F. Gookin of Martha's Vineyard. Quinn published his paper and Gookin's jointly in *The New England Quarterly* in 1957, five years after Gookin died.

The evidence for Pring's anchorage at Pamet Harbor, although indirect, is persuasive. In his narrative, Pring says he was in a "haven winding in compass like the shell of a snail," just as the tip of Cape Cod curves around on itself. He called his anchorage Whitson's Bay, a name that appears at the tip of Cape Cod on the "Velasco" map of 1610. John Whitson, mayor of Bristol, Pring's hometown, was one of the backers of his expedition. Pring says he went up a river, apt for Truro but not for Plymouth or Edgartown. Finally, Pring built a "small baricado," or stockade, which sounds very much like the "old fort or palisado" that the Pilgrims would find at Corn Hill next to Pamet Harbor. No other explorers are known to have visited Pamet Harbor, much less to have built a stockade there. (See appendix A.)

. . .

Martin Pring, twenty-three years old, had forty-four men under his command when his two ships left Bristol, England a few weeks after the death of Queen Elizabeth I. He obtained permission for his voyage from Sir Walter Raleigh, to whom the queen had granted rights of exploration in North America. His financial backers hoped he would bring back sassafras. He planned also to trade with the Indians for furs and perhaps establish a trading post that might be expanded later into a permanent settlement. If he found gold or other precious metals, that would be all to the good.

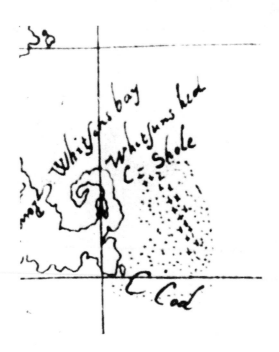

In his narrative, Captain Martin Pring named the bay where he anchored in 1603 "Whitson Bay," and this detail from the so-called Velasco map (circa. 1610) puts it at the end of Cape Cod. John Whitson, mayor of Bristol, Pring's port of embarkation in England, was a backer of the voyage. (Reproduced from the Collections of the Library of Congress.)

Pring's ships were small for ocean-crossing vessels. The *Speedwell* was only a third the size of the *Mayflower*, the *Discoverer* even smaller. Both ships were well provisioned with food for the crew and goods for trading with the Indians. The trading goods included hats of different colors, clothes of jersey and canvas, shoes and stockings, saws, pick-axes, spades, shovels, axes, hatchets, hooks, knives, scissors, hammers, nails, chisels, fish hooks, bells, beads, looking-glasses, thimbles, pins, needles and thread. Pring gave some of his goods to the Indians, but makes no mention of trading with them.

He also took along two powerful watchdogs, mastiffs named Gallant and Fool. Fool could carry a half-pike, a sizable iron-tipped spear, in his mouth. "And when we would be rid of the savages' company," says Pring, "we would let loose the mastiffs and suddenly with outcries they would flee away."

After coasting along Maine and northeast Massachusetts, Pring arrived in Cape Cod Bay in mid-June. On going ashore, he saw Indians and "thought it convenient to make a small baricado to keep diligent watch." The stockade, built of small logs driven into the sandy soil, provided a sense of safety for Pring's men while they worked in the forests, cutting firewood, hunting game, foraging for fruits and berries, and uprooting sassafras trees to be sent to market in England. At night, most or all of the men slept on board the two ships.

. . .

Pring's narrative dwells at length on the Indians–their gardens, weapons, canoes and an unsettling mix of pranks and menace. The Indians turned up periodically in groups ranging up to two hundred, almost all men. Pring thought the Indians were protective of the women for he saw only two.

He admired the Indians' stature, "somewhat taller than our ordinary people, strong, swift, well-proportioned, and", he adds abruptly, "given to treachery, as in the end we perceived." This seems exaggerated, although there was a certain wariness on both sides. The Indians must have wondered about strangely dressed men who arrived in enormous ships with sails, possessed of odd-shaped tools, trinkets and explosives and exhibiting a strange lust for great quantities of sassafras. Confronted by the interlopers with beards and light skins who could send forth thunderclaps, the Indians were remarkably trusting and accommodating.

Pring tells how the Indians took great delight in the "homely music" of a young man who played the cithern. During one of their visits, some twenty Indians formed a ring around him and danced to his music, "using many savage gestures, singing Io, Ia, Io, Ia, Ia, Io." When one of the Indians broke the ring, the rest would shout and knock him about in what appears to have been a friendly free-for-all. The Indians rewarded the musician with gifts that included tobacco, pipes, snake skins and deerskins. Neither spoke the other's language, but the language of music apparently united them on occasion. The festivities occurred near the stockade and thus may be imagined at Corn Hill or Tom's Hill at Pamet Harbor.

On another occasion, the men harvesting sassafras were taking their usual two-hour siesta in the woods when more than a hundred Indians armed with bows and arrows appeared. They surrounded the stockade and called to the four guards to come out, but the men refused. Captain Pring, alone with two men on his ship, became alarmed and fired a cannon to scare the Indians and waken the men sleeping in the woods. It took a second shot to bring his men to their feet. They picked up their weapons and let loose the mastiffs. As soon as the Indians spotted Gallant and Fool with his spear, says Pring, "they turned all to a jest and sport, and departed away in a friendly manner."

Pring's description of the Indians is observant and precise. He especially admired their arrows whose feathers were as tightly fastened "as any fletcher of ours can glue them on," and their birch bark canoes, one of which he took back to England. He marveled that it weighed less than sixty pounds, "a thing almost incredible in regard to the largeness and capacity."

Along the Pamet River, he found several unoccupied dwellings surrounded by gardens up to an acre in size, which were planted with Indian corn, cucumbers, squash and tobacco. In the open fields were quantities of beach peas and berries. To test the soil and growing conditions, the English planted an experimental garden of wheat, barley, oats, peas and other seeds they had brought from

The earliest–although totally fanciful–illustrations of Truro were inspired by Captain Martin Pring's narrative. An incident at Pamet Harbor is imagined in this engraving from Pieter van der Aa's book, "*Scheeps-togt van Martin Pringe* (1706). One of Pring's mastiffs, Fool, carries a half-pike in his mouth to frighten the Indians arriving in the center. Pring's ship fires a cannon to awaken his men, who are taking a mid-day nap at the right. The landscape is too mountainous for Truro, but the engraver had no description from Pring. Palm trees were not unusual in early depictions of North America.

England. The garden was a success, says Pring, "giving testimony of the goodness of the climate and the soil." The English vegetable garden was the first on record in the New World, although the men did not stay around for the harvest.

Cape Cod was heavily forested and abounded in wildlife when the first English arrived. Besides sassafras, Pring found a wide variety of hardwoods, including oak, ash, beech, birch, walnut, maple, cedar and cherry. The birds included eagles, vultures, hawks, herons, crows, gulls and "a great store of other river and sea fowl." In the near-shore waters were great quantities of cod, also mullet, turbot, mackerel, herring, crabs, lobster, and mussels with ragged pearls in them. The narrative mentions seals but no whales.

The wildlife they saw included deer in abundance, bears, wolves, foxes, lynx, porcupines "and (some say) Tygers." (Pring's qualified sighting of what must have been a mountain lion or puma prefigured a late twentieth century phenomenon. In 1980, 1981 and 1982, several Truro residents reported sighting what they thought was a large wild cat, which became known as the Pamet Puma. Among those who reported seeing a long-tailed cat the size of a big dog were a Truro policeman, a former school principal, and the noted sculptor Sidney Simon. Selectman Ed Oswalt was delegated to investigate the reported sightings. E. J. Kahn, Jr., wrote about them for *Boston Magazine* in 1982. Irving Tubbs, chief ranger at the Cape Cod National Seashore, told him that he had found not a shred of evidence to confirm what "some say" was a puma.)

At the end of July, Pring sent the *Discoverer* ahead to rush a load of sassafras to market; the *Speedwell* left ten days later. The day before Pring's departure, the Indians set fire to the woods, perhaps simply to clear underbrush as was their custom; and on the next day almost two hundred Indians gathered at Pamet Harbor, some of them going out to the ship in canoes. They wanted the English to return to shore, but Pring says he "sent them back and would none of their entertainment." To the end, ambiguity reigned in relations with the Indians.

Martin Pring, the young sea captain who discovered Truro in the year Shakespeare's *Hamlet* was first published, never returned to Cape Cod. He went on to become a famous mariner, sailing to Guiana, the East Indies, and back to the coast of Maine. After his death in Bristol at the age of forty-six, a monument to him was erected in St. Stephen's Church. If he had read the Pilgrims' account of their exploration of Truro, published a few years earlier, Pring would have learned that they had found the ruins of his "small baricado" at Pamet Harbor.

CHAPTER 3:
AMERICA'S MOST FAMOUS
SETTLERS ARRIVE IN TRURO

Although they were not the first Englishmen to spend time in Truro, the Pilgrims became the most famous. They were in the vanguard of one of the greatest events in recorded history, the trans-Atlantic migration of people from Europe to America. Their settlement at Plymouth was the first permanent European settlement in New England. Their first landing in the New World, however, was on Cape Cod, and the first place they explored for possible settlement was Truro. With winter imminent, the scouting party spent five days and nights in Truro, their longest time on shore before going across Cape Cod Bay to Plymouth.

The detailed account of the Pilgrims' exploration of Truro appears in a narrative published in 1622 in London. Historians called the narrative *Mourt's Relation* because its original title was long and rambling, the title page lacked an author's name, and the introduction was signed "G. Mourt." But no one named Mourt was with the Pilgrims or has been identified as the author. ("Relation" refers to a story someone relates.) Historians generally consider that William Bradford, who would become governor of Plymouth Plantation, and Edward Winslow were the anonymous authors and that Bradford wrote the section about the Outer Cape since Winslow is not mentioned in it. (See appendix B for text extracts.)

Mourt's Relation tells where the Pilgrims went in Truro and what they were doing for five days, day-by-day, in a narrative exceptional in early colonial history for its interest, suspense and literary qualities. In the early 1790s, the Reverend James Freeman, who had family roots in Truro, was the first to trace the footsteps of the Pilgrims. He wrote to a friend that *Mourt's Relation* "has now no obscurity. . . . I have seen how accurately every place is described."

• • •

The Pilgrims' ship, the *Mayflower*, was one of the first to carry families to the New World. One hundred and thirty-five men, women and children were crammed into the ship, which was only 113 feet long and 26 feet wide. The 102 passengers had all their worldly goods with them. Crossing the North Atlantic took two months. Storms battered the ship, which developed leaks. Most of the passengers were seasick much of the time. Landfall was a welcome sight, but in his memoirs Bradford nevertheless recalled their misgivings: "They had now no friends to welcome them, nor inns to entertain or refresh their weatherbeaten bodies, no houses or much less towns." They were, he said, "Englishmen who came over this great ocean and were ready to perish in this wilderness."

Their departure from England had been delayed, and their anchor splashed into the water of Provincetown Harbor on November 21, 1620, only a month before the start of winter. Bradford described their anchorage as "a good harbor and a pleasant bay, circled round, except in the entrance which is about four miles over from land to land, compassed about to the very sea with oaks, pines, juniper, sassafras and other sweet wood. It is a harbor wherein a thousand sail of ships may safely ride. There we relieved ourselves with wood and water and refreshed our people while our shallop [a type of longboat] was fitted to coast the bay to search for habitation. There was the greatest store of fowl that ever we saw. And every day we saw whales playing hard by us."

Before setting out on their search for habitation, the Pilgrims leaders had to deal with mutinous mutterings by some on board. They called a council, discussed their differences and finally all agreed "to combine together in one body and to submit to such government and governors as we should by common consent agree." Their one-page agreement was the *Mayflower Compact*, a singular act of democracy in an age of rule by kings and queens and feudal lords.

A few days later, fifteen men under the military command of Captain Miles Standish, and including William Bradford and two other men "for counsel and advice," buckled on their breastplates, armed themselves with muskets and swords, and went ashore to find a place to settle their families. Within an hour, they saw several Indians in the far distance. They went to meet them, but the Indians retreated and that was the only time they saw Indians.

For the rest of the day, they headed east and south toward Truro, tramping through a mature, hardwood forest that was largely free of underbrush. They found the woods "for the most part open and without underwood, fit either to go or ride in." They inspected the rich soil under the canopy of trees, not suspecting that under that thin layer of soil the Outer Cape was sand. In the centuries that followed, colonists harvested the trees, the top soil blew away and the hills reverted to mammoth, wind-blown sand dunes, the "walking dunes" that began their long, steady march southeast into Truro, a migration that continues today.

At nightfall, the scouting party reached the northern end of what would be called East Harbor (now Pilgrim Lake), near today's boundary with Provincetown. At that time, East Harbor was a salt-water lagoon connected at its northwest end by a narrow channel to Provincetown Harbor. The Pilgrims posted three sentinels to guard against an Indian raid, kindled a fire with flint and steel, ate some biscuits and cheese, drank some aquavit liquor and settled down for their first night on shore in the New World. Although their clothing was fairly substantial–made of wool, canvas and oilskin–they carried no bedrolls. They probably lay on a crude bed of leaves and pine boughs or sat propped up against a tree. Still, it was late November and the overnight low for Truro can drop below freezing. It would be a long night; the sun set around 4:15 and would not rise until 6:45–about thirteen hours of darkness.

. . .

The next morning, they would begin their survey of Truro. They had no plans to return to England. Husbands had brought their wives and children. They were looking for a place in the wilderness of North America to establish a community where they could build houses, feed and clothe their families, worship God in their own way and have their children carry on after them. Truro, and especially the Pamet River Valley, were the focus of the Pilgrims' first and longest quest for a place to settle.

The next day, the Pilgrims started out by following Indian tracks that ran between East Harbor and the Atlantic Ocean. At that time, the Atlantic shoreline was about six hundred feet farther out to sea. They went to the head of East Harbor's tidal creek and salt meadow, probably as far as the parking lot for Head-of-the-Meadow Beach before making a U-turn around the head of the marsh.

As the morning wore on, the Pilgrims were eager to find fresh water "as we were sore athirst." They had brought no water with them. About ten o'clock, they came upon a deep valley. They found little paths in the valley, probably game trails, and "there we saw a deer, and found springs of fresh water, of which we were heartily glad, and sat us down and drank our first New England water with as much delight as ever we drunk drink in all our lives." In his memoir, Bradford said the water of the now famous Pilgrim Spring was "as pleasant unto them as wine or beer had been"–high praise from the Pilgrims, who esteemed beer as much safer and healthier than water.

Despite its fame, attempts to identify the spring the Pilgrims found have been unsuccessful and have a left a residue of confusion. A small spring next to Pilgrim Lake's upper creek and marsh is marked by a bronze plaque on a granite block, but this spring is almost certainly not the right one. The plaque was put there in 1926 by Dr. William H. Rollins, a Boston dentist and a Pilgrim enthusiast. He bought one hundred square feet of land that included what he thought was the Pilgrim's spring and erected the monument. A trail leads to it from Pilgrim Heights above, and a paved bicycle path runs by it.

Rollins bequeathed the land and its spring to the Town of Truro, but the selectmen declined the offer for several reasons: There was no fund to maintain it; Rollins wanted his ashes scattered on the spot and a gravestone erected; and historians considered it impossible to designate as the Pilgrims' spring any one of several in the area.

Later, someone erected a memorial stone to Rollins, who died in 1929, and to his wife, Miriam, who had died earlier. The inscription read: "They tried to be useful in life and after death." When the Cape Cod National Seashore acquired the land, rangers removed the Rollins memorial stone but left the plaque marking the wrong spring. In fact, the plaque calls it "First Spring" not Pilgrim Spring, although it quotes from *Mourt's Relation*.

The more likely location of Pilgrim Spring is nearly a mile southeast of Rollins's site. In his narrative, Bradford says they went around the head of the East Harbor Creek and into the woods, crashing through the underbrush of hills and valleys until they came to a deep valley. His account shows that they had left the low, broad valley of the East Harbor creek and marshes, moved into hilly terrain and then found a deep valley. A relatively deep valley halfway between Route 6 and the Atlantic Ocean and about a mile north of Highland Road is probably the location of the spring that they Pilgrims found. In his edition of *Mourt's Relation*,

Freeman called the area Dyers Swamp. Cape Cod historians
Alexander Young and Henry Martyn Dexter, who also published
annotated editions of *Mourt's Relation* later in the nineteenth century, agreed with Freeman, although they said that two centuries
after the Pilgrims they found no springs. Samuel Eliot Morison
wrote in 1956 that he thought the spring must have been "the one
that feeds a little pond in Dyer's Swamp, surrounded by thickets."
In the end, however, Rollins achieved a measure of success. The
national seashore trail leading to his site is called the Pilgrim Spring
Trail and the U.S. Geological Survey identifies it as Pilgrim Spring.

. . .

After refreshing themselves, the Pilgrims headed south toward Cape
Cod Bay. Their route would have taken them across the Route 6
and Route 6A to the bayshore in the vicinity of Windigo Lane,
Twinefield Road and Pilgrims Path. When they reach the beach,
they built a bonfire to show their location to the *Mayflower*, which
was anchored several miles away. Continuing along the beach toward the Pamet River, which they had spotted from their anchorage, they turned inland and found "a fine, clear pond of fresh
water" just behind the barrier beach dune. This was the pond at
the future site of Pond Village in North Truro, one of the town's
three villages.

    The Pilgrims continued south on the uplands, where they
soon found "much plain [cleared] ground, about fifty acres fit for
the plow, and some signs where Indians had formerly planted their
corn." They crossed the Bay View Road area and dropped down to
the beach. Since they made no mention of Great Swamp in the
center of Shearwater, they were no doubt on the beach at that
point. They turned inland at Great Hollow and probably took the
gully that slants southeast up to what they would name Corn
Hill. There they soon came upon what were probably Indian graves,
the site of a dwelling, some old planks, a kettle they recognized as
European and fields of recently harvested corn.

Continuing south on Corn Hill, they found more cultivated fields, probably west of Old Colony Road on rolling land now occupied by the summer homes of Corn Hill Landing. From the heights, in clear weather the Pilgrims could have seen across the bay to the hills above Plymouth, where they would eventually settle. Beyond those hills was a wilderness the extent of which they could have hardly imagined.

Near the cultivated fields, the Pilgrims made a discovery crucial for their survival. They found baskets of corn buried in mounds of sand. At first, the Pilgrims were undecided whether to take the corn. Their stores of food were daily diminishing. Bradford and the other leaders had more than a hundred people to feed through the winter. After much debate, they decided to take thirty-six ears of corn and as much loose corn as they could carry in the kettle and stuff in their pockets. They promised themselves that "if we could find any of the people and come to parley with them, we would give them the kettle again and satisfy them for their corn."

The Pilgrims' appropriation of the Indians' corn is one of the best known anecdotes about the Pilgrims. Years later, Bradford was still trying to justify their action. In his memoir, he gave thanks to God that "they got seed to plant them corn the next year or else they might have starved, for they had none, nor any likelihood to get any until the season had been past." He wrote that the Pilgrims resolved to give the Indians "full satisfaction when they should meet with any of them (as about some six months afterward they did, to their good content)." Historians debate whether the Pilgrims should be censured for stealing the Indians' corn while protesting that they planned to pay for it, or should be excused for taking the corn to fill their needs while intending to pay for it later.

The Pilgrims named the spot Corn Hill, and two monuments mark their passage. The monument at the top of the hill is most unprepossessing. It is a plain granite post about eighteen inches high in the grass about forty feet west of the entrance to Corn Hill Landing. It carries the simple inscription "Cornhill 1620." Not a word about the Pilgrims. It marks the spot where the Provincetown Tercentenary Commission had erected a more elaborate monument. That monument was moved to the foot of Corn Hill, just off the beach parking lot, in 1976. The metal plaque on the boulder there carries the inscription: "Sixteen Pilgrims, led by Myles Standish, William Bradford, Stephen Hopkins and Edward Tilley found the precious Indian corn on this spot, which they called Corn Hill, on November 16, 1620, old style [of the calendar]. And sure it was God's Providence that we found the corn for else we know not how we should have done–*Mourt's Relation*. Provincetown Tercentenary Commission." Truro's citizenry had left it to Provincetown to take the lead on providing commemorative plaques. Town meeting refused to appropriate $100 for the observance of the Pilgrims tercentenary, understandably perhaps, since state and federal funds totaling $150,000 financed commemorative parks and plaques in various historic sites on the Outer Cape.

The Pilgrims' destination for this first excursion in Truro was the mouth of the Pamet River at the south end of Corn Hill. There, "hard by" Pamet Harbor they found the remains of "an old fort or palisado, which, as we conceived, had been made by some Christians." This was Martin Pring's "small baricado." From the wide mouth of the river two arms extended inland. The one farther south appeared to be twice as large and possibly suitable as a harbor for ships. The Pilgrims had no time that day to discover whether the Pamet was primarily a freshwater river or a saltwater tidal estuary, but they planned to return with their shallop to explore it.

At the end of their first day in Truro, the Pilgrims returned to the freshwater pond at Pond Village for the night. Their bivouac is commemorated by a plaque provided, again, by the Provincetown Tercentenary Commission: "1620-1920. Sixteen Pilgrims led by Myles Standish, William Bradford, Stephen Hopkins and Edward Tulley encamped on the shore of this pond for their second night on American soil, November 16, 1620, old style; drank their first New England water three miles northeast from here at the Pilgrim Spring; found the precious Indian corn two miles southwest from

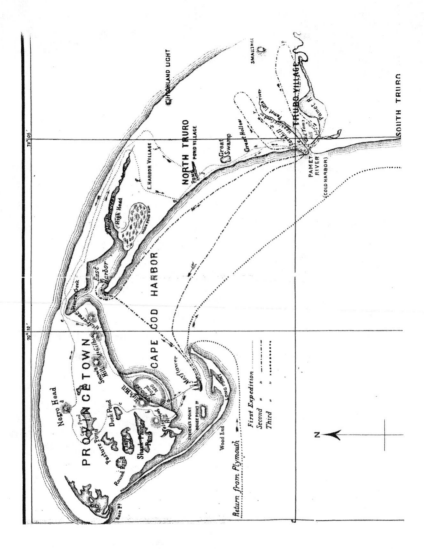

A map of the Pilgrims' two expeditions in Truro, the first beginning in Provincetown, skirting East Harbor (now Pilgrim Lake) and reaching Pamet Harbor. On their second expedition, they sailed their shallop to East Harbor, went on shore for about five miles (not shown) and then in the shallop to Pamet Harbor, from which they explored inland in two loops. Stout's Creek has long since been filled in by blowing sand. The inlet to East Harbor was dammed in 1869. (From Henry Martyn Dexter's 1865 edition of *Mourt's Relation*.)

here at Corn Hill." As was their custom, the Pilgrims built a temporary stockade for the night by driving long stakes into the ground and interlacing thick pine boughs to make a windbreak. They spent a long, cold, wet night huddled around a big fire. "It proved a very rainy night," wrote Bradford.

The next day brought the Pilgrims a bit of entertainment, although at Bradford's expense. At daybreak, they started back to the *Mayflower* and promptly got lost. They were heading north or northeast toward the head of East Harbor Creek and marshes. Their wandering took them across North Truro toward the Atlantic Ocean. The men at the front of the column came across a deer snare set by Indians. A young sapling had been bowed down to the ground, and amidst some acorns lay a noose and a hidden trip line to spring the trap.

The Pilgrim narrative, written by Bradford in the third person, describes what happened next: "As we were looking at it, William Bradford, being in the rear, when he came, looked upon it, and as he went about, it gave a sudden jerk up, and he was immediately caught by the leg. It was a very pretty device, made with a rope of their own making and a noose . . . as like ours as can be." The Indians' deer traps could be powerful. So well did the Pilgrims appreciate the pretty device that upended Bradford that they took the noose and found their way back to the Provincetown beaches and the *Mayflower*. "And thus," wrote Bradford, "we came both weary and welcome home and delivered in our corn to the store to be kept for seed, for we knew not how to come by any, and therefor were very glad, purposing so soon as we could meet with any of the inhabitants of that place to make them large satisfaction. This was our First Discovery."

. . .

The Pilgrims liked what they saw on their First Discovery. Ten days later, instead of scouting the rest of Cape Cod Bay, they returned to Truro "to make a more full discovery of the rivers." These were the Pamet and Little Pamet rivers, which shared a wide mouth to Cape Cod Bay at the foot of Corn Hill and whose environs the Pilgrims thought might be the best location for their settlement. They had to find a location soon. It was December, the weather was cold and stormy, and everybody was coughing. Twice in their narrative, the Pilgrims attribute deaths that occurred later that winter to the rainy, snowy, cold weather and to their wading ashore in the icy waters off Truro.

For this second trip ashore, the exploration party was almost twice as large. It was led by the *Mayflower*'s captain, who brought along some of his crew. Strong southerly winds and a snowstorm prevented them from reaching the Pamet in the shallop, so the boat dropped the men in shallow water near the beach, and sailors rowed the shallop through the inlet into the protection of a lagoon that would later be called East Harbor.

Cold and wet, the Pilgrims trudged through the snow toward the Pamet but had to camp for the night before reaching it. They probably got no farther than the Pond Village area. Their journal does not say where they camped for their third night in Truro, how they slept or what they ate. It does say that "it blowed and did snow all that day and night, and froze withal. Some of our people that are dead took the original of their death here."

. . .

The next day about eleven o'clock, their shallop picked them up, and the wind being fair they sailed into Pamet Harbor, which they called Cold Harbor. They thought it a good harbor for boats, but not for ships, since there was deep water only at high tide. The Pilgrims were thus the first to try to assess whether Pamet Harbor might work as an anchorage. Nearly four centuries later, the town was still debating whether the mouth of the tidal Pamet River could or should be maintained as a working harbor during low tides.

A replica of the shallop used by the Pilgrims on their expeditions from the *Mayflower*, anchored in Provincetown Harbor, to Truro's East Harbor, Pamet Harbor and up the Pamet River. (Courtesy of Plimoth Plantation, Plymouth MA, USA)

The shallop landed them at the base of Tom's Hill, and they started up the north shore of the Pamet River to see if it had a fresh water source, not realizing that it was salt water its entire length. By now six inches of snow covered the ground. The shallop followed them up the winding river, which at that time was probably much wider and deeper than today. Exploring the hills and valleys, the Pilgrims on foot would have gone along Castle Road and perhaps up as far as Town Hall. They crossed Route 6A and the Route 6 between Truro Center and Town Hall Road and continued along what is now North Pamet Road, perhaps ranging into the area of Avery Way and Rabbit Hill Road.

"At length night grew on," Bradford wrote, "and our men were tired with marching up and down steep hills and deep valleys." They made camp under pine trees, probably about half way from Truro Center to the Atlantic, and shot three fat geese and six ducks for their supper. Again there is no mention of shelter or sleeping arrangements. They likely built another wind barrier of tree limbs and crowded around a fire at the open end. It was one of the longest nights of the year.

The next morning, they abandoned their search for the headwaters of the Pamet River; the terrain was too hilly. They decided to head back to Corn Hill, where they had seen canoes, and to look for more corn. Backtracking toward the bay, they would have crossed Meetinghouse Road and Tom's Hill to reach the Little Pamet River somewhere along Corn Hill Road before the beach parking lot. There they borrowed the canoe they had seen and ferried the party across the Little Pamet to Corn Hill, where they raided the Indians' underground storage bins and collected more corn, a bag of beans and a bottle of oil.

The *Mayflower*'s captain wanted to return to the ship, but despite the snow and cold Bradford and other Pilgrims thought they should continue. The captain took the weak and sick with him. The remaining eighteen spent their fifth night in Truro on snow-covered, frozen ground.

On their last day in Truro, the Pilgrims marched several miles into the woods, following Indian paths and looking for Indian villages. Before reaching the Atlantic Ocean, which is never mentioned in their narrative, they turned back toward Cape Cod Bay and came across the cultivated fields they had seen on their second day in Truro. After their archaeological dig in the field and their examination of the two Indian corpses and the Indian dwelling, they returned to the *Mayflower* in the shallop.

• • •

On board the *Mayflower*, the question was whether or not to settle in Truro. Even though winter was upon them, they had used up five days exploring the woods and fields and the Pamet River valley. They had noted forests of valuable timber, rich black soil for crops, an abundance of game birds and great potential for fishing and whaling in the protected waters of Cape Cod Bay. They noted, too, the Indians' successful cultivation of corn and beans. Their immediate need, however, was for shelter against the winter cold and storms. They had to decide right away: "Having thus discovered this place, it was controversial amongst us what to do touching our abode and settling there; some thought it best for many reasons to abide there."

The tone of the Pilgrims' narrative suggests that a significant number of the leaders favored Truro as a place to settle. Bradford listed four reasons:

> First, that there was a convenient harbor for boats though not for ships. Secondly, good corn-ground ready to our hands, as we saw by experience in the goodly corn that it yielded, which would again agree with the ground and be natural seed for the same. Thirdly, Cape Cod was like to be a place of good fishing, for we saw daily great whales of the best kind for oil and bone come close aboard our ship and in fair weather swim and play with us. . . . Fourthly, the place was likely to be healthful, secure and defensible. But the last

and especial reason was that now the heart of winter and
unseasonable weather was come upon us, so that we could
not go upon coasting and discovery without danger of losing men and boat. . . . Also cold and wet lodging had so
tainted our people, for scarce any of us were free from vehe-
ment coughs . . . [that] would endanger the lives of many
and breed diseases and infection amongst us.

Others thought that they should search farther along the coast.
They argued that in Truro "the water was but in ponds, and it was
thought there would be none in summer, or very little"; and the
water would have to be carried up steep hills from the ponds.
They did not know that the ponds were full year-round.

A decision had to be reached quickly. Winter was upon them
and their food was running out. If the ship's stores ran too low,
they feared the captain might sail for England "and let us shift as
we could." The arguments for Truro appear to have been much
stronger than those against, but the Pilgrims decided to scout
around Cape Cod Bay and consider a place called Thievish Harbor, which was recommended by the ship's pilot, who had been
there on an earlier voyage. The scouting party rowed and sailed
their shallop to Wellfleet Harbor, south of Truro, and then to First
Encounter Beach in Eastham, where they had their first clash with
Indians, who tried to repulse the landing party but then retreated.
The Pilgrims then continued around the shore of Cape Cod Bay
to Thievish Harbor, also called Plymouth Harbor, which they very
quickly found suitable for their settlement.

A few months after the Pilgrims arrived in Plymouth, William
Bradford, thirty-two years old, was elected governor. In England,
he had been a weaver of a coarse cotton/linen cloth called fustian.
In America, he became a wealthy farmer and merchant, an investor in Truro and Provincetown land and fishing rights and author
of one of the classics of American literature, *Of Plymouth Plantation*. Although not as familiar in the popular mind as Miles Standish
and John Alden, William Bradford is described by his biographer

as "unquestionably the greatest of the Pilgrims, one of the greatest figures of seventeenth-century New England–indeed of our whole colonial period." He served as governor of Plymouth Colony longer than any other Pilgrim, thirty-two years, and was governor when he died at age sixty-nine.

Thus it was that Truro came close to winning the place in American history that went to Plymouth. The Pilgrim leaders seemed to favor Truro. If the *Mayflower's* pilot had not promoted Thievish Harbor, the first permanent European settlement in New England might well have been along the Pamet River.

CHAPTER 4:
EARLY LANDOWNERS AND
INDIAN ENCOUNTERS

The first landowners and settlers of Truro were Pilgrims from Plymouth and their immediate descendants. Most came by way of Eastham, which had been settled by Pilgrim families as Nauset in 1644. As early as the 1650s–just 30 years after the Pilgrims landed–colonists from the Nauset settlement were walking and riding north into the territory then known as Pamet to graze livestock, cut wood and gather salt marsh hay. These men and women were the first English to become familiar with Truro's hills, valleys, woodlands, meadows and salt marshes on a regular basis. They would have encountered as many as two hundred Indians, most of them at Corn Hill and High Head.

The settlers' early infiltration into Pamet Indian territory led to the laying out of a cart way. Durand Echeverria, a Wellfleet historian, found evidence that "the ancient Indian trail from Nauset to Pamet had by the 1650s been broadened into a rough cart way that ran north from the Eastham meeting house . . . [through Wellfleet and] . . . around the head of the Pamet River." The cart way would have been used to haul timber and hay from the end of the uninhabited Outer Cape and to drive livestock to and from pastures. It became known as the King's Highway when it ran the length of Cape Cod and in the twentieth century as Old King's Highway. Much of the rough cart way–Truro's first "road"–still exists today in stretches of a single-track sand road.

At about the same time, settlers established the boundary between Truro and Wellfleet. Boundary lines were of primary importance to colonists as they moved into undeveloped land. Truro's boundary with Wellfleet, which has remained unchanged for three and a half centuries, divided the Billingsgate land owned by Eastham "purchasers" from the Pamet land of "purchasers" who would become the Pamet Proprietors. The boundary is mentioned in an Eastham record of April 20, 1659, when a meadow that was right on the boundary line was granted to John Smalley.

In the next century, Truro selectmen would meet almost every year with selectmen from Wellfleet, and also with Provincetown after its boundary was set, to "perambulate" the boundaries and confirm the marks, which often were rudimentary. On May 6, 1712, for example, they met with Wellfleet selectmen at Bound Brook to perambulate: "But said oak tree with stones by it we could not find and judge that it may be washed away by the sea." They set a new mark, a pile of stones, farther inland. The boundary was and remains today a straight line from the precarious point at Bound Brook Island running due east to the Atlantic Ocean. Five granite columns mark the boundary today. Each has "W" on the Wellfleet side and "T" on the Truro side.

With a cart way from Eastham through what is now Wellfleet and into Truro, settlers from Eastham began in the 1650s to move north into territory occupied only by Indians. The settlers acquired meadow grants in Wellfleet, and by the end of the decade, according to Echeverria, "virtually all the good meadowland had been parceled out." Settlers then moved farther north into land that would become Truro. Thomas Prence of Eastham had already secured rights to this land.

. . .

Thomas Prence was Truro's first landowner. A founder of Eastham
and later a governor of Plymouth Colony, he had arrived on the
Fortune one year after the *Mayflower*, and he soon became a forceful Pilgrim leader. "A terror to evil-doers" was one portrayal. He
also became a major landowner throughout Plymouth Colony. In
Eastham, he had a two-hundred-acre farm that stretched from the
bay to the ocean. When William Bradford died in 1657, Prence
was elected governor of Plymouth Colony even though he insisted
on remaining on his Eastham farm, which he preferred to all his
other land holdings. He was re-elected to that post for sixteen
years until his death.

Prence's real estate interests in Pamet began five years after his
arrival in Eastham. On October 2, 1650, the General Court, Plymouth Colony's legislative body, granted a bass fishing monopoly
at the end of Cape Cod to Prence, Miles Standish and William
Paddy. Their monopoly included the right "to use lands, creeks,
timber, etc. upon the Cape land," and authorized the men to decide who among them would be first "to choose of the place to
build upon," suggesting that in the 1650s they or fishermen working for them built shelters on the bayshore of Truro and
Provincetown.

In the same grant, Prence was given the exclusive right on
behalf of Plymouth Colony to buy land at the end of Cape Cod
from the Indians, the land to be shared later by the three men.
The following year, the General Court added William Bradford to
the partnership; so Bradford, who traversed Truro for five days in
1620, was given land rights where he and the other Pilgrims from
the *Mayflower* had first set foot in America.

Within four years, Prence purchased land from an Indian whom
the English had named Sampson, paying him in knives, axes, hoes,
kettles, coats and a box. The transaction, which occurred sometime before 1655, is mentioned in "Sampson's Indenture" of 1680,
an agreement confirming Prence's deal with Sampson while set-

tling a claim on the same land by two other Indians, Peter and Joshua. The two received five pounds ten shillings, a considerable sum, to settle their claim. Captain John Freeman, who represented Plymouth Colony, said the colony wanted to "do no wrong to said Indians . . . and for maintaining peace and good agreement." The Indians also retained the right to pitch their wigwams and gather berries on the land and butcher whales that beached themselves on the bay shore. The boundary descriptions in Sampson's Indenture are difficult to interpret, but the land seems to have extended from High Head and East Harbor in what is now Truro to the end of the Cape. Sampson's Indenture documents the first recorded purchase of Truro land from an Indian.

At about the same time, the General Court extended Eastham's jurisdiction north to a point beyond East Harbor. Thus, for almost twenty years beginning in the early 1650s, Thomas Prence combined in his person governmental authority over the Pamet lands and a half-share ownership of them.

Prence's half-share ownership made him the first and controlling partner in a land development partnership that became known as the Pamet Proprietors. Such proprietorships were granted by Plymouth Colony to prominent men to assure the orderly development of the colony's land. For more than half a century, the Pamet Proprietors were not only partners in ownership of land held in common but were themselves principal individual landowners. They met periodically to divide partnership land among themselves, sell land to newcomers, settle land disputes and arrange for roads, fences and other matters of common concern. The Pamet Proprietors were, in effect, the local government before Pamet became the Town of Truro, and their leaders would become the town's first elected officials.

Thomas Prence never became a settler in Pamet; he preferred Eastham, where he had settled. Before he died, he sold "all my one-half-share of purchase land lying at Paomett . . . betwixt Bound Brook and the Eastern Harbor or Lovell's Creek" to Thomas Paine in 1670. This territory encompassed all of Pamet. Paine paid Prence twenty pounds and thereby became a Pamet Proprietor. Twenty years later, Paine, then in his seventies, would sell the half-share to his son Thomas for the same price. The son would become clerk of the Pamet Proprietors, founder of the Town of Truro and one of its two most prominent early citizens.

Over the years, other Eastham men acquired shares in the Pamet Proprietors' holdings through inheritance or purchase. One of them was Nicholas Snow of Eastham, who had arrived a year after the Pilgrims landed. He married Constance Hopkins, who had arrived on the *Mayflower* at age fifteen. Her grave is in Eastham. Their son inherited his father's share of Pamet lands; and their grandson, John Snow, became a leading citizen of Truro.

· · ·

Thomas Prence's purchase from the Indian Sampson set the pattern. The English would offer tools, trinkets and clothes, and the Indians would cede them ownership of vast acreages. The Indian concept of land use and acquisition, however, was quite different from that of the English. Tribes or clans might claim territory, but individual Indians had no need to "own"" real estate. In 1630, Francis Higginson, a Salem minister, described their disinterest in claiming ownership: "The Indians are not able to make use of the one fourth part of the land, neither have they any settled places, as towns, to dwell in, nor any ground as they challenge for their own possession, but change their habitation from place to place."

In contrast, the English had a hunger for land and a keen sense of property ownership; they staked claims, put lines on maps and built fences. Not until it was too late did the Indians learn that these transactions meant that they were giving up their long-held, traditional rights to use the woods, fields and marshes they knew so well. The English, of course, believed they were acting under terms of the Plymouth Colony charter from the king of England, which gave them the right to acquire land and distribute it among themselves and others. Sometimes they even made land grants to the Indians–for a price.

Although a few English took advantage of the Indians, leading settlers moved to stop abuses. In one of their first recorded actions in Pamet, dated June 4, 1700, the Pamet Proprietors appointed Thomas Paine as their purchasing agent "to buy all such lands of the Indians as they shall be minded to sell." This was renewed ten years later. They did this, they said, because they "were deeply sensible of the inconveniency of having many persons in their company buying of lands of the Indians for inconsiderable pay to their great damage."

For the most part, the settlers negotiated with the Pamet Indians and tried to settle any disputes, if only to avoid making enemies. Their early records include a number of agreements on land sales, boundaries and fishing rights. On July 24, 1697, nine settlers in Pamet and five Indians signed "an agreement and final settlement of the bounds and ranges between the lands now possessed by the English." The agreement confirmed an earlier record of unspecified date. In 1712, the English decided to give an Indian named Tonomatuk thirty shillings "to quiet his claim" to some Pamet land that four Indians–Jeremy, Anthony, Jediah John and David Peter–had sold to Nathaniel Atkins. The four Indians evidently had sold to Atkins land that Tonomatuk thought was his. And in connection with a real estate transaction in 1715, the English protested: "We are not willing that any Indian should suffer any wrong through our means or mistakes."

Generally, the Pamet Indians seemed to get along with the English. They offered no resistance to the settlers. Nothing in the records tells about any strife, crimes or threats of violence. They traded with the settlers, even buying horses from them. In 1671 Atamothaset bought a five-year-old horse from the elder Thomas Paine, and in 1692 Sequenyset, alias Sam, bought from Paine a brown horse with a white face and four white feet. Two years later, an Indian whom the English named Daniel Sam registered his own cattle brand, two slits on the top of the left ear.

About fifty to seventy-five Indians were in Pamet when the
settlers began arriving. This estimate is based on a 1698 survey by
the Plymouth Colony's Commission for the Propagation of the
Indians: "At East Harbor [in Pamet] and Billingsgate [Wellfleet] . . .
here are about twenty houses, in some of which are two families."
    Throughout the 1600s, the English recognized the Indians
not only as individuals but also as members of a tribe. This recognition was demonstrated in 1671 when Pamet Indian leaders signed
an elaborate treaty pledging the Pamets to side with the English
against plots or attacks by other Indians. The English had persuaded the Pamets, along with several other Cape Cod tribes, to
agree to fight alongside the English in any wars with Indians west
of Plymouth and Boston. The agreement was drawn up by the
Plymouth Colony for signature by the "poor Indians," and its ser-
vile and sanctimonious language reveals how the English imposed
their values on the native population:

> We, the Indians of Paomett, do engage our fidelity unto the
> government of New Plymouth, that we will submit our-
> selves unto their government and if we understand or hear
> of any plot or design contrived against the English, or any
> part of them, by any other Indians, we do hereby engage to
> reveal, declare or discover it to some one or more of the
> magistrates of New Plymouth. And further, if they have
> occasion to make use of our help, if any that shall or may
> come against the English living within the government of
> New Plymouth, we do engage to help them, if they desire or
> require our assistance, to the shedding of our blood or the
> loss of our lives; the like we engage for our posterity for ever
> that shall succeed us; and foreasmuch as the English and we
> poor Indians are of one blood, as Acts 17:26, for we do
> confess we poor Indians in our lives were as captives under
> Satan and our sachems, doing their wills whose breath per-
> ishes, as Psalms 146:3,4; Exodus 15:1,2, etc.; but now we
> know by the word of God that it is better to trust in the

great God and his strength, Psalms 118:8,9; and, besides,
we were like unto wolves and lions to destroy one another,
but we hope and believe in God; therefor we desire to enter
into covenant with the English respecting our fidelity, as
Isaiah 11:6, and this we further desire, that if the English
should hear any evil report of us, whereby there might be
any occasion of suspicion of our fidelity, we desire it might
not be believed or received until we might have the liberty
and opportunity to clear ourselves, for we desire to keep our
covenant, if God helps us so to do.

The Pamets were joined by six other Indian communities in pledging their fidelity for themselves, their neighbors and future generations. Nine Indians, led by two Pamets, went to the General Court in Plymouth and put their marks on the covenant. Four years later, during King Philip's War, the Pamet Indians along with others renewed their pledge to fight with the English. That devastating war, however, never came to Cape Cod or involved its Indians.

Despite their loyalty and friendship with the English settlers, or because of it, most of the Pamet Indians rapidly gave up their homeland to the English, usually for inconsiderable remuneration, and then found that they had no place to go. Their spirits demoralized, their friends and relatives dead of disease or victims of alcoholism, their way of life ruined, many of the surviving Indians wandered off to other parts of the country. A few became servants or slaves in Truro.

By the latter half of the 1700s, the Indian population had dwindled to a handful. In 1762, Ezra Stiles, who would be president of Yale University, wrote in his diary for June 4: "Truro has 180 Eng. Fam., not one Indian." Shebnah Rich, however, says that thirty years later, "in 1792, Rev. M. Damon [Truro's minister] wrote to the Massachusetts Historical Society that there was but one Indian family living in Truro."

PART II:

Settlers, Whalers and the Revolutionaries

CHAPTER 5:
FROM PAMET SETTLEMENT
TO TRURO TOWNSHIP

Few New England towns can state a year of settlement with certainty, and Truro is no exception. The best estimate for Truro is the 1680s or perhaps several years earlier. The evidence is contained in the earliest surviving record of the Pamet Proprietors. Dated May 22, 1689, the torn and faded document at Town Hall mentions the dwellings of Thomas Paine, who was a Pamet Proprietor, and John Savage, a squatter. One of Paine's meadow boundaries was "near where said Paine's dwelling house now standeth." Another meadow lot, which belonged to Joseph Rogers, was "at the place where John Savage hath built a cottage to live in."

Although pieces of the document are torn off, the words "settled by the proprietors" appear in its short preamble, indicating that the signatories considered themselves settlers in the 1680s. The document lays out eight lots of twenty acres each on the salt marshes and meadows along the Pamet River and ten upland lots at High Head overlooking East Harbor. The lot owners were Ensign Jonathan Bangs, William Twinning, Constant Freeman, Israel Cole,

Thomas Paine (two lots), Thomas Clark, Lieut. Joseph Rogers "deceased," John Snow and Caleb Hopkins.

The actual parceling of the land and the construction of the Paine and Savage dwellings certainly happened sometime before 1689, the date on the record. This is because the record is a duplicate of an original of unspecified date. At the bottom is written: "The persons named hereunto subscribed were written to the original copy and are therewith to be recorded in this book." The original, apparently lost, must have been written sometime earlier, perhaps several years or even a decade earlier, and Thomas Paine was copying it into a record book. The copy has nine signatures, including one by a woman, Mary Snow.

Mary Snow, the only woman among the Pamet Proprietors, seems to have signed her name as a witness on behalf of the family. She did not receive a lot in her name, but a parcel did go to her husband, John Snow, who had inherited his Pamet Proprietor holdings. He was one of three men who received lots but for some reason did not sign the record. Mary Snow was a person of stature and influence among the Pamet Proprietors. Three years later she witnessed another Pamet Proprietor record that granted two parcels of land in South Truro to Israel Cole. Although she signed as a witness to Pamet Proprietor records, Mary Snow herself did not become a landowner, and her name does not appear again in the records.

Other settlers may well have been living in Truro before Paine and Savage, but they are the first on record. Earlier settlers, if any, would have been squatters who arrived before the Pamet Proprietors began to assert their ownership and divide up their land into parcels for themselves and for sale to others.

Although the 1680s seems the most likely decade for the first permanent dwellings in Truro, at least one historian mentions an earlier date. Simeon Deyo's *History of Barnstable County, Massachusetts* includes a sketch map dated 1890 that gives settlement and incorporation dates for Cape Cod towns. For Truro is written "Set. 1670 Inc. 1709." Deyo, however, does not say how he arrived at

1670. As it happens, 1670 was the year Thomas Prence sold his half-share of Pamet to Thomas Paine's father, using Lovell's Creek as a boundary marker. The otherwise unknown Lovell may have lived there in 1670, or he may simply have owned meadows along the creek named for him. Nothing in the records indicates a permanent house or settlement such as the Paine and Savage houses. Another historian, Enoch Pratt of Eastham, picked 1680 as the year that "the settlement of Truro was also commenced by emigrants from this town," but he, too, does not cite evidence in his *Comprehensive History of Eastham, Wellfleet and Orleans* (1844).

In *Truro—Cape Cod, or Land Marks and Sea Marks* (1883), Shebnah Rich took an unusual position. He maintained that Truro was first settled, not by families from Eastham, but by unnamed people "in connection with the fisheries" long before the earliest Pamet Proprietor records. This notion echoes an assertion by his near contemporary, Frederick Freeman, that "there were merchants here [at Provincetown Harbor] periodically visiting and transiently residing from very early times." Neither writer gives any dates. Rich evidently assumed that merchants and fishermen from Europe stopped for extended sojourns on the Provincetown Harbor shoreline, which extends into Truro. If these sojourners existed, which does seem possible, there is no evidence they established permanent settlements. They left no trace for recorded history.

By 1700, the Pamet Proprietors were well-established; and although the settlement was still quite small, probably only twenty or thirty families, it was growing steadily. The Pamet Proprietors continued to divide land among themselves and sell lots to new settlers. They bought land from Indians, who probably numbered fewer than fifty by then. In 1703, they designated land for a permanent commons, "which shall never be divided or disposed of to any man's or men's own particular use," a stricture eventually abandoned. They voted to charge six shillings a sloop-load for hay taken from East Harbor by men who "come from other parts," and they laid out what they called a "Drift Highway," a right-of-way from the head of the Pamet River northwest to East Harbor. Anticipating the need to attract a resident minister, they set aside upland and meadow acreage for his use, and in 1704 they built their first meetinghouse on the Hill of Storms, which was just about in the middle of their lands. The site is now Old North Cemetery on Route 6 across from the police and fire station.

Initially, squatters were a major issue for the Pamet Proprietors. About a dozen settlers had arrived independently and claimed land for themselves even as the Pamet Proprietors were carving out lots for themselves. One of the squatters was Thomas Smith, and in 1699 the Pamet Proprietors took up the issue of land rights. Smith said he had bought his land from two Indians. The Pamet Proprietors, however, asserted their rights to the land. Smith offered to pay them for their rights, whereupon the Pamet Proprietors decided on the traditional, candle-timed auction. "Methods being agreed upon," their minutes say, "the candle was lighted and money bid." When the candle sputtered out, Smith had made the highest bid–fifty pounds–which went into the Pamet Proprietors' treasury. For the next two decades, land and boundary disputes would be a regular item on their agenda.

Other squatters were a physician, Dr. William Dyer, a native of Barnstable, who, along with his wife, Mary, died in 1738; and a Mr. Gold, who appears in the records only because his cellar was a landmark even though it had collapsed. The record of July 24, 1697, on land boundaries refers to "the point of upland where Mr. Gold's cellar formerly was." Several records of 1700 recognize unnamed inhabitants at High Head, and the Pamet Proprietors seemed to have generally accepted them. At one meeting, they agreed on a conservation measure to pay "the neighbors at Pamet" to build a fence "below Eastern Harbor Pond sufficient to stop the sand and keep the tide out of said pond."

From its beginning and throughout the history of Truro, conservation of natural resources would be a major concern, and conservation was the subject of a measure voted on June 30, 1696, at one of the Pamet Proprietors' earliest recorded meetings. The measure, which might well be considered the first bylaw, levied fines

on anyone who cut trees for cordwood or timber on their undi-
vided land. Another conservation concern that would continue
into the twentieth century was the preservation of meadows, rivers, and harbors from silting by wind-blown and water-borne sand.

· · ·

Besides conservation of natural resources, a recurring concern
throughout Truro's history has been enemy incursions and the threat
of attack by enemy forces. The first of many for this town with its
vulnerable position on the Atlantic coast occurred in 1690 when
the English were just getting settled in Truro. Frenchmen from
Canada landed at the end of Cape Cod and marched through Pamet.
The only record of it is in the diary of Judge Samuel Sewall of
Boston. In his entry for July 8, 1690, he wrote that the government leaders "are alarmed by a post who brings a relation of Frenchmen being landed at Cape Cod [that is, at the end of the Cape]
and marched within 10 miles of Eastham." The French incursion
alarmed the government in Boston because this was at the start of
King William's War (1689-1699) between the English and the
French. In America, the French and their Indian allies were raiding settlements all along the Atlantic Coast. "The frontier was in
grave danger," writes the historian Samuel Eliot Morison; and the
Pamet settlers found themselves on this dangerous frontier.

Seven years later, enemy Frenchmen again landed at end of
Cape Cod. This time Indians loyal to the English fought and de-
feated them. According to a Plymouth Colony record, ten Pamet
Indians "did repel, kill and take some of the said enemies and did
thusly defend the effects of the English which might otherwise
have been taken and carried away by the said French enemies."
The Indians were rewarded for their loyalty and success. Plymouth
Colony gave "a good gun" to the Indian leader, Hugh, and cloth
coats to the other nine Indians. Even after the official end of the
war, the French from Canada continued their depredations. In

early 1703, Sewall got word from Eastham that "three sloops and a whale boat or two [were] taken at Cape Cod by a French sloop."

Unfortunately, the Pamet Proprietors did not leave any records about these French incursions; their primary concern was management of their properties.

· · ·

Securing township status for Pamet was not easy. The settlement was small. It was part of Eastham, which extended to the end of Cape Cod and which seemed at times to have some interest in keeping Pamet in its domain. It took the Pamet Proprietors almost a decade to achieve their goal. At one point, they threatened the Massachusetts Bay Province that they would "pluck up stakes and be gone" if conditions imposed for township status were too onerous.

The settlers' first move came in 1700 when they set aside land for a minister, and in 1704 they built their first meetinghouse. Although they issued calls to two prospective ministers in 1701 and 1705, both declined, probably because the settlement was so small and remote.

Having a resident minister and township status was important for several reasons. Pamet was too far away from the Eastham meetinghouse, three or four hours away by horseback. A round trip on the Sabbath must have been wearisome, especially for the women and children. The settlers also chafed at the cost of being governed and taxed by distant Eastham. In 1702, Eastham agreed to cut in half the charges that the Pamet settlers had to pay for the distant meetinghouse and minister. The tax cut was contingent on the Pamet Proprietors hiring a minister. The following year, they told Eastham that they intended to petition Boston to be a town, and Eastham did not contest it.

Two years later, in a reversal of sentiment, Eastham offered Pamet two seats on its expanded five-man board of selectmen, no doubt an attempt to persuade the Pamet settlers to remain part of

Eastham. The Pamet Proprietors would have none of it; they took their case to Boston, and within a few months the provincial legislature was considering the first of three bills and ordering a survey of Pamet "which the inhabitants pray may be made a township by the name of "Dangerfield," a name that would not survive.

A bill to establish a town to be called Dangerfield was introduced in the House of Representatives on June 8, 1705. It noted that "a competent number of inhabitants" was settled on enough land and that they therefore deserved encouragement to form a town. The bill required that the town maintain a "highway" (really just a right-of-way) sixty feet wide running from the new town to the tip of the Cape, a provision that was ultimately dropped. It would also give the town police responsibility for all of what is now Provincetown. That idea, too, was dropped, although it would be revived several years after the Town of Truro was created. The bill went back and forth between the two houses, failed to pass the Governor's Council (the upper house) and died. The council then ordered a survey of the Pamet territory to be presented at the fall session of the legislature.

In the fall session, the same bill again bounced back and forth between the lower and upper houses for three weeks. Then on November 13, 1705, both chambers passed a new bill that contained a number of conditions, one of which would prove to be unacceptable to the Pamet Proprietors. This second bill opened by stating that there were at the time about thirty families living in Pamet, not considered enough to qualify as a town. The Pamet settlers' petition would be granted on three conditions: that the settlement have forty families; that they have "an able, orthodox minister within three years;" and that the Indians be allowed free use of any unclaimed land or land held in common by the settlers.

The Pamet Proprietors balked at the third condition. Thomas Paine, who had emerged as their leader, sent a compelling letter to Boston on April 15, 1706, conveying Pamet's rejection of township status if they had to comply with the third condition. Paine declared that if the Indians were to be "fellow commoners" in the

lands that the Pamet settlers bought from them, many of the settlers would "be forced to pluck up stakes and be gone;" and Pamet
would never reach forty families nor be able to maintain a minister. Paine's letter, which has not heretofore been considered by
historians, is the only example of his writing that has been found,
aside from his official minutes as clerk of the Pamet Proprietors
and the town. His writing is simple and direct, forceful yet diplo-
matic. (See appendix C.)

The only known letter of Thomas Paine protests a condition for township
status. Appendix C gives a transcription of the text. (Photostat courtesy of the
Massachusetts Archives.)

Whether any Pamet Indians sought a share in the Pamet lands or why the provincial legislature thought they should have a share has not turned up in the records. The provision was quite unusual in Massachusetts Bay Province as a requirement for township status. In any case, the Pamet inhabitants rejected it. Three years passed. Pamet remained Pamet, a district of Eastham. Nobody said anything about the request for Dangerfield as the name of the town. Thomas Paine continued as clerk of the Pamet Proprietors. A few more settlers arrived.

Then, in a whirlwind of governmental activity over three days in July 1709, Paine renewed his efforts. Working with an official in Boston, he submitted a petition on July 14 noting that Pamet had "forty families, daily increasing," had built a meetinghouse five years earlier and had visiting ministers for seven years. Without township status, however, the Pamet leaders could not levy taxes to support a resident minister. "The burden," he said, "lies very heavy upon such as are willing to contribute thereto." Paine's petition is not in his hand, but his signature is at the bottom. Not previously considered by historians, the petition also provides dates for two significant events: visiting preachers were in Pamet as early as 1702, and the first meetinghouse was built in 1704.

The Governor's Council approved the petition on the same day and ordered that a bill be drafted, "provided the inhabitants procure and settle a learned, orthodox minister among them within the space of three years." The Council also added at the end of its one sentence order, "the town to be called Truroe." This is the first mention of Truro as the name of the town.

The next day, the House of Representatives tried to delay action on Paine's petition in order to give Eastham time to register any objections. The order to consult Eastham, however, was crossed out and "concurred," was written in. At the same time, the final bill creating the Truro township was drafted and approved by both houses. If Eastham had any objection, there is no record of it. Governor Joseph Dudley signed the bill into law the following day, July 16, and the Town of Truro was established.

The act was clearly the work of professional lawmakers in Boston. It was in the usual two parts. The first half–the "whereas" part–notes that Pamet consists of "forty families, and daily increasing." The boundaries are given as extending "from the Province lands reserved for the fishery" to Eastham (Wellfleet today) and "from sea to sea across the neck of land commonly called Cape Cod." A minister in residence was a requirement, and the act, reflecting Thomas Paine's petition, acknowledges that the inhabitants "have built a convenient house to meet in for the public worship of God, and have for some time had a minister among them."

The second half of the act creates the new town: "Be it therefor enacted . . . that the tract of land called Pawmet . . . is erected into a township . . . and shall be called by the name of Truroe." The inhabitants were to elect selectmen and other town officers. And there were two conditions. First, the town was obligated to "procure and settle a learned orthodox minister" within three years. The second condition was a transition measure. Truro's citizens, now independent of Eastham, must pay their share of the provincial taxes due from Eastham for the year. Years later, the township act came to be known as the act of "incorporation," although that word does appear in the act. (See Appendix D.)

. . .

The new town was named Truro, not Dangerfield as the inhabitants had suggested. Dangerfield is a strange name for a town, and historians to date have misunderstood its origin. Frederick Freeman, writing in his *History of Cape Cod* (1858 and 1862), was the first to surmise that the name reflected "the dangers that beset navigation at this locality." Shebnah Rich ignored that surmise, but Deyo's history in 1890 went along with the idea of it as "a name given by early navigators." Henry C. Kittredge suggested in *Cape Cod: Its History and Its People* (1930) that it "was not thought to be a name likely to attract newcomers; so the settlers wisely changed it." The meaning

TRURO: THE STORY OF A CAPE COD TOWN

of Dangerfield for the Pamet settlers, however, had nothing to do with the perils of navigation. The settlers were not mariners, and their records say nothing about shipwrecks or the dangers of navigation. There is no "danger field" in the *Oxford English Dictionary*, although it lists dozens of words that start with "danger."

A more likely source for Dangerfield is the West Midlands of England, where it is a surname. *The Dictionary of Surnames* defines Dangerfield as an "English (Norman) habitation name," an English version of "Angerville," a place name in Normandy, with the French preposition "de," signifying "of" Angerville. A genealogist may someday find an early Truro family with connections to a Dangerfield clan in the West Midlands.

Even though the inhabitants reportedly asked that the town be called Dangerfield, and the first bill in the House designated Dangerfield, there is no record of who suggested it, or why. It does not appear in any records of the Pamet Proprietors. Nor was Dangerfield mentioned in the law that finally granted "Pawmet" township status as Truro.

Someone picked Truro as the new name for the new town. The Pamet settlers might have suggested Pamet, which would have been an appropriate and historically accurate name. It was the name of the area for at least a century. The English settlers, however, were subjects of the British Crown, and the custom was to name colonial towns after English towns or prominent colonists. Truro was a town in England, and its name had not yet been adopted for a town in New England.

Shebnah Rich thought that Thomas Paine might have suggested Truro as the name. Rich visited Truro, England, in 1878 and found Paine and other Truro family names in the city directory; but nothing in the records suggests that the Paines of Cape Cod and the Paines of Truro, England, were related. The first time the name Truro turns up in any colonial records is in Boston two days before passage of the act establishing the town.

Geography suggests why the town was named Truro. The geography of Truro, Cape Cod, and that of the small English city in

Cornwall are remarkably similar. The Cornish city is situated on a short tidal river flowing into a large harbor, Falmouth Harbor, located not far from Land's End of Great Britain. The Pamet settlement was also located on a short tidal river, the Pamet, flowing into a large harbor, Provincetown Harbor, not far from the "land's end" of the Massachusetts Bay Province.

The man who selected Truro as the town's name may have been the governor himself. It was customary for officials in Boston to name towns on Cape Cod. The inhabitants of Monomoy, for example, asked for a proper English name and got Chatham. Whoever selected Truro would have been in a position of power and would have known something about the geography of Truro, England. An official fitting this description was Governor Joseph Dudley, who signed the act naming Truro. Born in America and a Harvard graduate, Dudley nevertheless lived in England thirteen years and was a member of parliament. For eight years, he was lieutenant-governor of the Isle of Wight, close off the south coast of England and not far from the Cornish Truro that would give its name to the new town on Cape Cod.

· · ·

The inhabitants of the Pamet lands, given township status and a new name from the Old World, moved quickly to form their government. Just sixteen days after gaining township status, the leading citizens of the new Town of Truro, most of them Pamet Proprietors, gathered in their meetinghouse for their first town meeting: "Pursuant to an order of the general court, the inhabitants of Truro were warned and met on the first day of August, 1709, and chose officers for said town for the remaining part of the present year. That is to say: for town clerk, John Snow; for selectmen, Thomas Mulford, Jedediah Lumbert and John Snow; for constable, Benj. Small; and for tithing man, Hezekiah Purington; for town treasurer, Constant Freeman; for

fence viewers, Thomas Mulford, Thomas Lumbert and Beriah
Smith; for surveyors of highways, Thomas Mulford and Joseph
Young, senior." For whatever reason, John Snow, not Thomas Paine,
was elected clerk even though Paine had been the Pamet Proprietors' clerk and would serve as Truro's town clerk for many years
after his election to that position six months later.

Although the Pamet Proprietorship ceded its governmental power to the Town of Truro, the Pamet Proprietors continued to own and manage land well into the nineteenth century.
Purchases by individuals of land owned in common began to
accelerate after Pamet became Truro, and by 1720, they had
carved out more than a hundred additional parcels for themselves and for sale to others. In the second half of the 1700s,
only a few meadows, marshes and adjacent beaches remained
in common ownership. The name had changed to Truro Proprietors, and they met once a year to arrange for the sale of the
hay from their land and for the maintenance of fencing. One
year, somebody came up with an idea that may have resulted
in an unusually festive meeting. On April 23, 1781, they voted
"that whoever would make up the fence belonging to the proprietors' meadow this year and pay the charges of setting the
bounds between said proprietors and the common meadow and
would give the most liquor should have the grass growing therein
this year, and it was let at vendue [auction], and Elisha Snow
bid four and half muggs of todde, and it was struck off to him."

In time, only a few parcels of land remained in partnership, and the name changed to the Eastern Harbor Meadows
and Beaches Proprietors. The company must have been dor-
mant for several decades, for in 1834 the Town of Truro, as-
suming ownership of the beaches, sold at auction Beach Point,
the narrow spit of sand between what is now Pilgrim Lake and
Provincetown Harbor. The town anticipated ownership claims
and voted in advance to refer any claims to the county court.
The eight parcels sold for a total of $828 and four years later
the town and the remaining proprietors split the proceeds. With

that settlement on April 28, 1838, the successors to the Pamet Proprietors put their land development company out of business—nearly two centuries after it was formed by the original Pamet Proprietors.

CHAPTER 6:
THE FOUNDING FATHER,
THE MINISTER AND SLAVERY

If anyone can be designated the founder of the settlement that became Truro, it would be Thomas Paine. He was one of the first two settlers on record to build a homestead in what was called Pamet. He soon became the leading landholder and the most influential citizen in governing the town. He was also the town's blacksmith and its first miller. His greatest achievement was obtaining township status for the Pamet settlers. The early history of Truro revolves around Paine; and when he died at age 64, he left Truro a thriving community of farmers, fishermen and whalers with their own minister and local government. The entire Paine family was grandly prolific and devoted to public service; six sons followed him in public service. A grandnephew was one of the signers of *The Declaration of Independence*.

Thomas Paine was born in 1657, the year William Bradford died and Thomas Prence of Eastham succeeded as governor of Plymouth Colony. He was born in Eastham, the third of Thomas and Mary Snow Paine's ten children. His mother's mother was on the *Mayflower* with her parents, the Hopkins. Tradition holds that his paternal grandparents and his father, who was then a boy of 10, arrived in Plymouth a few years after the *Mayflower*.

The elder Paine became a leading citizen of Eastham, following his arrival six years after the settlement was established. He was a successful craftsman, owner of livestock, respected public official and real estate investor. By trade, he was a cooper and millwright. He was making barrels for his neighbors when there were only two dozen homesteads in the tiny outpost of the Plymouth Colony. Later on, at least one of the grain-grinding mills he designed and built was powered by the current in a tidal creek. His fellow townsmen named him to many Eastham town offices, including selectman, treasurer, and tax "ratemaker." For at least four years, Eastham sent him to Plymouth as its representative to the General Court. In 1670, he became a Pamet Proprietor by buying the half-share of his neighbor, Governor Prence. In the same year, he was appointed by Plymouth Colony to enforce the regulations controlling fishermen who dried their catch on shore at the end of Cape Cod. He also seems to have had a financial stake in the fishing privileges and profits there. A recent widower at his death, he left seven sons and two daughters. All six sons served regularly as public officials, five in various Cape Cod towns and one in Connecticut. Their parents had given them all excellent training in reading, writing and arithmetic and set good example for the importance of public service in their towns.

The younger Thomas Paine grew up in Eastham and married Hannah Snow of Plymouth, who bore him fourteen children during their long marriage. Sometime in the 1680s, perhaps earlier, Paine built his house in Pamet. The new home was not far from Pamet Harbor, probably at the head of the Little Pamet River valley, where it turns into Long Nook. The ruin of a cellar hole east of Castle Road, where it crosses the Little Pamet, is thought by some to be the site. Two later records confirm the general location of his homestead. In 1703, the Pamet Proprietors laid out a roadway that went next to "Thomas Paine's land where he now lives" before swinging southeast to get around the head of the Pamet River.

And a few years later one of his sons was given "a bit of land to sit his house upon" next to Paine's land and near a salt-marsh meadow that was "known by the name of Long Nook."

Paine became one of the Pamet Proprietors in 1690 by purchasing his father's half-share in the land development partnership. The purchase made him the majority shareholder among more than a half-dozen others. He served as their clerk—in effect their chief administrator—for more than two decades. Over the years, Paine would acquire land from the Pamet Proprietors until he and his sons owned large tracts on the Pamet River and Little Pamet and into the Long Nook valley.

At the time, Pamet was still a district of the town of Eastham, and Paine was also active in its affairs. He served as an Eastham selectman for nine years; he was Eastham's representative to the provincial legislature in Boston in 1691; and in the late 1690s he was Eastham's town clerk.

As new settlers arrived in Pamet in the first decade of the 1700s, the Pamet Proprietors found themselves in charge of local affairs. Paine was named to most of the three-man committees that were directed to certify boundaries, lay out highways, supervise fencing, purchase land from the Indians, set aside land for a minister, and settle land disputes. When they needed a schoolmaster, Paine was authorized to find one.

. . .

Thomas Paine was a busy man in the early 1700s. Someone would have had to represent the Pamet settlers at the Eastham town meeting in when they won a reduction in taxes, and he would have been the most qualified. He probably was at the Eastham town meeting in 1703 that approved Pamet's separation from Eastham after a heated and unruly debate that led to fines for "persons disorderly or tumultuously speaking." He was also best qualified to represent Truro in Boston in 1705 when the settlers were seeking township status. He was back in Boston in July 1709 when

Pamet's final and successful petition was put before the legislature. When the House of Representatives hesitated and wanted to see if Eastham had any objection to giving up Pamet, he could have called on his brother John, who was Eastham's representative in Boston.

At the first annual town meeting, in 1710, the fifty-four-year-old Paine was elected town clerk, a position he would hold, along with other offices, for most of the rest of his life. In December, town meeting granted him sixty pounds toward construction of a grist mill and specified how much he could take for each bushel of grain he processed. The next year, a vote of town meeting recognized his efforts in "getting a township . . . and getting a minister" and paid him three pounds to cover his expenses. As town clerk and treasurer, Paine entered the order, signed it and paid himself the three pounds.

In addition to the grist mill, Paine had other income-producing occupations. His town duties provided some income, both in cash and in occasional land grants. As the major shareholder among the Pamet Proprietors, he received a share of the proceeds from the sale of lots. Some of his land was in salt marshes, which produced hay for sale or barter. He was a blacksmith, and he and his sons made barrels. His wife and children grew flax and vegetables, including corn and other grains.

· · ·

Most valuable, however, was his skill at building and operating a grist mill, a windmill that ground grain into flour. He learned the trade from his father, who is thought to have built the first grist mill on Cape Cod. David Freeman Hawke in *Everyday Life in Early America* calls it a highly specialized craft combining the skills of carpenter, cooper, joiner, blacksmith and mason. A grist mill was a major capital investment. The grinding stones had to be imported from Europe, then assembled and dressed by an expert. As the miller, Paine had to judge the particular quality of each batch of

grain and adjust the stones accordingly. Millers were given a contract specifying what they could charge. "The grist-mill, in short,
was treated as a public utility," writes Hawke.. A committee of
three was appointed to oversee the performance of the contract. As
clerk, Paine entered and signed the record of the agreement.

Thomas Paine continued to be at the center of town affairs
until his final days. Besides serving as town clerk, he was also a
selectman for six years, treasurer for six years and representative to
Boston five years. He was named to the committee that planned
and supervised the construction of a new meetinghouse, although
he did not live to see the building completed. He died on January
23, 1721, at the age of sixty-four. His gravestone is one of the
oldest in Truro. The oldest is that of his first wife, Hannah, who
had died seven years earlier. Paine's stone in Old North Cemetery
is considered most unusual for Cape Cod. In their book on burying grounds, Diana Hume George and Malcolm A. Nelson say it
is "apparently the work of the North River school of carvers, with
its ominous, lopsided skull, fearsome teeth, and wings that look
more like the legs of a spider than angelic feathers."

He died a wealthy man; his estate was valued at 4,722 pounds,
12 shillings and 9 pence. Almost 90 percent of it was in Truro real
estate. By present-day standards, he was a millionaire. The inventory of his estate, evaluated by three neighbors, contained sixty-
four groups of items, ranging from horses, sheep, lambs and pigs
to horse collars, fish hooks and tobacco. He also owned some
"apothecary stuff" and two spinning wheels. He evidently was an
elegant dresser. The personal goods with the highest value were
"the gentleman's wearing apparel, woolen and linen, silver and
leather, all wigs and snuff," valued at twenty-eight pounds, fourteen shillings and fourteen pence.

Books valued at nine pounds were also among his personal
goods. Paine had no formal education, but the clear, precise, liter-
ate records he wrote as clerk of the Pamet Proprietors and the Town
of Truro testify to his success in educating himself. His books and
his visits to Boston formed his university. The inventory does not

say how many books he had or their titles, but one of them must have been his Bible. The books had about the same value as his nine pair of sheets and six pair of pillowcases.

He divided his extensive real estate holdings among his six surviving sons and four daughters. Two sons, Joshua and Barnabas, inherited the homestead and his blacksmith tools. Paine's oldest surviving son and namesake inherited his windmill, but on condition that he also accept inheritance of two elderly blacks.

Thomas Paine can fairly be considered the founding father of Truro. Not only was he among the first settlers, he also owned or controlled more land from the beginning. As clerk-administrator for the Pamet Proprietors, he had an authoritative voice in virtually every decision. He secured township status for the settlement. With his grist mill, smithy, real estate and elective offices, Thomas Paine was a commanding presence in business and civic affairs. Midway in his career, he was joined by an equally imposing presence, the town's first permanent minister, young John Avery.

. . .

On the first Sunday of November in the year 1711, the inhabitants of Truro, as many as two hundred by then, crowded into their small meetinghouse on top of the Hill of Storms. The meetinghouse was located in the graveyard now called Old North Cemetery. It would be a memorable day; their first minister would be ordained. Among the visitors from out of town were ministers from Harwich, Falmouth and Plymouth. The new town government had allocated ten pounds "to defray the expenses of entertainment of elders, messengers, scholars and gentlemen at Mr. Avery's ordination." The ordination ceremony confirmed the twenty-five-year-old Harvard graduate as the town's first minister. The three visiting ministers performed the laying on of hands; Thomas Paine and six other men "embodied" the new church; and the Avery then preached the first sermon of his long tenure as Truro's minister.

The selection of John Avery proved to be most fortunate both for himself and the town. He served the town for forty-three years as its minister, longer than any other clergyman in the town's history; and he also served as physician, lawyer and blacksmith. His library was the first in town, and he helped hire the first schoolmaster, also a graduate of Harvard.

John Avery was born in Dedham, southwest of Boston, on February 4, 1686. His father and his grandfather, who were born in England, were both blacksmiths; and his father also operated a sawmill. His mother, who had five children, lived to the age of ninety-one. John graduated from Harvard College, which was as much a theological seminary as a liberal arts college in those days. As did most ministers, Avery began his career as a substitute or visiting preacher; and he was in Truro in that capacity just five months after it was established as a town. "Mr. John Avery came to Truro to Preach the Gospel Nov. 11, 1709," says the church record. He was still single, but he may have already been courting Ruth Little of Marshfield, a town halfway between Plymouth and Boston. She knew about young men who aspired to the ministry; her brother was the minister at Plymouth.

The young bachelor made a good impression on the town. The following February, town meeting voted unanimously to hire him as their first resident minister at sixty pounds a year in salary plus twenty pounds toward the construction of a parsonage. Avery, however, wanted to consult with friends and did not immediately accept their offer. Two and a half months passed, and then the town fathers, meeting as the Pamet Proprietors, agreed to offer him thirty-four acres at Highland and ten acres of meadow at East Harbor. They also suggested a ten-year contract. Three weeks later, meeting this time as the town government, they unanimously confirmed their invitation.

Avery, however, now had some concern about his comfort at the pulpit; and the voters had some concern about how long they would be sitting in their hard, wooden pews listening to his sermons. Both concerns were satisfied. The voters directed that the treasurer "as soon as he can with conveniency, buy a cushion for the pulpit and an hourglass and a box to put them in." At the services, a deacon would turn the hourglass so the minister (and the congregation) would know how long he had been preaching.

In May 1710, Avery accepted Truro's call. A committee of three, including Thomas Paine, drew up a contract, which did not include the contemplated ten-year clause. Avery had a contract, but he would not be ordained as minister for more than a year. In November, John Avery and Ruth Little were married. She was a great-granddaughter of a *Mayflower* passenger, Richard Warren, who was assistant governor of Plymouth Colony under Governor William Bradford. Her wedding day was also her twenty-fourth birthday. Newlyweds can use money, and as it happened the provincial government voted in the same month to pay Avery for his services as a visiting preacher in Deerfield the previous year. Ruth and John Avery would have ten children in eighteen years, and forty-four grandchildren. In the generations to follow, five successive John Averys graduated from Harvard.

Within a few months of Avery's ordination, the young couple had a new road from the meetinghouse through the woods to a plateau near the ocean, where they built their house and where the first lighthouse would be built at the end of the century. Their house at Tashmuit, an Indian word for a spring, was probably next door to the present-day Highland House, which houses the museum of the Truro Historical Society. Shebnah Rich wrote in the early 1880s that the Averys' house was located "a short distance north of Highland House and near the well-known spring. It was a two-story house, with ell. The old plaster, hard as granite, and bits of thick English glass can now be found on the spot. The smithy, where the good minister, clad in leather apron, shaped the glowing iron with muscular arm, stood just southwest of his house by the road." The site of the house appears to have been on what is now the ninth green of the Highland Golf Links or just to the north of it.

Avery was also the town's physician, and in his will, he left "a Doctor's chest, Case Drawers, Instruments, bottles and Medicines" valued at more than five pounds. Besides being a blacksmith, he was reputed to be a cabinetmaker. He served on town committees, and he helped to settle disputes in neighboring towns. He and his wife ran a farm and wood lot with the help of several slaves.

When Ruth Avery died in 1732 at the age of forty-six, she was eulogized by Eastham's minister, the Reverend Benjamin Webb. Most of his long *Discourse . . . on the Much Lamented Death of Mrs. Ruth Avery* urged his readers to live a Christian life and die a Christian death. At the end, he praised her piety: "She was a person of bright parts, considerable knowledge, a steady and agreeable temper, uncommon prudence, aptness and industry in governing her household, but what I principally aim at is that she was a person of serious piety." He concluded that she was "a most agreeable and delightful yoke-fellow, a tender, useful and lovely parent, a good neighbor, a pleasant and profitable companion upon all occasions."

As the minister's wife, she had been active in church affairs. She gave the church two pewter tankards for its communion service. On the handles is inscribed, "Ruth Avery to Truro Church, 1721." Minister and wife were one of the two leading couples of Truro at the very beginning of the town's existence.

With the Reverend John Avery as minister, the town in the early 1700s experienced a burst of growth. Not only were the original settlers having large families, but the Pamet Proprietors were dividing their land holdings among themselves at a more rapid pace and selling parcels to newcomers. The congregation soon outgrew its first meetinghouse, and on October 3, 1720, town meeting agreed to build a new one.

. . .

The first meetinghouse had been built in 1704 by the Pamet Proprietors, but nothing beyond its existence is known for sure; even its location has to be deduced. The historian Frederick Freeman said in 1857 that tradition put the meetinghouse and an "ancient graveyard" near the present Christian Union Church in the village of North Truro.

The present Scope, and future Gain of the Christian Life.

A

DISCOURSE

Deliver'd at *Truroe*, October 8. 1732.
Occasioned by the much lamented DEATH
O F

Mrs. *Ruth Avery,*

The vertuous and pious Consort
O F
the Reverend
Mr. 𝔍𝔬𝔥𝔫 𝔄𝔳𝔢𝔯𝔶,
Pastor of the Church of CHRIST there ;
Who deceas'd, *October* 1. 1 7 3 2.
In the 46th Year of her Age.

By *BENJAMIN WEBB*, M. A·
And Pastor of the second Church of CHRIST
in *Eaſtkam.*

Pſal, xxxvii. 37. *Mark the perfect Man, and behold the Upright, for the End of that Man
is Peace,*

Printed at *boſton* in *New-England,*

1 7 3 3.

The eulogy for Ruth Avery, wife of the Reverend John Avery, was preserved in print by the Eastham minister who delivered it. (Photo courtesy of the Department of Rare Books and Manuscripts of the Boston Public Library.)

Shebnah Rich analyzed the records and concluded that the first meetinghouse had been on the same site as its successor–in Old North Cemetery on the Hill of Storms. He gave several reasons. A town record of 1712 says the new road made for Avery went from the first meetinghouse "northeast through the woods" to the Avery house at Highland. Highland, however, is much more easterly from the Christian Union Church. The town laid out a graveyard at the first meetinghouse in 1713, and 1713 is the date of the oldest gravestone in the Old North Cemetery. Finally, Rich noted that town records make no reference to a different site for the second meetinghouse, despite precise details of its construction.

In keeping with the austere custom of the Congregational Church, the second meetinghouse was a simple frame structure forty feet by thirty-six feet and twenty-two feet high. To pay for it, town meeting directed the selectmen to raise 350 pounds through taxes and assessments. Less than a year later, however, the town shifted part of the financial burden from taxpayers to worshipers. This was done by giving each of about a dozen men "the privilege of building a pew" and paying for the "sites of the pews in the new meetinghouse." In this way, thirty-nine pounds of the 350 pounds were raised. Town meeting then went further, directing that "contributions be regularly taken up as soon as the new meetinghouse is finished, and that the inhabitants as often as they contribute, enclose the money so contributed in a piece of paper, with his or her name written thereon." This was a major step toward the separation of church and state finances.

Avery's new and much larger meetinghouse must have been an impressive structure for its day. It served the community for well over a century. Shebnah Rich knew it in his youth and wrote: "For one hundred and twenty years the old meetinghouse in Truro, standing on the 'wind-swept plain,' was the great landmark of Cape Cod . . . seen first as the mariner strained his eyes toward the desired land. . . . The heavy white-oak frame was cut on the spot, and when the old meetinghouse was demolished in 1840, the

The second Congregational meetinghouse stood for 120 years on the Hill of Storms, where it was a prominent landmark for ships at sea. Built in 1720, it replaced the first meetinghouse, which had been built sixteen years before at the same spot. The engraving is from John Warner Barber's *Historical Collections* of 1839, the year before the second meetinghouse was torn down.

timber was as sound as when raised." The meetinghouse was the center of the town. There was no town hall, no post office, no store. The settlers got together at the meetinghouse for religious services on Sundays, and town meetings were held at the meeting-house when they were not held in someone's house.

. . .

When young John Avery arrived in Truro four years out of Harvard, he left behind the libraries and intellectual life of Cambridge and Boston and suddenly became one of the leaders of a few hundred people in a frontier settlement of farmers, fishermen and whalers far out on Cape Cod. Indian families still lived in the town. No one else in town had a formal education until a few years later when he helped the selectmen hire another Harvard graduate as the town's first schoolmaster.

He evidently found time to maintain contacts with intellectu-als in Boston and to collect books for his library. Although noth-ing that he wrote has been found, he might be called the first man of letters in a town that would become a writer's colony in the twentieth century. His personal library, valued at more than thir-teen pounds at his death, represented almost 10 percent of his total estate. Ancient money values and book prices are difficult to estimate, but the library may have been worth several thousand dollars in present-day valuation.

Only four of his books are known. The first, of course, was his own Bible. A second copy was added as a gift to his church. It was inscribed, "The gift of Mr. John Trail, merchant in Boston, to the Church of Christ in Truro, whereof the Rev. Mr. John Avery is Pastor. Dated in Boston N.E., April 27, 1738." The Bible, now held by the Christian Union Church in North Truro, was printed in London in 1708 and re-bound in calfskin. Second in impor-tance to the law of the Bible was civil law, and town meeting voted in 1714, that "Mr. Avery should have the old law book that was bought by the town."

The other two titles were books of American history. He was a
patron of *A Chronological History of New England in the Form of
Annals* (1736) by Thomas Prince of Boston. Prince's slim volume
covered the early explorations of America up to 1633, including
Captain Martin Pring's voyage and the Pilgrims' arrival and settlement. The other was *De Orbe Novo*, a history of voyages of discovery by Christopher Columbus and other navigators, written by
Peter Martyr, the first historian of the Americas.

Martyr's book was a gift of Judge Samuel Sewall, one of Avery's
literary and political acquaintances in Boston. Sewall knew Avery's
parents well and had dined with them in Dedham. A merchant, a
colonial magistrate and the only judge at the Salem witchcraft
trials to repent publicly, he must have been a fascinating dinner
companion for the young minister from Truro. He was also the
first prominent abolitionist. In 1700, he published an eloquent
anti-slavery tract, but he was too far ahead of the times. Mainly, he
is remembered for his voluminous diaries. His entry for March 20,
1718, reads: "Mr. Avery of Truro dines with us. I gave him a volume of Peter Martyr."

Avery had bookplates that said: "John Avery. His Book. 1741."
It's likely that he loaned books to his neighbors, and although his
library was a private collection, it might be seen, without much
exaggeration, as Truro's first lending library.

· · ·

Except for Avery's library, books were scarce and public libraries
non-existent in colonial Truro. The New England colonists, nevertheless, put high priority on public education, and Avery would
be involved in selecting a schoolmaster for Truro. Plymouth Colony
required towns of fifty families or more to hire a schoolmaster.
Towns with twice that number were to include Latin and Greek in
the curriculum. For a time, Plymouth reserved the taxes on fishermen working at the end of Cape Cod to help pay for education in
the colony.

Before Pamet became Truro, the settlers were authorized by Eastham to hire their own schoolmaster "to teach their children to read the Bible." Thomas Paine, who lived in Pamet and who was the Eastham town clerk, was directed to engage a schoolmaster, but he was not successful. Six years after it became a town, Truro still had no schoolmaster, and Barnstable County officials ordered it "to answer . . . for not having a schoolmaster in said town according to law." The town reacted quickly. Town meeting in 1715 voted to ask Avery to join the selectmen in the search for a schoolmaster. In the first three months of the following year, no fewer than four town meetings were held on the subject, and the town hired as its first schoolmaster, Samuel Spear, twenty years old and a graduate of Harvard.

Spear held his first classes in two Truro homes, one south of the Pamet River and the other north of it. Soon he was teaching in four different homes in four different neighborhoods, with classes running two or three months in each house. Public education in Truro was launched, although it would be almost ten years before the first schoolhouse was built.

For the next decade, Spear and his successors taught sessions at houses in three or four neighborhoods. The kitchen-dining room was the classroom. A schoolmaster might find before him anywhere from ten to twenty pupils, ranging in age from six to twenty. That would indicate a total enrollment of about forty to eighty pupils, representing about half the town's boys. Schooling was primarily for boys. Although there were only sixty or seventy families in Truro in the early 1700s, many were quite large. Hannah and Thomas Paine had fourteen children; Ruth and John Avery had ten.

The one-room, neighborhood schoolhouse celebrated in American history would be the rule for more than two centuries, whether in a home or in one of the many schoolhouses that were built beginning about 1725. Efforts for the first schoolhouses began on April 29, 1724, when the Truro Proprietors set aside two parcels of land for school buildings, one just south of the Pamet River and the other at the northerly side of Long Nook near the Paine family property. The town was divided into neighborhood school districts, and each district built its own schoolhouse or used someone's kitchen-dining area. As the pupil population grew and shifted, the number of districts would vary from three or four in the early 1700s to as many as eleven in 1858.

. . .

The Reverend John Avery died on April 23, 1754, in his sixty-eighth year. His gravestone in Old North Cemetery is one of the few that carries a descriptive epitaph:

> In this dark Cavern, in this lonesome Grave,
> Here lies the honest, pious, virtuous Friend;
> Him, kind Heaven to us Priest & Doctor gave,
> As such he lived; as such we mourn his End.

Instead of usual death's-head skull with wings, symbolizing the body's death and the soul's flight to heaven, his stone bore the customary round face with expressive eyes and eyebrows and a wide, flat nose.

A half-century later, the Reverend James Freeman, a Boston minister whose parents came from Truro and who knew Truro well, wrote a short characterization: "The inhabitants of Truro who personally knew Mr. Avery speak of him in very respectful terms. As a minister, he was greatly beloved and admired by his people, being a good and useful preacher, of an exemplary life and conversation. As a physician, he was no less esteemed. He always manifested great tenderness for the sick; and his people very sensibly felt their loss in his death."

Avery was the first of three Harvard graduates whose ministries spanned the town's first 118 years, from 1710 to 1828. His successor was the Reverend Caleb Upham, an outspoken patriot, who was in turn succeeded by the Reverend Jude Damon. Damon served forty-two years, one year short of Avery's record. Very few colonial towns enjoyed such long-lasting relations with their ministers.

After Ruth's death, Avery married another Ruth. She was Ruth Knowles, a great-granddaughter of Governor Thomas Prence, one of the first Pamet Proprietors. And in 1748, three years after his second wife died, he married his third, the widow Mary Rotch of Provincetown and Boston.

Of the seven surviving Avery children, only Job stayed in Truro, and he had already been designated the principal beneficiary of his father's real estate: "To my son Job Avery I have already given by deed of gift my Lands in this Town of Truro my Dwelling-house and buildings appertaining thereto, my Pew in the meetinghouse, as also my young negro man named Larned, nevertheless it is my will that my son Job take care to make out to Mary, my beloved wife, the privileges expressed to her in this my last Will and Testament."

Mary Avery and her twice-widowed husband had signed a pre-nuptial agreement that provided for her, and in his will he bequeathed to her the use "of my westerly bedroom and study" and the use of a wood lot as long as she was his widow. She died, however, the following year. Job and his wife, Jane Thatcher Avery of Eastham, brought up nine children on the family homestead at Highland. Job served several years as a selectman and as town clerk and treasurer.

The other Avery children had moved off-Cape. John, the eldest, was a prosperous merchant and distiller of liquors in Boston. He exported provisions to the West Indies and imported slaves. Well-established in Boston, he did not share in the bequests of real estate but did inherit his father's silver tankard. His son, also John, was an influential revolutionary in the War of Independence and the first secretary of the Commonwealth of Massachusetts, a position he held for thirty years. The Avery family has kept track of its genealogy, and more than two centuries after the Reverend John

Avery died half a dozen direct descendants of Truro's first minister were living in town.

Avery's material success is evident in his will. The long inventory of his furniture, clothing, linens, tools, livestock and other household goods comes to a total value of 148 pounds. A quarter of it was in livestock, including twenty-nine sheep, four cows and five steers. Among the household goods were a pair of tobacco tongs, an eight-day clock and three wigs.

He also left bequests of a number of slaves. His eldest daughter had died at age twenty-nine, and to her three children he gave the household goods that he had given their mother and also "my Negro girl named Phillis." His second daughter, Elizabeth Draper, could keep the household goods she had already received "together with my Indian girl Sarah, who now lives with her."

At the very end of his will, he provided for two more blacks in a way that indicates that he did not want them sold out of the Avery family, although he stops short of freeing them: "Further it is my will that my two Negroes Jack and Hope have the liberty to choose their master among all my children, and they with whom they shall live give nothing for them, and that they shall not be sold from my children to any person whatsoever, and this was added before I signed this will and testament." Which families Jack and Hope chose is not known.

. . .

The word "slave" does not appear in Avery's will or that of Thomas Paine, nor in town records. The slaves were referred to as "servants" and were called "my Indian," "my Negroes," or "his" man or woman. They often lived in the same house with the families that owned them, sometimes in an outbuilding. They worked alongside whites as domestics, farm hands and laborers. Anecdotes about Truro slaves that were passed from generation to generation, however, were patronizing; and, in fact, the only recorded descriptions of any

Truro individuals of the time are anecdotal recollections about three blacks named Pomp, Joe and Hector. No surnames were ever given.

The apparent lack of concern for fellow human beings who had been sold into slavery and the casual acceptance of the practice are difficult to accept. Historians, however, note that in the 1700s slavery was considered a legitimate institution protected by law and that no concerted opposition developed until just before the American Revolution. In their 1994 history of slavery, John Hope Franklin and Alfred A. Moss, Jr., write that while there were some anti-slavery protests in the mid-1700s "even in the Northern colonies, where there was no extensive use of slaves, the majority of the articulate colonists paid little attention to slavery." The same no doubt held true for Truro. If, for example, Avery, a slave owner, subscribed to the abolitionist sentiments of Judge Sewall, he left no record of it.

Indians could lose their freedom and become slaves in several different ways. Some were prisoners of war who had been assigned or sold to families. They could also be put into bondage as punishment for crimes and non-payment of debt. As early as 1674, Plymouth Colony passed a law ordering that an Indian who stole from the English must make a four-fold restitution in payments of some sort or must work it off as a servant or farm hand. If he failed to make restitution, he could be sold for his theft at the discretion of two of the magistrates. Legislation in the same year made it lawful to sell Indians if they ran away while working off their debts.

Young Indians who "spend their time idly" could be forced into a kind of slavery by the selectmen or town constable acting on a complaint. Indian idlers would be assigned "to some persons that shall keep them to work and not abuse them" for some unspecified time. If they ran away they would owe twice the time they were away. The unscrupulous colonist who wanted free labor could take advantage of these Plymouth Colony laws. The records, however, do not indicate how Indians became slaves in Truro.

At least seven Truro families had a total of eighteen slaves or more, over two or three generations. The family names were Avery,

Paine, Collins, Mulford, Lumbert, Snow and Dyer. Nathaniel Dyer owned a black woman named Peggy, who died in 1805 at age forty-two; she was probably the second-last slave in Truro. John Snow sold a black woman named Moll Hector to Captain Thomas Lumbert; the bill of sale was read in town meeting on January 30, 1753, because of a claim for expenses by Samuel Dyer. Moll Hector was described as "the Negro woman, deceased, about whom there has been so much controversy." The issue seemed to have been whether the town should reimburse Samuel Dyer for taking care of Moll in her final years after she had been freed–or abandoned.

The Reverend John Avery had seven slaves at various times, two of them Indians. His eldest son became a slave trader in Boston, and other sons and daughters inherited five slaves. Job Avery, who inherited a black man named Larned with the homestead, also owned a black woman named Violet. She was baptized on August 24, 1760, and was accepted as a full member of the Truro church. Job Avery also took possession of a black man who was on the British warship *Somerset* when it went aground off Truro during the Revolutionary War. John Greenough of Wellfleet, who was supervising the salvage, reported that "there is in the keeping of Job Avery of Truro a Negro man formerly of Virginia or North Carolina who came ashore in the *Somerset*; Mr. [Job] Avery will not deliver him." Job Avery was exercising salvage rights in keeping the black man.

Religiously inclined slaves were regularly admitted as full members of the Congregational Church. Besides Violet, four others became church members. They were "Pegge, Indian servant to Rev. J. Avery," "Hope Negro servant," probably the Hope named in Avery's will; "a Negro servant of Elder Mulford," whose name, perhaps "Casse," is difficult to decipher; and "Ezra, Negro," who appears in the records because he was twice assigned to work for a time at the Brattle Street church in Boston.

Three generations of Paines had at least six black slaves. Thomas Paine, the long-time clerk of the Pamet Proprietors and the

Town of Truro, bequeathed in his will two elderly slaves in a way that would ensure their care. He noted that they "are now grown in years and more likely to be charge than profit to him or any that shall take said charge of them." To induce his heirs to take care of them, he specified that his windmill–a most valuable asset–would go to his eldest son provided he accepted responsibility for the slaves. If he declined, then one of the other sons could have the windmill and the two slaves. His will names them but the handwriting is not clear.

Shebnah Rich relates anecdotes about the Paine family slaves, in particular Pomp, who came to a tragic end, and Hector, a beloved local character who was the last slave in Truro. Rich heard the stories from oldtimers whose memories went back to the 1700s. He says Pomp was purchased by Jonathan Paine from the captain of a Truro whaling ship. Pomp "performed his duties as a slave faithfully" but was morbidly homesick. He believed in "metempsychosis, or transmigration of soul." Rich relates Pomp's final hours: "One day, when the longing for kith and kin and home was deep in his heart, he took a jug of water, a loaf of bread and a rope, and went into a thick woodlot belonging to his master. Selecting a high tree, the stump of which may yet be seen [in the 1880s], he placed his jug of water and loaf of bread at the foot of the tree to sustain him over the journey for Africa's sunny fountains. Many days after, his body was found hanging to the tree; his soul had gone to the God who gave it, in whose merciful hands we leave him." The wood lot, located in Long Nook, which was the Rich family neighborhood, became known as "Pomp's Lot."

In the same passage, Rich terms slavery "unaccountable and irreconcilable in our day." He deplores "the villainous traffic in African slaves" but notes that in the 1600s and well into the 1700s slavery was generally accepted as a "fair field for enterprise" and was "defended by the press, the pulpit, the platform and the sword of this Christian nation." He cites a distant relative, Captain Matthias Rich, a native of Truro, as one who made a fortune in the cruel business of trading and shipping slaves. Captain Rich, who died about 1810, lived for many years in Boston but moved to Baltimore, when, Rich says tellingly, "public sentiment became too strong to face." The captain's son, says Rich, had large plantations in Mississippi.

. . .

The slave named Hector lived a long and legendary life in Truro, but only after what must have been a wrenching separation from his mother in childhood. Like Pomp, he was owned by the Paine family, although only for the first three years of his life. Rich heard Hector's story from a Paine descendant who was in his eighties when Rich was writing his history.

As Rich tells it, Jonathan Paine had a black named Joe who hinted that he wanted a wife. Paine bought one for him in Boston. Joe's introduction to the woman is described by Rich in a melodramatic way, but the anecdote is at least third-hand. Joe's wife soon gave birth to Hector. But when Hector was still a child he was sold to Benjamin Collins for thirty pounds. In a bill of sale dated October 7, 1726, Paine agreed to "sell one negro boy named Hector, about three years of age, unto said Collins . . . his heirs and assigns." children.

Hector became a famous local character. Rich says that for a long time "as black as Hector" was a local saying. Places were named after him: Hector's Bridge, Hector's Nook and Hector's Stubble, but these names have all faded with time. When Hector was about twenty-four years old, he was baptized by Avery. A devout Christian, he prayed aloud while working in the fields.

Hector was remembered in a paper read before the Truro Lyceum by Joshua Dyer in the mid-1800s: "There are those now living who remember Hector, an old man, with bleached locks and dim eyes, struggling amid the last waves of a toilsome life. He sighed not for Africa. Truro was his home, and he knew no other. During a long life he had scarce wandered beyond the sound of his lowing herds, or the meanderings of the Pamet, which he had paddled so often in his little canoe." Collins may have sold Hector to someone named Sawyer, for Hector has that surname at his death. The Reverend Jude Damon, Truro's minister at the time, recorded it as: "Sawyer, Hector, a. 83y.6m, a black man, Feb. 1, 1807." According to Rich, Hector was the last slave in Truro. His burial place is unknown.

CHAPTER 7:
TRURO COPES WITH PROVINCETOWN

From its very beginning, and on and off for most of its history, Truro has found itself at odds with Provincetown on a variety of issues ranging from cattle grazing on the wrong side of the boundary in the eighteenth century to schooling and municipal water in the twentieth. In the early 1700s, the problems stemmed mainly from geographic and demographic conditions that made the Province Lands, later to be Provincetown, hard to reach and hard to govern.

Geographically, the Province Lands, even though adjacent, were remote from Truro. East Harbor was a barrier to direct travel by land. There was no bridge across its inlet from Provincetown Harbor. The only way to reach Provincetown was to go cross-country around the north side of East Harbor over the wind-swept, ever-shifting sand dunes along the Atlantic Ocean. Ocean breakthroughs in big storms could block the route. The blinding sand storms and impossibility of maintaining a roadway across miles of barren dunes would shock travelers of the early 1800s, who left records of their experience.

Demographically, Truro's settlers were farmers and artisans who were tied to their land. Families arrived and stayed. Truro's population grew steadily, and the town became a tightly knit community. The inhabitants had little to do with their neighbors to the north. The Province Lands people were different. They were mainly itinerant fishermen, the "sojourners," who came and went with the fishing seasons. Some may have built houses and stayed for several years, perhaps as traders or boatbuilders, but often enough they, too, would move on to other fishing spots. They were not the kind of men who improved their property, paid taxes, performed civic duties and left estates to their descendants.

The visiting fishermen were a rowdy bunch, shocking to the God-fearing citizens of Truro. Samuel Spear, Truro's first schoolmaster, who later became the first minister in the Province Lands, described it as a tough parish: "A seaport place whereto there is great resort by fishermen and others who frequently carry it very disorderly amongst us by excessive drinking, quarreling, profanation of the Sabbath, etc., the like vicious practices being very much to the dishonor of Almighty God, a grief to all sober persons." The Province Lands neighborhood near a small harbor behind Race Point was called "Helltown."

Truro's long history of troubles with Provincetown began soon after it won township status. The main issues were not only environmental but maritime, a perceived threat to navigation in Provincetown Harbor. At East Harbor, over-grazing and deforestation was exposing the top soil and sand to the winds off the ocean. The blowing sand was silting up the shallow harbor East Harbor and its marshes, and it was thought that silting was shrinking Provincetown Harbor near the entrance to East Harbor. (See map in chapter 14.) Both towns appealed to the provincial legislature in Boston. In 1714, the legislature enacted the first and most significant of dozens of laws passed during the 1700s to settle disputes between the two towns. It also put a reluctant Truro in charge of the Province Lands.

The act of 1714 covered three different issues. It prohibited taking turpentine from pine trees around Provincetown Harbor, a practice that killed the trees, denuded the land and let the wind blow sand into the harbor, which was "in danger of being damnified, if not made wholly unserviceable." It also ordered the Province Lands inhabitants to hire a "learned, orthodox minister of good conversation" at sixty pounds a year. To help pay the minister's salary, the act levied a tax of four pence per man per week "coming to abide or sojourn there." And it made the Province Lands a district annexed to Truro. If the tax revenues fell short of the sixty pounds a year, Truro could try to tax the Province Lands inhabitants to make up the difference.

A boundary between Truro and the new district was needed, so eight Truro men met to lay out the line from Provincetown Harbor to the Atlantic Ocean by compass sightings. Lacking any permanent landmarks, they did their best with a stump, the remains of a whale's carcass and trees:

> Beginning at the easterly end of a cliff near the cape harbor, called by the Indians, Ketsconcoyet and by the English Cormorant Hill, at the jaw bone of a whale, set in the ground there by the side of a red oak stump, and thence running by a marked range trees near on a north and by west line about half a point more westerly to a marked pine tree standing by a reedy pond called by the Indians Weochnotckcoyisset, and from thence by marked range trees to a high hill on the back side near the North Sea [Atlantic Ocean] with a red cedar post set in the said hill.

Their line was well northwest of East Harbor and almost a mile into what is now Provincetown. In the early nineteenth century, Truro would give up land to Provincetown three times. The boundary was moved in 1813, 1829, and finally in 1836 to a line that crossed the end of East Harbor, a more natural boundary.

In the first year of its responsibility for the Province Lands, Truro had a mini-rebellion on its hands. Some people in the Province Lands refused "to do their duty or be governed" by Truro.

They no doubt balked at paying the taxes. Truro petitioned the legislature "that Cape Cod [i.e. the Province Lands] may be declared and made a part of the town of Truro so that the inhabitants thereof may be under the government of the said town, or that Cape Cod may not belong to Truro and so the inhabitants thereof are not under the jurisdiction and government of the said town." Truro had had enough and was ready to give up its jurisdiction over the Province Lands. Boston directed the inhabitants of the Province Lands not only to respond to Truro's petition but to explain why they had not hired a minister.

But the mini-rebellion faded; and two years later, Truro received a grant of 150 pounds from the provincial government in Boston to build a meetinghouse in the Province Lands. Thomas Paine was one of three men who would see to the construction.

Eventually, the inhabitants of the Province Lands won their independence from Truro—and won it on their own terms. The legislature in Boston in 1727 created a township called, appropriately enough, Provincetown. (The fishermen in residence had suggested "Herringtown.") The short act conceded almost everything to the inhabitants, who were complaining that they labored under "difficulties and inconveniences." It put no restrictions on fishing, whaling, or cutting down trees for lumber. It also repealed the prohibition against tapping pine trees for turpentine. Probably with the aid of Boston merchants, the fishermen and whalers had won over the legislators. Provincetown was founded. Truro's responsibility for the district had lasted just thirteen years.

Despite the generous autonomy given Provincetown, the new town went into a decline. In a little more than a decade, it was petitioning for help to support a minister. The petition said the town was still "a place of great resort of people [fishermen] at some seasons of the year," but its inhabitants were "exceedingly reduced . . . both in numbers and estate." There were only twenty families, "and those generally very poor." By 1748, Provincetown would have only two or three families, according to the historian Frederick Freeman. Recovery began in the mid-1700s, and

Provincetown would eventually surpass Truro in population and commercial activity.

And there were boundary disputes. Provincetown asked the Boston legislature for a law to stop Truro farmers from letting their cattle graze in the Province Lands. The proprietors in Truro countered by seeking legislation to protect their meadows at East Harbor. An act passed in 1739 prohibited Provincetown cattle from grazing on Truro beaches and meadows. The proprietors could seize errant cattle and horses and hold them for damages. Provincetown farmers countered the following year by complaining to the legislature that Truro farmers were "driving down vast herds" of cattle to feed in the Province Lands. Truro town meeting asked to be heard on the matter, citing the damages done to them. The charges and counter-charges continued through most of the century.

The silting of Provincetown Harbor was an issue not only for both towns but especially for Boston merchants, who recognized its great importance to navigation and the fishing industry. In 1743, they petitioned the provincial legislature to take some action. Provincetown and Truro had also sent in petitions about the condition of the harbor. The legislature directed a committee to do an on-site inspection and, while they were at it, to tell the inhabitants of Truro "that they do not drive any cattle on the beach to the northward of East Harbor meadows in the meantime."

The committee reported that beach grass prevented loose sand from blowing into the salt-hay meadows if livestock were kept off it and recommended that Truro's proprietors fence in their cattle, but it came down harder on Provincetown. Provincetown was ordered to impound wayward livestock, share no more than three yoke of oxen and one bull, and limit each family to one horse and one cow. Two cows, however, could be kept by anyone who had "a license to keep a house of public entertainment." These laws were renewed every few years throughout the 1700s, apparently without much effect.

. . .

Coping with Provincetown, while bothersome for town officials, could not have been a major preoccupation for most of Truro's citizens. Like most colonists in New England towns in the early 1700s, they were hard at work farming their fields and orchards, cutting timber and tending to livestock. In addition, many farmers also became fishermen, whalemen and boat-builders. They caught fish in Cape Cod Bay, harpooned whales there and harvested oil and blubber from the pilot whales that beached themselves or were driven ashore. The more intrepid sailors joined the off-shore fishing fleets and whaling ships, and Truro mariners would be notable for their adventurous whaling voyages to distant seas–some became well-known captains–as well as for the disasters that often befell their fishing boats.

Truro was a typical farming community with the usual problems. Livestock owners let their animals loose on land set aside as commons for grazing and had to begin branding horses and cattle. Some allowed their swine and rams to roam free, and the town tried year after year to control the troublesome animals by fines or confiscation. The issue continued even into the 1930s. Troublesome, too, were wild predators–crows, wolves and foxes–and the town paid bounties to hunters who killed them.

With Thomas Paine as town clerk, the records of the early 1700s became more detailed about town affairs, from bridges across the Pamet to bounties on crows. Bridge construction and maintenance were controversial. Town meeting decided in 1737 that Truro was too poor to build one and maintain it against the strong tidal flows. Besides, it would hinder scows carrying wood and hay to Provincetown. Within a few years they did build a bridge across the Pamet, but disputes about who would maintain it went on for decades.

The only personal record of life in the new Town of Truro is a fragment of diary kept by Moses Paine (1695-1764), who was a son a Thomas Paine. His entry on the drowning of Captain Doane

and his crew of five is the first record of fatalities in Truro's long
history of maritime disasters. The following diary entries survived:

May 27,   Being Lord's Day I went to meeting at Truro, and Mr.
           Avery's text in the forenoon was Psalms 66:18 verse and
           the afternoon it was Genesis 50:5. This day I was re-
           ceived into full communion with the church. O my
           Lord, my God, help me, poor unworthy creature, to
           keep covenant with my God. There was also Isaac Cole
           and Robert Freeman taken into the church and also
           Joseph Smalley. Be pleased O Lord to help us and pre-
           serve us by thy mighty power through faith unto salva-
           tion.
May 30,   this day my uncle John Paine's wife died and that very
           suddenly.
July 2,   this morning Joshua Doane's wife died.
Aug. 6,   this day at night was a great storm of wind and rain,
           which did much damnify Indian corn.
Aug. 10,   this day Mr. Hubbard came to my uncle John Paine's
           to keep school [in Eastham].
Oct. 14,   being Lord's Day, and an excessive wind so that there
           was no meeting in Eastham.
Nov. 29,   this day Capt. Joshua Doane, Thomas Pitty, George
           Vickerie, William Ghustan, Joseph Sweat and Sam
           Charles were drowned in going from Eastern Harbor to
           Billingsgate.
Dec. 16,   this day was a public thanksgiving throughout this prov-
           ince.

The official records kept by Town Clerk Thomas Paine and by the
Pamet Proprietors testify also to the environmental damage to Truro's
fragile fields, forests, and marshes caused by ever-increasing farming and grazing. In one instance, the Truro Proprietors acted to
preserve the salt marshes they owned at East Harbor, which they
often called meadows, by ordering fencing put up against the blow-

ing sand at East Harbor. In 1718, they said it was "evident that if some speedy course not be taken, the meadow would all be lost." A decade later, they were still ordering that fences be built. Hay from tidal salt marshes was a major crop for the early settlers and would be important even into the twentieth century. Salt-marsh hay grows, not throughout the marshes, but around the edges that are flooded only twice a month by the highest of the high tides, which occur at the time of new and full moon. These salt-marsh edges were vulnerable to being buried by blowing sand..

· · ·

In the mid-1700s, Truro's colonists again found themselves not only threatened by enemy invasion but entangled with Provincetown over what to do about defenses. In the French and Indian War, known in Europe as the Seven Years War, the British were contending with the French over territory in North America. Truro was drawn into an uneasy alliance with Provincetown to defend against invasion by the French from Canada. The French were once again threatening the New England coastline, and Cape Cod was an obvious objective. Truro found itself bound to the fortunes of Provincetown because of the strategic value of Provincetown Harbor.

Provincetown's few inhabitants petitioned Boston to direct Truro to help them stand watch. Truro petitioned Boston for five cannons and ammunition "to secure the navigation frequently at anchor in said harbor as also to protect the inhabitants of the towns of Truro and Provincetown." Boston agreed on April 2, 1757, to fund gun emplacements to be built by men from the two towns. There's no indication, however, that the emplacements were ever built or that the cannons ever arrived. Truro did agree to provide men to share the watch for French warships or raiding parties.

The town also agreed to take custody of a French Acadian family for the duration of the war. The British had deported thousands of French Acadians from British-held Nova Scotia. Most of them were wandering the American colonies, some as far as Louisiana where they became known as Cajuns. Three dozen turned up in Sandwich in 1760 in seven small boats. The Acadians were arrested as enemy aliens and distributed to towns from Plymouth to Truro, where they were interned for the rest of the war. One Acadian family, Peter Trahone, his wife and two children, were assigned to Truro.

The threat of enemy raids was serious enough that Truro men made sure their guns were ready even on Sunday, which was strictly a day of rest and worship. The town fathers agreed that "a suitable number of guns and ammunition be brought to the meetinghouse on the Sabbath to be ready in case there should be an alarm." The town fathers would recall their parents' tales of French raiding parties during King William's War. French ships could drop anchor in Provincetown Harbor at any time. The town also provided soldiers, paying $15 to anyone who joined the British to fight the French. In less than two decades, the alliances would be reversed: Truro men would be fighting the British, and the French would eventually join the colonials in their Revolutionary War.

CHAPTER 8:
A PIONEER WHALING TOWN

The Truro of Thomas Paine and the Reverend John Avery was a whaling town in their time and for several generations after them. Even though its harbor could not accommodate the large whaling ships that hunted in distant oceans, Truro's whaling men became renowned for their skill; three of them became famous captains. Many had undoubtedly honed their skills harpooning whales close to home in Cape Cod Bay. They were adventurous boys and men who signed on with long-voyage whaling ships sailing from Boston, Provincetown, Wellfleet and other New England ports. Cape Cod historian Henry C. Kittredge said the history of Truro, Wellfleet and Provincetown "comprises the bulk of the history of the Cape long-voyage whale-fishery," and Truro was "the pioneer in this hazardous business" on Cape Cod.

Truro's reputation as a pioneer rests primarily on the exploits of Captain Henry Atkins, a Truro proprietor who began whaling voyages as early as 1720. He went to distant oceans in search of whales at about the same time that Nantucket was building up its long-voyage whaling fleet, the first in the colonies. Atkins emerges from the records as a major figure in early whaling and a colorful character who knew how to draw attention to his exploits.

In 1729, Captain Atkins took his ship, the *Whale*, from Boston into Davis Strait between Greenland and Baffin Island, near the Arctic Circle. His voyage was probably the first from the colonies that reached that far north. On his return passage, he explored the coast of Labrador and traded with Indians. He would make a second trip to Labrador thirty years later. Accounts of both voyages by an unknown narrator turned up in the papers of Francis Bernard, governor of Massachusetts Bay Province. In the accounts, Atkins noted the Indians' beaver furs, the forests and the harbors. He suggested the area could support trading posts.

On a whaling voyage to Davis Strait in 1732, he brought back a polar bear cub, the first ever seen in the colonies. He exhibited the bear at a Boston wharf and gave the *Boston Weekly News-Letter* a lengthy, lurid account of the capture that dramatized the ferocity of the mother bear. (In his *History of the American Whale Fishery* Alexander Starbuck says that this voyage by Atkins was "probably the first voyage to this locality from the colonies." But the account of his 1729 voyage, found in the governor's papers, puts him there three years earlier.)

Soon, Provincetown whalers were also working in Davis Strait. In *Follow the Whale* Ivan T. Sanderson says, "Provincetown specialized in the northern fishery, and by 1737 she had a dozen 100-ton vessels trespassing upon the Dutch sea domains in Davis Strait." Truro probably supplied crew members for Atkins's ship, which sailed from Boston, and for the early expeditions from Provincetown and other ports as well, although that has not been confirmed.

One of the first American whaling captains to take sperm whales, Atkins contributed to a research paper published in 1725 by the Royal Society of London. Paul Dudley, author of the paper, said that Atkins provided "the best and most exact account of ambergris." Atkins described the peculiar substance and how he extracted it from the bowels of sperm whales. Ambergris, used as perfume fixative, was a very valuable product for whalers.

Back in Truro in 1760, Atkins, sixty-four years old, was credited with a vivid description of whales in abundance in

Provincetown Harbor. Ezra Stiles, a visitor to the Outer Cape, heard about it and wrote in his diary that Atkins had seen as many whales "at one time as would have made a bridge from the end of the Cape to Truro shore, which is seven miles across and would require two thousand whales." Allowing for a bit of tongue-in-cheek exaggeration by the ancient mariner, the observation still suggests there were a lot of whales off Truro's bayshore in the mid-1700s.

. . .

Two other Truro captains won fame as the first whalers to reach the Falkland Islands off the tip of South America. James Freeman, who called Truro whalers "some of the most dextrous whalemen in the world," tells of the captains' achievements in his description of Truro, published twenty years later: "Two inhabitants of Truro, Captain David Smith and Captain Gamaliel Collings, were the first who adventured to the Falkland Islands in pursuit of whales. This voyage was undertaken in 1774 by the advice of Admiral Montague of the British Navy and was crowned with success. Since that period, the whalemen of Truro have chiefly visited the coasts of Guinea and Brazil." Admiral John Montagu, who had served in the Bay of Biscay whaling waters, commanded the British fleet in the American colonies from 1771 to 1774, just before Smith and Collings voyaged to the Falkland Islands.

Their achievement was praised (if not by name) by the British orator Edmund Burke the following year in his famous speech to Parliament that defended the rebellious colonies' rights. British whalers lagged, he said, while New Englanders "penetrated to the deepest frozen recesses of Hudson's Bay and Davis Strait" and made the Falkland Islands, too remote for the British, a stopping-place for New England whalers "in the progress of their victorious industry." (Throwing some doubt, however, on Freeman's claim that the two Truro captains were there first is a comment by Hector St. John de Crèvecoeur seven years earlier about Nantucket whalers:

"Would you believe that they had already gone to the Falkland Islands?")

. . .

Deep-sea whaling may appear in popular literature to be a roman-tic adventure. Certainly, some young Truro farmers readily signed on for the sailing adventure, the thrill of the hunt, and especially a chance to get rich with a share in the profits. That may have been true in the early days of long-voyage whaling. Later on and into the 1800s, however, they found themselves thrown into close liv-ing quarters with ruffians and criminals. In the quest for profits in a dirty, dangerous business, ruthless captains turned whaling ships into floating prisons. Working conditions were so bad that some crews were driven to mutiny, the most serious crime at sea. Only the desperate and the hardened could make a career of it.

Long-voyage whaling could also lock the farmer-sailor into a cycle of debt. Edward Augustus Kendall, a British writer who toured America and stopped at Truro in 1807, took pains to debunk the illusion of whaling supporting happy, prosperous families. As he describes it at some length, a Truro whaleman would sign on for a share of the voyage profits and use that as security for a line of credit with merchants for his outfit and for his family to draw on while he was away. His debts, however, were rarely covered by his share of the whaling profits and the farmer-sailor would be obliged to sign on again to try to catch up. Kittredge saw the evils of long-voyage whaling, too. He went so far as to celebrate the wreck in 1925 of the *Wanderer*, New Bedford's last whaling ship. "The world," he wrote, "is a better place without long-voyage whaling than it ever was with it."

Long-voyage whaling flourished in the 1700s and early 1800s, but whales and whaling have figured in Truro's history from the time of the Pilgrims to the present day. The Pilgrims saw whales near the *Mayflower* in Provincetown Harbor in 1620 and wished they had harpoons to catch them. The ship's captain and mate thought the whaling in Cape Cod Bay would be better than at Greenland; they planned to return the next year. When the Pilgrims had to decide whether to homestead in Truro or look further, their arguments for staying included good whaling: "For we saw daily great whales of the best kind for oil and bone come close aboard our ship and in fair weather swim and play about us."

The Pamet settlers witnessed the strange phenomenon of groups of small whales that swam onto the bay shore beaches and died. They harvested these whales on the beaches just as the Indians had done before them. In one of their earliest official acts, the Pamet Proprietors drew up an agreement with Indians that confirmed the settlers' rights to one-eighth of the whales the Indians found on the beaches that they had sold to the Pamet Proprietors. The mass strandings every few years would provide Truro inhabitants with a rich harvest of whale oil for more than two centuries.

The beached whales were pilot whales, which later were also called blackfish. For reasons still unclear, groups of pilot whales from time to time swim onto beaches and expire. They do this in various parts of the world on beaches that usually face west. Such strandings have occurred every few years on the bayshore beaches of Truro and other towns on the Outer Cape. Despite their names, these mammals of the ocean are actually large dolphins about twelve to eighteen feet long. They seem to be gregarious, and early observers thought the pods followed a leader, or pilot. Their fatal strandings occur in groups from half a dozen to several hundreds. Scientists still do not understand why they do it, although there are many theories.

Harvesting stranded pilot whales on the beach quickly led to harpooning whales offshore. By the early 1700s, Truro settlers were whaling on Cape Cod Bay. First they went out in small boats to drive pilot whales to shore by smacking their oars on the water. Later, they began chasing down and harpooning larger species and towing the carcasses to shore. This near-shore whaling lacked the romance of the high seas, but it could be done at home and was much safer. Throughout the 1700s, Truro men not only went out on long-voyage whaling expeditions but harpooned whales in Cape Cod Bay.

Both harpooned whales and whales that beached themselves were the subject of many disputes. As early as 1690, Salem whalers complained that whales that escaped after they harpooned them near Truro were turning up in the hands of people from the Outer Cape. Everyone tried to claim beached whales. In England, they belonged to the Crown. Plymouth Colony and then Massachusetts Bay Province made vague claims on behalf of the Crown or for themselves. Town governments also claimed jurisdiction over beached whales. When the beaching was near a town line, the number of claimants multiplied. They could include both town governments, the provincial government, ministers or others granted a share by the town, whoever found the whale, and the whaleboat crews who claimed they had driven the whales ashore.

Most of the early settlers worked as farmers and whalers. Eastham, which included Pamet until 1709, noted in a petition to Plymouth Colony in 1706 that "all or most of us are concerned in fitting out boats to catch and take whales . . . [and] to cut them up and take away the fat and the bone . . . and afterwards let the rest of the body . . . lie on shore in low water to be washed away by the sea, being of no value nor worth of anything to us." Cape Cod Bay was yielding scores of whales, seventy to a hundred every season, according to Ezra Stiles. Eastham's petition was in support of a request by a Boston entrepreneur who manufactured saltpeter. He wanted to process the remains of butchered whales left on the beach. Eastham argued that there would be trickle-down benefits to the Outer Cape economy: more employment, more barrel-makers who would need houses to live in, more shipments on local sloops to Boston, and possibly more exports from New England to the rest of the world.

One whale hunt off Truro in 1725 turned into a dispute recorded by the town clerk. A Barnstable man told Truro's town clerk that he and his men were the first to strike a whale off Pamet Harbor. Another whaleman declared that he was the second. Both affidavits stated that a third man, perhaps from Truro, then wounded the whale, "and they and we soon killed said whale." The dispute was over who should get how much of the carcass, which would have been towed ashore in Truro for butchering. Later on, Truro men would mark their lances to strengthen ownership claims; Joshua Atwood registered with the Truro town clerk that his lance "that he hath made on purpose to kill fin-backs with, hath a three-square head marked W.R."

Whether stranded or harpooned, the whales were butchered on the bayshore beach. (No whaling was done off the Atlantic Ocean shore.) The whalers boiled the blubber in big kettles over wood fires and skimmed off the oil, a process called "trying out," which continued even into the twentieth century. The rest of the carcass was left to be washed away at high tide. The proliferation of try works and whale houses led the Pamet Proprietors, who owned many of the beaches and marshes, to regulate the rendering operations as early as 1701. They named two men "to look after all such persons as shall set up whale houses [on their land] . . . or that shall cut wood or timber," for firewood. The two men were to collect a fee of one shilling per visiting whaleman or order them to leave.

The town also tried to regulate the division of spoils when many were involved in driving the pilot whales to shore. In a town meeting in March 1753, the men voted that "when any blackfish or porpoises shall be drove on shore and killed by any number of boats of the inhabitants of this town, if one man or men shall insist upon having the fish divided to each boat, it shall be done." The voters also ordered that boys younger than ten could not share in the spoils.

Truro's farmer-whalers in the 1700s were also experienced fishermen who sailed boats to catch cod, mackerel and herring during the fishing seasons. Early in the century, herring were so abundant that Marblehead fishermen appealed to Massachusetts Bay Province to stop over-fishing. Outer Cape fishermen, they complained, were netting so many herring that they left great quantities to rot on the beach. In 1762, about a hundred men went on fishing voyages from Truro, according to diarist Ezra Stiles. That represented about a third of Truro's men. Several town records of the time mention fish houses and fish flakes for drying and curing the catch.

Whales, however, were an especially rich resource; and when whales were sighted off the bayshore, Truro men dropped everything to launch their whaling boats and row out to be first to put a harpoon into the prize. One February day in 1755, news of a whale reached Truro's church elders just as they were about to hear whether the Reverend Caleb Upham would accept their offer to be their next minister. They adjourned the meeting and the whalemen headed for the harbor. Reconvening the next day, they raised their salary offer and added twenty cords of wood a year delivered to Upham's door. He accepted the improved offer from this prosperous and dedicated whaling town.

· · ·

By the end of the 1700s, over-hunting had greatly reduced the number of whales in Cape Cod Bay. The Reverend James Freeman observed that "formerly whales of different species were common on the coasts and yielded a great profit to the inhabitants who pursued them in boats from the shore; but they are now rare." In addition, the Revolutionary War had disrupted both offshore and long-voyage whaling. Although Truro's whaling never again reached the level of the mid-1700s, shore whaling and some harpooning in Cape Cod Bay and shipping out on long-voyage whaling continued into the 1800s.

One day in 1810, according to Shebnah Rich, whalemen from South Truro plunged a harpoon into a right whale just offshore but could not get close enough for the kill. They sent for a retired whaler, Captain Tom Atwood, who "was rowed on to the safe side and sent his lance to her life." Rich wrote in 1883 that "early in the present century, nine large sloops from Truro were engaged in whaling" and that the *Lydia and Sophia* was probably the largest vessel built in Truro up to that time.

Pilot whales continued to strand on the beaches, providing extra income for Truro's farmers. One farmer driving his cows to pasture spotted scores of pilot whales on the beach. He marked seventy-five and sold them that day for $1,900, an enormous sum for the time. In 1834, when Rich was ten years old, he watched fishermen chase a pod of pilot whales toward the beach at Great Hollow: "It was a time of intense excitement. . . . The vast school of sea monsters, maddened by frantic shouts and splashing oars, rushed wildly on the shore, throwing themselves clean on to the beach; others, pursuing, piled their massive, slippery carcasses on the first, like cakes of ice pushed up by the tide, till the shore presented a living causeway of over six hundred shining mammals, the largest number at that time ever driven ashore in one school."

Henry David Thoreau was in Truro in July 1855 when a pod of about thirty pilot whales, which he called blackfish, was driven onto the bay beach, also near Great Hollow. A fisherman slashed one of them to show Thoreau the blubber and flesh. The blubber was about three inches thick and looked like pork. "As I passed my finger through the cut," Thoreau said, "it was covered with oil. . . . [the flesh] firm and red like beef." The fisherman said he preferred it to beef. Another pod of pilot whales appeared in the bay. "We saw several boats soon made fast," said Thoreau, "each to its fish, which, four or five rods ahead, was drawing it like a race-horse straight toward the beach, leaping half out of water, blowing blood and water from its hole and leaving a streak of foam behind." One of the largest pods of pilot whales was driven ashore in 1874, again near Great Hollow. Rich says that there were 1,405 on the beach and that they yielded 27,000 gallons of oil.

Dead pilot whales, however, soon became a nuisance rather than a resource. Anthony L. Marshall, author of *Truro, Cape Cod, As I Knew It*, recalled that in the early 1920s they stranded occasionally and "once ashore, they had to be gotten rid of as soon as possible as the stench from their decomposing bodies was horrible." Only one Truro man, Charles W. Snow, who was also super-intendent of town streets, was still processing blubber. He had his try works near Town Hall. The purest oil, which came from the "melon" of the bulbous head, was prized by watchmakers as a lubricant. Disposal of the carcasses became a more serious problem, and the board of health ordered that they be buried or towed out to sea.

In December 1992, seven pilot whales swam about a mile up the narrow, twisting Pamet River to Truro Center. They thrashed in circles just twenty feet from the post office, where they were stopped by the embankment that carries Route 6A across the Pamet River. Townsfolk picking up their mail watched wildlife rescuers in wet suits try to save the whales, which refused to swim back to the bay. They captured four and trucked them to the tip of Cape Cod, hoping the whales would be able to swim out to sea. Only two made it alive to the launching, and one of those soon returned to the Pamet where it was found dead in a marsh. No one claimed any of the dead whales for their oil. The whaling industry in New England waters was long gone. By the end of the twentieth century, stranded pilot whales were victims to be rescued, not beasts to be butchered.

CHAPTER 9:
A TEA TEMPEST,
BOMBARDMENTS AND 460
BRITISH PRISONERS

Truro didn't dump any tea into Pamet Harbor, but the town fathers almost had their own "Boston Tea Party" at the start of the American Revolution. Just six days before the Boston Tea Party in late 1773, one ship in a fleet of four British vessels carrying tea to Boston was driven ashore at the end of Cape Cod during a storm. The Boston merchant whose tea was on board and the Boston revolutionaries who wanted to prevent it from landing raced to get control of the shipwrecked tea. Tea, a favorite beverage in the colonies, had become political dynamite, and Truro would feel the repercussions.

When she went aground, the British vessel *William* was carrying fifty-eight large chests of tea being shipped to Jonathan Clarke, a Boston merchant and British loyalist. Clarke heard about the wreck and rode to Provincetown to try to salvage his tea. On the way he picked up his cousin, John Greenough, a Wellfleet schoolteacher, merchant and Barnstable County justice of the peace. An energetic and commanding figure, Greenough could bring some governmental authority to salvage operations before the Cape Codders made off with the ship's cargo.

Greenough supervised moving the tea from the hulk to Provincetown Harbor. A few people turned up and bought small quantities of the duty-free tea, and among them were Wellfleet's minister and "several persons" from Truro. All, including Greenough, would be called to account by their fellow citizens.

While the loyalists Clarke and Greenough in Provincetown were salvaging the tea from the shipwreck, a mob of revolutionaries in Boston, inspired by inflammatory rhetoric and dressed as Indians, boarded the three other British ships and dumped 342 chests of tea into the harbor. Tea had suddenly become a symbol of the malevolence of British tyranny. The pretext was the British Tea Act of 1773. Although one goal of the act was to lower the price of tea in the colonies, the act also retained the controversial duty on tea carried by British ships to America. Focusing on tax enforcement and ignoring the prospect of cheaper tea, Samuel Adams and the agitators for revolution in 1773 turned the Tea Act into a burning issue of liberty versus despotism. Not insignificantly, they also had the support of America's tea smugglers, whose prices would have been undercut.

The day after the Boston Tea Party, Samuel Adams's committee of correspondence hastily dispatched letters urging Cape Codders to do the same with the tea from the wreck of the *William* for a Cape Cod version of the Boston Tea Party. Clarke and Greenough, however, were already on the scene and moving quickly to have the tea carted to the Provincetown waterfront for shipment to Boston. The men who helped to move the fifty-eight chests were paid handsomely in tea.

Clarke's efforts to save his tea did not go smoothly. In a New Year's Eve letter to his partners, he said that word of the Boston Tea Party reaching Truro and Provincetown had "greatly obstructed" sending the tea on to Boston. "As the people of Boston have themselves been at liberty to destroy what tea was there," he wrote, "I fear the people in this place think themselves licensed to steal what is here." Clarke managed to keep control of the tea, but he had to get a schooner from Salem to take it to Boston. Cape Cod's shipmasters would not cooperate.

When Samuel Adams heard that Clarke had secured his tea, he railed in a letter to a friend that the Boston raiders who dumped the tea into Boston Harbor "would have marched on snowshoes . . . to have done the business for them [the Cape Codders]." He thought it "strange," too, that Clarke could ride the length of Cape Cod and "not meet with a single instance of contempt."

The Boston Tea Party and the wreck of the *William* with its cargo of the now infamous tea galvanized the revolution-minded citizens of Truro and Wellfleet. Truro called a town meeting on February 28, 1774, to examine the "several persons" who had purchased the "baneful" tea. The meeting, however, exonerated them, finding that "their buying this noxious tea was through ignorance and inadvertence, and that they were induced thereto by the base and villainous example and artful persuading of some noted pretended friends to government from the neighboring towns, and therefore this meeting thinks them excusable with an acknowledgment."

Town meeting then moved immediately to support the Boston revolutionaries against Great Britain. The voters named a committee of nine citizens to draft a declaration of solidarity to be sent to Boston. The draft, however, had no doubt already been written, for within half an hour all nine men signed off on the long text. The principal authors may well have been the Reverend Caleb Upham, Truro's minister, and Dr. Samuel Adams of Truro, who later joined the Continental Army as a surgeon (and who is not to be confused with the Boston agitator and revolutionary of the same name). Upham and Dr. Adams were close friends and ardent American patriots.

Town meeting adopted the declaration of solidarity, which reveals the hand of someone who knew well the rhetoric of the American revolutionaries. (See appendix E.) In it, Truro pledged

to join the Boston revolutionaries to defend "our rights and privileges" so as to avoid "the deplorable state of wretched slavery" caused
by unlawful measures by the British, in particular "their late and
detestable scheme of sending teas to the colonies by the East India
Co. subject to unrighteous American duty." The sale and consumption of tea would not be encouraged, and anyone involved in
selling the offending tea would be treated "as the meanest and
basest of enemies." Finally, the resolution observed that no one
from Truro would help the British transport to Boston the tea
from the shipwreck in Provincetown "despite liberal promises of a
large reward." Stung by the waywardness of a few of its tea drink-
ers, Truro was not going to leave any doubt in the minds of its
Boston brethren about its devotion to liberty and the resistance.
In Truro, tea was proscribed.

John Greenough and the Wellfleet minister were in trouble
with their townsfolk, too. Wellfleet's committee of correspondence
confiscated most of a three-hundred-pound chest of tea that
Greenough had taken from the shipment as his pay. He managed
to get it back, however, and defended his actions at a Wellfleet
town meeting. The Wellfleet minister who bought the baneful tea
had been in Provincetown for the ordination of its minister, which
was attended by some men Greenough called "incendiaries." On
his way home, the minister was waylaid in the Wellfleet woods by
three men who seized his tea and scattered it on the ground. A
Boston newspaper reported the incident: "At first he thought they
were Negroes who had been to see the ordination but soon discovered that they were persons disguised." (Just as the Bostonians
were disguised as Indians for the Boston Tea Party.)

· · ·

Truro had been drawn into the revolutionary movement almost a
year before the Boston Tea Party. The newly formed Boston committee of correspondence led by Samuel Adams had written to
Massachusetts towns seeking their support to resist the threat of

British oppression. Adams's committee was the first of a network of such committees throughout the thirteen colonies. One of the Boston committee's letters, accompanied by a pamphlet, sought Truro's support in the face of "our common danger."

Truro's selectmen met on January 25, 1773, to approve a reply. In revolutionary rhetoric, they complained of "intolerable grievances," although without specifying any, and said they concurred "with our brethren in every part of the province in all legal and constitutional measures to recover our legal rights and liberties and in defense of those we still enjoy." Thus, two years before the shots heard around the world were fired at Lexington and Concord, Truro declared its solidarity with those resisting what they saw as British encroachments on their liberties.

The war itself came to Truro in the fall of 1775 when a British ship lobbed cannonballs into the town and British marauders came ashore. The hostilities are mentioned in a letter by the Reverend Caleb Upham, an outspoken American patriot who scorned the British as piratical "buccaneers." In a letter of November 7, 1775, to his friend Dr. Samuel Adams, who was with the Continental Army, Upham wrote: "Here we live in constant fear of the *buccaneers* [his emphasis] who are often coming into the harbor and have fired upon this town. I have stripped my house of furniture and got it to Treat Collins together with yours. I have three times left my house and gone further south to lodge, upon account of these sons of _____, what you please. Would move myself and family this day if duty did not require my longer stay." (The discreet blank is the minister's.)

Upham expressed his outrage, but he did not indicate where the British cannonballs landed or whether the British commandeered supplies. His letter does suggest that the British may have carried off furniture or household goods. Truro had a militia of sorts and had petitioned Boston for gunpowder, but a local militia could not be very effective against the British navy, which controlled the waters off the Outer Cape and kept Truro "in constant fear."

Twenty-eight of Upham's letters to Dr. Adams survive. Written between 1775 and 1781, they have not heretofore been cited by historians. Most of them fairly explode with indignation at the British and their loyalists in Truro. In a letter from Truro, dated July 22, 1779, he writes to Dr. Adams:

> When, my dear sir, will this more than savage war be over? When will the bloodhounds of [King] George Whelps be restrained from glutting themselves on this country's blood. Their [illegible] barbarities in Connecticut are a disgrace to humanity. Call not such creatures men, but call them D_____, but sooner or later they shall receive their reward. . . . Excuse these effusions. Language is too feeble to express my abhorrence of their infernal ravages and depredations.

Upham, who was in his fifties, had succeeded the Reverend John Avery two decades earlier. He was a well-respected, somewhat intimidating minister of Truro's Congregational Church, whose writings showed "a taste for poetry," according to the Reverend James Freeman, who said Upham left a poem in manuscript when he died.

Upham had been an American patriot as early as 1774, and this caused him trouble at a time when most colonists thought of themselves as loyal British subjects. Some of his parishioners reportedly abused him "in a most scurrilous manner" for entertaining in his home men they considered rebels to British rule. The incident and a boycott of the equally patriotic Dr. Adams are reported by Charles F. Swift, a nineteenth-century journalist and Cape Cod historian. He cites a letter of December 5, 1774, from Dr. Adams to Thomas Paine of Eastham, but the letter has not been found.

Upham was equally exasperated by his loyalist neighbors. In 1776, he wrote to Dr. Adams about a British warship "trading with their good friends, you know where; an enemy within the

walls more dangerous than numbers without." The loyalist sentiment in Truro that enraged Upham was not unusual; historians
find little evidence of nationalism or separatist feeling before 1775
in the American colonies. Truro's colonists had been law-abiding,
God-fearing citizens of the British empire for several generations.
They shared a common heritage and a common religion, and many
had relatives in England.

At one point, Truro's militia officers seemed to side with the
British loyalists. In the months between the skirmishes at Lexington and Concord and the battle of Bunker Hill, Truro named three
men to lead its militia. The three responded with a confirming
note on June 1, 1775, in which they were careful to "acknowledge
King George the Third of Great Britain to be our king and sovereign" and to "use our best endeavors to guard the town from suf-
fering any [ill-minded persons?] to land in said town in order to
deprive us of our rights or liberties, and we will use our best endeavors to keep peace and good order in these difficult times against
mobs and riots." There was no mention of the British, nor any
expression of support for the revolutionaries in Boston.

Loyalist sentiment in Truro persisted years after the Declaration of Independence. In a 1778 letter, Upham railed sarcastically
that a British "lying speech . . . is much admired by the wise men
of a certain place . . . strange infatuation that men should be fond
of slavery."

Exulting in a crucial American victory, Upham wrote in 1781:
"My dear friend, glory to God and salvation to my country. I heartily
congratulate you on the capture of [General] Cornwallis, chief
hangman to George Whelps and his gang of banditti. What a glorious acquisition of fame and profit to these dispirited states. What
an éclat it will make through the courts of Europe."

Rambunctious in life, Upham was more subdued about his
death. The words on his gravestone in Old North Cemetery say
simply, "I have been and that is all."

. . .

Throughout the Revolutionary War, Truro had to balance not only
the conflicting views of American patriots and British loyalists but
also the conflicting demands on their meager resources: what to
do about the threat of British warships bombarding the town,
whether to try to resist British landing parties looking for supplies, how to arm and supply the Truro militia for the defense of
the town, how to meet the constant requisitions by the Continental Army for men and supplies, and, not the least, how to secure
the salvage rights to British shipwrecks.

Truro was vulnerable to British warships in Provincetown Harbor for two reasons. Truro's shoreline formed the eastern end of the
harbor, which was not fortified, and any attempt to defend the
harbor shores fell to Truro since Provincetown's population was
only a fifth the size of Truro's. Upham noted in June 1776, a month
before the Declaration of Independence, that "a fleet of enemy
ships were seen yesterday . . . I am afraid they will make a visit and
we are far from being prepared to give them a proper reception."
Truro faced not only the occasional bombardment but also the
prospect of Royal Marines raiding the town for water, firewood,
supplies, booty or even manpower.

Town militias, greatly out-manned and out-gunned by the
British, had to be ingenious. One anecdote purports to tell how
the Truro militia foiled a British landing party. Historian Frederick
Freeman was the first to print the story of the militia's ruse on the
bay shore. As in the scene in the opera *Aida* where the soldiers
parade across the stage, into the wings, around backstage and again
across the stage in the triumphal march, the few men of the Truro
militia are supposed to have marched again and again across the
front of a dune. "It was naturally supposed by the enemy," says
Freeman, "that an immense force was assembled . . . It was not
judged prudent, therefore, by the British commander to attempt
a landing." Freeman gives no source for his anecdote, which he
relates without any qualifications. He was writing in the 1860s,

about eighty-five years after the supposed ruse. At best, he would have heard about it only second-hand. One Cape Cod historian, Henry Kittredge, calls it a yarn.

Truro's leaders also had to adapt to the uncertainty of British intentions. British warships could lie quietly at anchor off Truro, or they could open fire on the town, as Upham described. The British might send raiding parties ashore or simply arrive as peaceable visitors and potential customers for farm products. Early in 1776, town meeting named a committee of three men "to discourse with the men-of-war, should they come with a flag of truce, to know what their requests are, and to do what they shall think best for the town and province." British shore parties may not have received a warm welcome in Truro, but their visits probably were tolerated, if only because it would have been futile to resist.

The advantage to the British of Provincetown Harbor had come to the attention of General George Washington, and he sent Peleg Wadsworth to see if it could be defended. Wadsworth reported on December 16, 1775, that the harbor was so large that ships could anchor out of reach of cannon on shore but that fortifications could "prevent their watering, rendezvous, etc. etc." No gun emplacements, however, were built.

Truro's vulnerability was also described in early 1777 when the town sought relief from conscription of its men. Its petition to the Boston authorities protested that Provincetown Harbor "is unfortified, and the enemy still continue to make it their rendezvous, which, exposing them [Truro's inhabitants] to ravages and insults, keeps them often in alarms . . . and under the necessity of keeping a constant watch." As a result of its petition, the town was excused from the most recent call for conscripts.

In the end, however, the town's official position was to join the revolution against the British. Five days after the Declaration of Independence, town meeting voted "to fall in with the provincial and continental congresses." Come what may, the Town of Truro would support the Boston revolutionaries and General George Washington's Continental Army.

. . .

During the war, two British ships—the passenger ship *Friendship* and the warship *Somerset*—went aground and were seized by Truro men. The *Friendship* was wrecked near Truro's boundary with Provincetown in a storm on February 19, 1776. The records suggest that her passengers were loyalist families traveling from Boston to Canada. A British warship tried to retrieve the passengers and crew but could not because of violent winds. "The pilot of her is the only person secreted from the rebels," the British captain wrote in his report. The other survivors made it to Truro without harm.

The government of Massachusetts Bay Province in Boston, by now under the control of the revolutionaries, moved to seize the wreckage of the *Friendship*. It ordered Truro's selectmen and committee of correspondence to take charge of rigging, sails and contents until the courts could determine to whom they belonged. The order warned that "as embezzlement in cases of this nature is highly disreputable and altogether unjustifiable and every species thereof ought to be discouraged, that all persons be directed to use their utmost endeavors to prevent the same." Boston wanted all the armaments and supplies from the wreck for the Continental Army. Its rhetoric was aimed at keeping Truro from exercising its traditional rights of salvage. Truro, however, would prevail.

The provincial government also directed that a strange assortment of supplies—one cask of vinegar, two boxes of tin, eight bolts of canvas and five kegs of paint—be sent immediately to the Continental Army. An army major took four cannon for the defense of Martha's Vineyard and the Elizabeth Islands. Finally, the order from Boston recommended that the captors restore to the captain his clothes and personal papers. The captain, crew and passengers of the *Friendship* remained in Truro for four months. Then, because they were "suspected of being inimical to the rights and liberties of America," the men were sent to Boston for court hearings. The women and children were permitted "to repair to their respective places of abode."

The wreck of the *Friendship* was Truro's first experience claiming salvage rights to an enemy ship in wartime. The provincial government ultimately recognized nineteen Truro men as "captors of the ship *Friendship*" and even paid them eighty pounds for the four cannon taken by the army major. Truro had control of the money aboard the ship, too; the town was directed to use it to pay for carting baggage of the prisoners from Truro to Plymouth. The men may also have succeeded in keeping 150 pounds of gunpowder and selling it to the Continental Army; a record concerning the *Friendship* mentions the purchase of gunpowder from unidentified persons by three mid-Cape men.

. . .

Defense of the town was a primary concern throughout the eight years of war. As was the case in other colonial towns, Truro maintained a "committee of correspondence, inspection and safety" to coordinate military activities. Men were assigned regularly to stand watch for British ships. Even while responding to a dozen calls for more men and supplies for the Continental Army, the town was seeking weapons and even soldiers from Boston to reinforce its militia. In early 1776, town meeting went so far as to request twelve cannons, powder, cannonballs and two hundred men—a formidable defense force. Shortly thereafter, the town reduced its requirements to two or three field pieces. There's no indication they received anything. Some months later, they made mention of two small cannons but no ammunition, and without indicating where the cannons came from. Ammunition of all kinds was in short supply, and the town voted to fine anyone firing a gun "except to defend the town."

For most of 1776, the town's militia was reinforced by "regular army" soldiers. A garrison of troops from the Continental Army was stationed in Truro for ten months. Sea-coast defense forces were assigned to most of New England's coastal towns, and Truro got "one company of fifty men and a commissary to supply them with provisions and money." Two Truro men ran the commissary. Nothing in the town records describes this encampment or its effect on the townspeople. The garrison, along with others in New England, was disbanded in November.

On one occasion, Truro men used a small cannon to re-take an American merchant vessel captured by a British man-of-war, and they did it without firing a shot. British seamen had seized the American brig *Compte d'Estaing* after it ran ashore on the Atlantic beach to escape capture. The American crew came ashore, and their captain, Richard James, sent a letter from Truro to Boston on June 18, 1777, asking for instructions. He said that Truro men "mustered very early" but were unable to repel the British. Then, he said, "we had a small cannon brought, at the sight of which they [the British] left the brig." The Truro militia must have hauled the cannon to the top of the cliff and aimed it down on the British boarding party.

At high tide, Captain James ran the ship higher on the beach and quickly unloaded canvas, powder, and small arms. He says he "had it trucked round to Truro town, in the care of one of the committee, Mr. Ephraim Harding," a selectman. Captain James planned to unload the ship's cargo, about six hundred bushels of salt from the West Indies, and sell it to Cape Codders, "as the people are in great want of it and the expense of trucking and re-shipping it will be considerable." The authorities in Boston, how-ever, instructed him to transfer the salt to a sloop they were send-ing from Boston, and the British lost interest in the empty brig on the beach.

Two months later, the provincial government furnished two more field pieces, along with grapeshot, cannonballs and gunpow-der "for the annoyance of our enemies" and "for effectually pre-venting all intercourse with the British men-of-war." The two ad-ditional cannons brought the town's arsenal to four, but they were smaller and could fire grapeshot or cannonballs weighing only two or three pounds. Truro was to enlist up to thirty men as gun crew, and town meeting named officers for it; but the records do not tell whether the cannons were ever used. In any case, they were not needed during the town's most momentous engagement with the enemy–dealing with the wreck of the British man-of-war *Somerset* and its survivors, 460 British sailors and marines taken prisoner by a handful of unarmed Truro militia men.

. . .

With sixty-four cannons and a gun deck 160 feet long, HMS *Somerset* was one of the largest warships in the British navy. Her crew, including a contingent of Royal Marines, numbered about 480 men. Under the command of Captain George Ourry, the *Somerset* was part of a fleet of sixteen British warships hunting French ships off the coast of New England.

On Sunday, November 1, 1778, when she was north of Cape Cod, the weather turned stormy. On Monday, the gale increased, probably with gusts of hurricane force. Waves broke over the ship's deck, and several of the sails blew to pieces. The heavy seas and the gale-force winds, which shifted to the north, were driving the *Somerset* toward the shoals off the end of Cape Cod.

At his court martial, Captain Ourry described the ship's final minutes just before nightfall: "It blew a very hard gale of wind at this time; very soon after six in the afternoon, saw the breakers to leeward at about a half a mile distance and soon after the ship struck, which knocked away the rudder, and she bilged [broke open] right under the counter [at the stern]." The *Somerset* was hard aground stern-first on the southeast end of the Peaked Hill sand bars. The pounding breakers would soon demolish her. The beach was about six hundred feet away.

The 64-gun H.M.S. *Somerset*, one of the largest warships in the British fleet during the Revolutionary War, was wrecked on a sand bar off Truro's ocean beach in a northeast gale in 1778. The watercolor drawing, made more than a century later, is an artist's conception of the British fleet. The lead warship is believed to be similar to the *Somerset*. (Courtesy of the Mariners' Museum, Newport News, Virginia.)

Night fell. The crew manned the pumps, but the hold filled with sea water. To lighten the ship, Ourry had the crew cut away the masts and sails and throw overboard cannons and heavy chests of arms in the hope that wind and waves would drive the ship off the sand bar and closer to shore so it would be easier for the men to save themselves. All night, huge waves poured over the deck, where the men waited for dawn to see if they could get to safety before the ship broke up.

The next morning, word spread on shore about the wreck, and men from Provincetown and Truro arrived at the beach, which was strewn with masts, rigging, and sails. The storm, a typical three-day "nor'easter" with its on-shore winds, was still raging. What happened next is told by John Greenough of Wellfleet. He was the schoolteacher, merchant and county official who had been in trouble two years earlier for accepting shipwrecked tea. He had won back the respect of the revolutionary leadership and would be put in charge of salvaging the *Somerset* wreck for Massachusetts, which was trying to collect arms, ammunition and supplies for the Continental Army.

In his report, Greenough told how the British officers surrendered to Captain Atkins of the Truro militia: "The weather was boisterous, the surf so high that no person could then board her. A boat was carted by the people of Province[town] about five miles to the shore nearest the ship. In the afternoon two boats came safe from the ship, with the third [rank] lieutenant, who surrendered himself a prisoner to Mr. Isaiah Atkins, one of the selectmen of Truro; in the second boat the captain came, who also surrendered in like manner." A third boat with twenty-one men tried to reach shore but foundered in the surf, and the men were lost.

Details of the British surrender to Atkins and the Truro militia were later confirmed in the proceedings of a maritime court judging salvage rights. Jonathan Collins of Truro testified that he "heard the captain of the *Somerset* ask for the principal man and Isaiah Atkins being named the captain gave him his sword and said save the men and ship shall be yours." Dr. William Thayer of Truro testified that "the captain and crew submitted to the Truro militia and marched off under their orders."

The storm began to subside on Wednesday, and the rest of the British survivors came ashore in small boats and rafts. Several hundred Truro men and women were on the beach to greet and grab. Greenough describes a tumultuous scene of rescue, salvage, bargaining and plundering: "Almost all the inhabitants of Truro came down to the wreck, they say as militia, although I could never learn that they were in any military arrangement nor under any command, order or discipline. . . . Others were trading with the seamen for clothing, etc., brought from the ship; and a great number [of people were] cutting up and carrying off sails, rigging, etc."

On Thursday, the Truro militia had their prisoners to "guard" while trying to do some salvaging for themselves. More booty continued to come ashore. Greenough said there were chests of tools, leather hides, bolts of cloth, "and many other valuable articles." That night a guard was posted over the goods, but "a great part [was] embezzled before the next day." When the salvage operations came to the attention of General Joseph Otis of Barnstable, he wrote: "From all that I can learn there is wicked work at the wreck—riotous doings. The Truro and Provincetown men made a division of the clothing . . . Truro took two thirds and Provincetown one third. There is a very plundering gang that way."

There was no shelter on the beach, and before nightfall on Thursday, Greenough said, "The prisoners were conducted off the shore to town by three or four unarmed men." That night, Truro's 250 families provided for 460 prisoners of war. Captain Ourry found pen and paper and wrote to his superiors that the ship "is all to pieces, myself and Officers, with the seamen are now going to march off to Boston, where I hope you will be able to negotiate for an exchange." It's doubtful that in any other engagement with the British any American military unit took more British prisoners with fewer men than did the tiny militia of Truro.

On Friday, Captain Ourry and his men began the long walk to Boston "under the care of Mr. Atkins" of the Truro militia. Atkins

took them through Wellfleet to Eastham, where they spent the
night. The militia of towns from Cape Cod to Boston then picked
up the guard duty and accompanied the long line of prisoners.
Some of the prisoners escaped simply by strolling away. Captain
Ourry and most of the British prisoners were exchanged for American prisoners held in New York. At Captain Ourry's court martial,
his fellow captains cleared him of any negligence in the loss of his
ship and twenty-one men.

The dramatic wreck of the *Somerset* gave rise to more than a
dozen legends, which Marjorie Hubbell Gibson was able to expose as untrue in her 1992 book, *H.M.S Somerset 1746-1778*, a
chronicle of the ship's history. One legend had the *Somerset* stationed in Provincetown Harbor and its captain and crew socializ-
ing on shore with the inhabitants. The ship's log, however, shows
that the *Somerset* never anchored in Provincetown Harbor. Another
legend had Truro's Dr. Thayer as the ship's surgeon and had him
marrying Lucy Rich and staying in town to practice medicine. Dr.
Thayer, in fact, was the husband of Susanna Rich and one of the
Truro men who claimed salvage rights to the *Somerset*. The ship's
surgeon was Henry Watson.

Several weeks later, another gale drove the wrecked ship onto
the beach. Upham wrote to his friend that it was "as violent a
storm as has been known in the memory of man, which drove two
vessels ashore on the Cape [the end of Cape Cod], one from Salem
to [the] West Indies, wholly lost . . . the other [a sloop], three
men lost, two escaped and vessel may be got off. These, including
the *Somerset*, make eight wrecks on Cape since October, glorious
harvest for mooners." Mooners was shorthand for mooncussers,
who, according to maritime lore, cursed the moon and prayed for
moonless nights so they could lure ships onto sand bars with false
signal lanterns and make off with salvage from the wreckage.

After the wreckage had reached the beach and the militia had
taken away the British prisoners, Greenough had eighty-two men
on salvage operations for the revolutionary government. They carted
provisions, powder, iron and a variety of weaponry and ship's gear

to East Harbor for shipment to Boston. Greenough complained that even though he tried to recover booty taken from the wreck he was unsuccessful. He noted in particular that Job Avery took charge of a black man from the *Somerset* and would not give him up.

In addition to Greenough's efforts, six small ships anchored near the *Somerset* to salvage what they could at low tide and carry it to Boston. Sixteen cannons were entrusted to Lieutenant Colonel Paul Revere to fortify Castle Island in Boston Harbor, where they could be used against their former owner. The townsfolk of Truro, however, had made off with as much as they could salvage. Three months after the wreck, the revolutionary government ordered the Barnstable County sheriff to collect everything taken from the *Somerset* and deposit it with the Board of War for use by the military. The order gave the sheriff the authority to "break open in the daytime" dwellings or other buildings, if necessary and directed that he identify those who do not cooperate.

The issue between the Truro townsfolk and the revolutionary government was whether a shipwrecked enemy vessel was the property of the government or of the men who found her, boarded her, and brought the booty to shore. Truro people had been salvaging wrecks on the Atlantic shore for a century or more. They had prevailed in the case of the *Friendship* wreck in 1776, and they would not willingly give up their claims to the *Somerset*. They contended that wrecks abandoned by captain and crew on Cape Cod, or anywhere in the world, belonged to whoever got there first and had the strength, skill and persistence to seize the ship or carry away its gear and contents.

The dispute over the *Somerset* went to Massachusetts maritime court, and an auction of "sundry articles" salvaged by Greenough's men from the wreck brought 32,510 pounds for the salvagers. The court split the proceeds between the state and the claimants from the Outer Cape, almost two hundred Truro men and three from Provincetown. The awards, which were divided and sub-divided, ranged from about 1,300 pounds to 25 pounds.

The *Somerset* was one of the two largest British warships destroyed during the Revolutionary War. (The other was the *Augusta*, which had blown up in the Delaware River the year before.) The *Somerset* had served the British well. After the skirmish at Lexington and Concord, she covered the British retreat to their Boston Harbor stronghold; and she was at the battle of Bunker Hill, firing red hot cannonballs that set Charlestown afire.

The remains of the *Somerset*, stripped of almost everything of value and buried over the years by the shifting sands, have surfaced three times after storms, most recently in 1973. Shebnah Rich wrote that the hull was exposed in the 1870s. Several cart loads of timbers were hauled away and Captain Sears Rich had "a handsome cane made from the timber of the *Somerset*." She surfaced again in 1886 and the cathead from her bow, now on display at the Provincetown Monument Museum, was recovered along with a cannon and other items from the wreck. E.A. Grozier, an eyewitness to this re-emergence of the *Somerset*, wrote an article for the *New York World*: "I can see a score or two of men and boys at work on the *Somerset* with the evident intention of rending her limb from limb. They come to the beach well equipped with saws and axes and shovels, crowbars and wedges . . . The especially enterprising individuals will cart off a cord or more of wood." In 1973, another storm uncovered the last remaining timbers of the *Somerset* wreck, the largest of the many shipwrecks in Truro's history.

Truro's encounter with the *Somerset* occurred three years after the start of the war, which would drag on for almost five more years. Although wrecks of warships were a source of supplies and even income, the burden of the war was heavy on Truro. Most of the able-bodied men were either in the army or on American privateers. Fishing boats stayed in the harbor rather than risk capture

The bones of the British man-of-war *Somerset*, wrecked in 1778, have surfaced from time to time after storms rearrange the ocean shoreline in North Truro, most recently in 1973. (Photo by Nat Champlin.)

by the British. All around Cape Cod, the British were capturing American merchant vessels and fishing boats and forcing the sailors to serve on British ships.

Calls for conscripts continued, and town meeting voted manfully "to try to get soldiers for the Continental Army." The following year saw no less than three calls for a total of thirty-three men. After four years of conscriptions, this quota would have been very difficult, if not impossible, to fill. Truro families were also expected to respond to periodic requisitions for blankets, shoes, stockings, shirts and at one point 3,680 pounds of beef.

Adding to its problems were a ruinous inflation, a shortage of currency and frequent tax levies. *The Commonwealth History of Massachusetts* selected Truro to illustrate the predicament of Massachusetts towns: "The [Truro] inhabitants petitioned the legislature that it was impossible for them to pay their taxes. The harbor was open to the enemy to land and rob them of their stock and burn their buildings. For four years 'our constables cannot gather enough to support our revered pastor;' the town treasury was empty; the schools had been closed for six months; necessary town charges were unpaid; poor families, widows and fatherless children depended on the charity of the town; and 'the greatest part of our men have gone into the war.'"

The calls for men and supplies continued even after the British army surrendered at Yorktown in 1781. Although the land war had ended, the British navy continued its depredations of coastal towns for three more years. For example, in 1782, town meeting named a three-man committee "to go aboard the British ships when they come into Cape Cod [i.e. Provincetown] Harbor." What the committee would do was not specified. Since the land war was over, they might have been offering to sell fresh water and supplies.

Many of Truro's men did not return from the war, although the number was not recorded. Shebnah Rich, writing a century later, said that twenty-eight men from twenty-six houses north of Pond Village "were either killed, died by sickness in camp or on board prison ships." Lieutenant Ebenezer Collins, twenty-five years old, was "killed at the siege of Boston and buried on Prospect Hill." Collins wrote in his last letter: "We are about to move on the British, and may the Lord of hosts go with us." And thirteen men from Truro and Wellfleet were imprisoned in England after the capture of their privateer *Resolution* in 1780.

Disease was at least as deadly as British gunfire; many died in a prison ship at New York. Three sons of Jonathan Paine died during the war—one in a British prison, another in a hospital in New York and the third at home "of army sickness," according to Rich. The three were great-grandsons of Thomas Paine, Truro's founder.

At least one story from the war had a happy ending. Rich recounts the odyssey of David Snow and his teenage son, also David, who were missing for seven years. A British privateer captured the Snows in 1775 while they were fishing from a small boat near Truro. They were carried to Nova Scotia and then to a prison in England, the same one that held the crew of the *Resolution*. They escaped, made their way to France, the Carolinas, Boston and finally back home to Truro in 1783 for a reunion with family and friends just as the war ended.

CHAPTER 10:
TRURO IN 1794, ITS HARBORS
AND FIRST LIGHTHOUSE

During George Washington's second term as president, a thirty-four-year-old Boston minister and writer toured Truro and wrote the first full description of the town. He was the Reverend James Freeman, a prominent Unitarian minister, whose parents and ancestors had come from Truro when it was still a colonial town.

Although he lived in Boston, Freeman had strong ties to Cape Cod and Truro. He crisscrossed the town in the decade after the Revolutionary War and wrote a profile of it in "A Topographical Description of Truro, in the County of Barnstable, 1794," which was published in *Collections of the Massachusetts Historical Society*. He also followed in the footsteps of the Pilgrims in Truro and published an annotated edition of *Mourt's Relation*. He was responsible for the construction of lifesaving huts along the Atlantic shore of the Outer Cape, and he wrote a pamphlet on how shipwrecked sailors could find the huts. He also was the leader in a campaign to persuade the U.S. Congress to build a lighthouse in Truro, the first on Cape Cod.

James Freeman (1759-1835) was born in Charlestown, Massachusetts, a son of Constant and Lois Cobb Freeman, both natives of Truro. A great-grandfather was Constant Freeman, the Pamet Proprietor who was Truro's first treasurer and one of its earliest selectmen. Freeman made liturgical history when he led the congregation of King's Chapel in Boston, which was the first Episcopal Church in New England, to reject the Trinity and become the first Unitarian church in America. Many of his sermons and speeches were published. A founder of the Massachusetts Historical Society, he was for many years its recording secretary and a contributor to its publications.

Freeman was a plain-spoken intellectual who was ahead of his time on many issues and wrote about them in a clear, precise prose. His profiles of Cape Cod towns are free of rhetorical flourishes and civic boosting. His sermons were considered models of forceful clarity. An activist, he was in the habit of identifying problems and recommending solutions, whether theological, navigational or educational.

"He had a genius for friendship," according to the *Dictionary of American Biography*, "and his intimate circle embraced ministers of all shades of doctrinal belief," including even the first Roman Catholic bishop in mostly Protestant Boston. He also had many friends and relatives in Truro. When he was a twenty-three-year-old Harvard graduate, he wrote to his sister, "While I was upon the Cape I endeavored to visit all my friends; for being now engaged in the church I expect not to go there again for many years."

Despite his misgivings, he was able to visit Cape Cod and write more than a half-dozen articles about its towns.

Truro's poor soil and barren landscape struck him forcefully: "Except for the salt marshes, the soil of the township is sandy, barren and free from rocks and stones . . . The soil in every part of the township is continually depreciating, little pains being taken to manure it." And again, "The soil is not only injured by inattention and bad husbandry, but also by the light sand which is blown

The Reverend James Freeman, who wrote the earliest description of Truro, was the son of Truro natives and the first Unitarian minister of King's Chapel in Boston. He spent considerable time in the 1790s in Truro, where he had friends and relatives. His portrait hangs in the Massachusetts Historical Society building in Boston. (Illustration courtesy of King's Chapel, Boston.)

in from the beach." The farmers grew some corn, rye, turnips, potatoes and pumpkins, but not enough to supply their needs. The
town had to import much of its food from Boston. And because
the soil is deep sand, he says, "the roads are universally bad."

From hilltops, Freeman observed a mostly treeless landscape:
"From those in the north part of the township, nothing can be
discerned, except the meetinghouse, a few windmills and here and
there a wood." One clear day, he admired the unobstructed view
from the meetinghouse, "which commands an extensive prospect
of the ocean, Cape harbor and the opposite shore as far as Monument and the high lands of Marshfield."

Truro was mostly treeless for most of its history. The Pilgrims
had found the Outer Cape "all wooded," but the colonists harvested nearly all the trees for firewood, buildings and ships, and
then used the cleared land for farming and grazing. The town's
landscape continued treeless into the twentieth century. Early
photographs show broad, open vistas punctuated by church steeples
and windmills. Not until the 1930s and 1940s would the pitch
pine and scrub oak take hold on the abandoned farmland. They
soon covered most of Truro. By the end of the twentieth century,
stands of aging pitch pines, attacked by a pine tip moth, were
giving way to a variety of oaks and locust. The hardwood forest
that the Pilgrims described was slowly returning.

"A traveler . . . observing the barrenness of Truro," says Freeman, "would wonder what could induce any person to remain in
such a place. His wonder would cease when he was informed that
the subsistence of the inhabitants is derived principally from the
sea." He then provides a long list of fin fish, shellfish, whales and
sea fowl.

Freeman has little say about Truro's inhabitants or government;
his subject is topography. He does note that able-bodied men were
away on whalers, fishing ships and merchant vessels two-thirds of
the year. "Young men are sent to sea very early in life," he says. "In
general they go at the age of twelve or fourteen and follow the sea
until they are forty-five or fifty years of age." The older men and

small boys remained at home to work the farms, he says, and "the women are generally employed in spinning, weaving and knitting."

. . .

In 1794, Truro's population was by Freeman's account about 1,300 in 165 houses. If correct, each house sheltered more than seven people, although a large number of boys and men would have been away at sea much of time. Only three houses had two stories. "The houses being small are in general finished immediately after they are erected," he says. "The meeting house is painted and in good repair. The inhabitants in general are very constant in their attendance on public worship. There is one water mill [powered by tidal currents] and three windmills." One of the windmills was undoubtedly the grist mill built by Thomas Paine in the early 1700s. Another may have been the big windmill that stands today in Eastham on Route 6. Local lore says that it was built in Plymouth, moved to Truro and then moved again to Eastham sometime around 1800. Accounts differ.

The largest village, with forty houses, was Pond Village, now North Truro, where the Pilgrims spent their second night on shore. Freeman noted that a low spot in the coastal dune afforded the villagers "a convenient landing place" on the bayshore and suggested that a breakwater would improve the anchorage off the beach. Pamet Harbor, which would become a thriving fishing port in forty years, had only a few houses scattered near the river.

East Harbor, one of the earliest settlements, had only fourteen houses, the harbor being "shoal and of little use," according to Freeman. He also noted that the salt marshes around East Harbor were "continually diminished by the blowing in of the sand." By the end of the nineteenth century there would be only three houses at East Harbor.

He estimated that blowing sand had moved the shoreline nearly a half-mile into the East Harbor marshes and Provincetown

Harbor in less than sixty years; and he guessed that the ocean might have equally eroded the beach. That would be about forty-five feet a year, a rate of erosion and silting that sounds greatly exaggerated. In response to fears about the fate of the town, he was reassuring: "There is no probability, however, that the township will soon be overwhelmed by the ocean as some apprehend, the land being so high that it must during many ages resist the force of the waves."

．．．

Harvard-educated and a member of Boston's first board of education, Freeman editorialized about the state of education in Truro: "But though education is more attended to of late than it was some years ago, yet it is much to be wished that the importance and advantage of it were still more considered. Only four persons from Truro have had a college education."

What school was like when Freeman was there is described by another Freeman, Eben Freeman of Wellfleet, who was born in 1790. He went to a private school that was only a few yards from the boundary with Truro. Parents had joined together to build the schoolhouse, which had seats for thirty-two pupils, who came from Truro as well as Wellfleet. The schoolhouse was the first in Wellfleet; a monument in the woods marks the spot. Eben Freeman left his recollections of it in a manuscript he wrote when he was seventy-five years old. In his *History of Wellfleet* (1920), Everett I. Nye provides a partial transcript of Freeman's vivid account:

> In those days there was always someone who went to sea in summer and stayed home in winter. The neighbors would select some such one to teach their boys, hire some kitchen in an old house, fit it up with rough seats and tables. . . . Those with slates and writing books sit at the tables or benches, and readers only sit on low benches. . . . The schoolmaster brings Pike's Arithmetic, the Bible and

Westminister Catechisms. The scholars bring the same if
they have them. Some bring a book called the Psalter [the
Book of Psalms from the Old Testament]. In some schools
there was no arithmetic but the master's. The custom then
was for the master to write his sums down on each scholar's
manuscript so called. The scholar went to his seat and puzzled
it out to prove it by reading the rule. A scholar who could
read a chapter in St. John's Gospel without spelling the
words was thought a good reader; and if he could cipher as
far as the rule of three he was then considered finished, left
school and went to sea for a living. That was the case of the
writer.

There was always plenty of work at home for boys and girls, and
Eben Freeman described the difficulty of making time for schooling: "When I was a boy of ten summers, being the fifth in a family
of eight sons, four older than myself, I was reserved to make up
lost time, perhaps one day a week, when the others were absent
[presumably totaling four days a week], so I lost my winter school
in the new schoolhouse." He also indicated that girls had been
receiving some education: "Summer schools were kept by female
teachers." And he tells how women in town deplored the introduction of spelling books. A teacher from out of town brought a
dozen and sold them for twenty cents apiece. "Some of the old
women, and some others, said it would undo the country. They
never, never read in anything but the New Testament and the
Psalter."

. . .

Six years after the Reverend James Freeman's description of Truro,
Timothy Dwight, the president of Yale College, stopped in Truro
during his tour of Cape Cod and New England. Wondering at the
"dry, sandy, barren" landscape, he noted the use of beach grass to
anchor the shifting sands of the dunes in North Truro. With the

thoroughness of an academic, Dwight went on at length about the "enormous mass of sand" in North Truro and the beach grass planted to hold it in place. The sand, he observed, "is blown into plains, valleys and hills. The hills are of every height, from ten to two hundred feet. Frequently they are naked, round and extremely elegant, and often rough, pointed, wild and fantastical." He marveled at the tenacity of beach grass, which inspired "the admiration and gratitude of man." He was told that the inhabitants of Truro were required by law to plant beach grass every April. One of the planting locations was on the ocean dune where storm waves in the mid-1700s had broken through into the tidal creek above East Harbor. That ocean breakthrough and others after it, which were thought to threaten to carry sand through East Harbor and into Provincetown Harbor on the bay side, would lead to a controversial decision in the late nineteenth century to close East Harbor with a large dike.

Dwight had dinner at Well's tavern, the only one in Truro, and his son had nothing good to say about it in his journal: "This fellow, who is a Frenchman, charged us most enormous bills, nearly double to what we had customarily been charged before. The bill was brought in, in the lump; we requested to have it separate and to see the grounds for the charge; upon this he began to swear and curse and in short to treat us with the true French spirit."

If innkeepers were rude to travelers, Truro's selectmen found it impossible to accommodate a large group of travelers who arrived in May 1792 to settle in the town. There were twenty men and women, most of them with children, some of the women widows. The selectmen did not see how the town could or should receive them. On May 23, they signed an order regarding these "transient persons with their families . . . who have lately come into the town for the purpose of abiding therein, not having obtained the town's consent therefor" and ordered that all of them "with their children and others under their care" leave town within fifteen days. This was an example of the old colonial practice of "warning out," by which small communities defended against a sudden influx of newcomers who might not share their values. The transients may have been gypsies or refugees from political or religious turmoil. Who they were, whence they came, whether they traveled by boat or by land, why they were wandering the countryside and where they went remain unknown.

• • •

The Reverend James Freeman not only provided the first full description of Truro, he also recommended ways to improve Pamet Harbor and make a protected anchorage at Pond Village. The centuries to come would see many such recommendations and some attempts to provide fishing vessels with safe anchorages.

Pamet Harbor, like all Cape Cod harbors, is subject to continual silting. It's a slow, almost imperceptible process but inexorable. The tidal currents pull sand from the banks; offshore currents shift sand from the beach beside the harbor mouth; and the wind blows a fine shower of sand from land into the harbor waters. Although Pamet Harbor was briefly successful in the early 1800s as a fishing port, ever since then the town has alternated between trying to maintain sufficient, round-the-clock depth in the harbor and its channel and accepting the futility of trying to change or stop the effects of wind, wave and tidal flow in a harbor that is barely more than a tidal inlet.

Captain Martin Pring was the first on record to make his anchorage in Pamet Harbor, but he made no comment on its size, depth or usefulness. The Pilgrims thought at first that it might make a suitable harbor for ships. In *Mourt's Relation*, William Bradford said that he stood "right by the cut or mouth which came from the sea" and noted that the river was "not unlike to be a harbor for ships."

When the Pilgrims saw it, the mouth of the Pamet River was much wider and was more than a quarter of mile farther north, almost under the end of Corn Hill. (The present entrance, farther south, was dredged in 1919.) They found it "not navigable for ships, yet . . . a good harbor for boats, for it flows there twelve foot at high water." More than a century later, Freeman would persuade some town leaders to revive the name the Pilgrims gave it, "Cold Harbor," as a richly historical name, but the change did not catch on.

Pamet Harbor is rarely mentioned in the surviving records for most of the 1700s, when Truro was beginning to flourish as a town. The river itself must have been important for the real estate along its banks and especially for its salt-marsh meadows, which were quickly parceled out by the Pamet Proprietors. It seems to have served as an inland waterway for the riverine colonists. Scows and small boats carried hay, firewood, timber and other goods. It almost cut Truro in half, hindering travel, until the first of several bridges was built, probably in the 1720s. At mid-century, at least one wharf was built. The town authorized Jonathan Paine, a descendent of Thomas Paine, to build one "below the bank at Indian Neck [now Tom's Hill] somewhere against the land of Esq. Paine." That would be near Pamet Harbor. But there is little mention in the records of the 1700s of boat traffic, boat-building or shipping in Pamet Harbor or the winding river.

Pamet Harbor, if it could be called a harbor, was described for the first time in any detail in the 1790s. Freeman wrote in *Massachusetts Magazine* (1791) that Truro "has no harbor of any consequence, and but few vessels. Their seamen are employed in other places. Here is an inlet or creek, called Pamet." It was about a hundred feet wide at the mouth and up to twelve feet deep at high tide but with only a foot or two of water at low tide. In the same year, town meeting considered raising money by issuing chances in "a lottery for the purpose of making a harbor at Pamet River so-called in this town." Presumably, making a harbor would require some dredging. If so, this proposal in 1791 was the first time the citizens of Truro thought about improving the mouth of the Pamet River as an anchorage. There is no record, however, of any dredging.

Three years later, Freeman was more optimistic, and he had a new idea: breakwaters. In his "Topographical Description of Truro," he made his recommendation for Pamet Harbor, including the estimated cost:

> At the mouth of this river is a tide harbor. The river divides itself into three branches, on which are three bodies of salt marsh, viz. the Great Meadow [on Pamet River], Hopkins's Meadow [on Little Pamet] and Eagle's Neck Meadow. These branches give a water communication to a great number of the inhabitants with boats, scows, etc. The situation of this harbor is such as justly claims attention; and if repaired, would be of public utility . . . In heavy gales of wind at the northwest it would be a safe retreat for vessels either driving from their anchors in Cape harbor [Provincetown Harbor] or drifting into Barnstable bay [Cape Cod Bay]; and would prevent their running on Truro shore, which has been the fate of many . . . and it might thus be the means of saving much property and perhaps some lives. Pamet Harbor is about a hundred yards wide at the mouth but wider within. A wharf sixty yards in length, fourteen feet wide on the ground and sharp on the top, and ten feet in height would make a safe and good harbor, and by estimation would cost, built with timber and filled up with stones, about eighteen hundred and fifty dollars. Though the top of the wharf would be covered with high water, yet it would break the sea in twelve or thirteen feet of water.

By "wharf" Freeman evidently meant a breakwater in the bay beyond the mouth of the Pamet River and parallel to the shoreline. His 180-foot structure never received serious consideration within his lifetime, although in 1839, according to Shebnah Rich, the Truro Breakwater Company, Inc., applied for but failed to get a federal grant to build one.

. . .

Even the tiny pond at Pond Village was seen as a potential harbor with an anchorage just offshore in Cape Cod Bay. The coastal bank was low at that point, and Freeman noted that it made a convenient landing place. He added, however, that "when the wind blows directly on shore, it comes across a bay nearly eight leagues wide." In rough seas, landings would be decidedly difficult. Freeman reported that there were several proposals to create a suitable anchorage at Pond Village, the town's largest village at the time; and his suggestion in 1794 was a breakwater nearly a quarter-mile long. But, he said, nothing was built because of lack of money and enthusiasm.

A decade later, the Pond Villagers made a small harbor by dredging the pond and digging a channel to Cape Cod Bay. Dr. Jason Ayres led the Truro Pond Harbor Corporation, which undertook the project, but it failed. Seventy-five years later, Shebnah Rich wrote: "This work was accomplished at considerable expense; a few small vessels entered, but the heavy westerly winds soon filled the channel with sand, and it proved a total failure." The pond itself was silting in, too. Alexander Young was there in August 1841 to research his edition of *Mourt's Relation*. He found "the upper or eastern part of it overgrown with flags and bushes. It was no doubt formerly much larger, and has been gradually filling up." In the next decade, Thoreau would meet a farmer who "raised potatoes and pumpkins there where a vessel once anchored."

Yet another attempt to construct a breakwater at Pond Village was made in 1848. The Truro Wharf and Breakwater Co. planned one eight hundred feet long with a wharf extending five hundred feet out almost to the breakwater. Fishing boats could tie up at the wharf behind the breakwater. No sooner had construction started, however, than worms began to destroy the wood pilings. Isaac M. "Mort" Small, resort owner, town official and chronicler, told how chains and anchors held the breakwater in place, but not for long: "Then there came a terrific gale and unusual sea which twisted the thing around, tore it away from its anchorage and practically smashed it all to pieces, and that was the end of the breakwater."

Even in the twentieth century, after the railroad embankment along the shoreline had cut access from the bay to the pond, interest revived in a breakwater. The issue came up in 1920 and again in 1939 when town meeting authorized two thousand dollars towards the expense of a breakwater at North Truro. The idea probably was to shelter fishing boats and the beachfront shacks used by the weir fishermen, but again no action was taken.

. . .

The Reverend James Freeman was also the leading advocate for a lighthouse in Truro, the first on Cape Cod. The idea seems to have arisen around 1790 from the newly formed Massachusetts Humane Society, of which Freeman was a founder. The January 1791 issue of *Massachusetts Magazine* carried a one-paragraph, anonymous item, probably by Freeman, reporting that "much has been said upon the fitness of erecting a lighthouse" at the Highlands in Truro. The next year, the Humane Society petitioned the state to build a lighthouse, preferably with federal funding, "to preserve the lives and property of those who navigate the Bay of Massachusetts."

Freeman may well have inspired the petition. Both he and his friend, the Reverend Levi Whitman of Wellfleet, argued the need for a lighthouse. In his "Topographical Description of Truro," Freeman noted: "The eastern shore of Truro is very dangerous for seamen. More vessels are cast away here than in any other part of the county of Barnstable. A lighthouse near the Clay Pounds, should Congress think proper to erect one, would prevent many of these fatal accidents."

Two years later, Freeman, the Humane Society and the Boston Marine Society sent a petition to the U.S. Congress, then meeting in Philadelphia, recommending a lighthouse as "perhaps the only measure that could aid the navigator in this respect, upon that dangerous winter coast." Congress agreed, and Isaac Small sold ten acres at the Highlands to the United States of America for $110 and was named the first lighthouse keeper. His grandson, Mort Small, would become the marine reporting agent at the lighthouse.

"Clay Pounds" is a curious designation for the area at the Highlands, or Highland. A deep vein of clay runs from the cliff face across the sandy cape almost to the bay, but the term pounds has puzzled historians. The designation dates to the 1600s, turning up first in a town record of 1700 that set aside land for a minister. (The area also went by the Indian name of Tashmuit, referring to the springs there.) Early historians thought that "pounds" referred to the pounding taken by ships that went aground there. Thoreau doubted that derivation. He noted that small ponds there were "upheld by the clay, which were formerly called the Clay Pits." The word "pounds" may have designated depressions in the clay that impounded rainwater.

The contract award to build Cape Cod's first lighthouse should have caused a major scandal and Congressional investigation. The man in charge of building the lighthouse and keeper's dwelling was General Benjamin Lincoln, collector of the port of Boston and superintendent of lighthouses; and the low bidder on the project was none other than his son, Theodore, who managed his father's lumber interests in Maine. The son supplied the lumber, but the father personally supervised the construction. He also borrowed blocks and rigging from a government shipyard. He used a government boat to travel to Truro and probably to bring over stone for the foundation. He used his own team of oxen, rather than pay for Truro oxen, to haul materials to the job site. Midway through the project, he wrote to his son that even as the low bidder their cost would be only half their bid. His son, the nominal winner of the contract, apparently never set foot in Truro. The father managed the project and also managed to escape investigation into his award of the contract to his son.

General Lincoln and his son finished building Cape Cod Light, as it was officially called, by the end of 1797; but lighting the lamps was delayed for several months by the search for an eclipser. This was a semicircular screen that rotated slowly around the array of whale-oil lamps, making it flash periodically. The eclipser mechanism used big weights to power it around a track much as the small, hanging weights in a grandfather clock power the hands. A flashing light was thought necessary to distinguish Highland Light from the steady lights at Boston Harbor and Cape Ann, each about forty miles away. Isaac Small, the first lighthouse keeper, had his salary increased from $150 to $200 a year because of the additional work required to crank the weights up every day and to maintain the eclipser. Historian Larry Lowenthal says that "Cape Cod probably has the distinction of housing the first eclipsing mechanism in an American lighthouse."

The source of light was quite primitive and smelly. Donald W. Davidson describes it in *America's Landfall*: "The light was from a lantern room of spider lamps. These were little more than shallow pans of whale oil, each containing four solid, tubular wicks without any chimneys. Simple as these were, they caused a mess, because the spider lamps gave off a pungent smoke that not only soiled the lantern glass throughout the tower, but also prevented the keeper from staying very long within the lantern room to clean them."

The wooden lighthouse at Highland, an octagon forty to forty-five feet high, soon began to deteriorate. Less than a year after it was completed, an inspector reported that twelve panes of glass had fallen out, the copper dome leaked and the high winds blew sand from around the foundation. Moreover, the eclipser did not perform as intended. The man who succeeded General Lincoln as superintendent of lighthouses concluded later that the lighthouse built by his predecessor was "wretchedly constructed." Nevertheless, Cape Cod's first lighthouse, which became known in Truro and the Outer Cape as Highland Light, lasted nearly thirty-five years on the windswept bluff of clay at the edge of the Atlantic Ocean before it was replaced.

At the same time that he was lobbying for a lighthouse, Freeman recognized that shipwrecked sailors needed shelter from the cold even when they made it to the uninhabited shore. In his position with Humane Society, he led its program to construct huts to provide shelter. The urgency for such huts and their maintenance impressed Freeman when crewmen from the wreck of the *Brutus* in March 1802 froze to death not far from a hut north of East Harbor that had been blown down. The sailors managed to reach shore but died in a snowstorm. Only five survived. The hut had been built "in an improper manner," according to Freeman. "If it had remained, it is probable that the whole of the unfortunate crew of that ship would have been saved, as they gained the shore a few rods only from the spot where the hut had stood."

The Humane Society built a new hut, and several Outer Cape citizens, including the Reverend Jude Damon of Truro, promised to keep it in good repair and supplied with hay or straw. Truro's hut was the first of six the society built between Race Point and Chatham in the early 1800s. They stood on piles and were eight-foot square. The Humane Society (which was not concerned with animal welfare) had been founded in the 1780s to encourage construction of these huts as well as lighthouses and lifesaving stations along the Atlantic Coast. The society also assisted shipwrecked mariners and the survivors of men who died in rescue operations.

Three men with Truro connections were leaders of the Humane Society in its early days. Freeman, a founding member, not only led its efforts for the lighthouse but was authorized to build lifesaving huts on Cape Cod. In 1802, he published a guide to the huts and other shelters from Provincetown to Chatham along the Atlantic shore. He described where there was access inland through the high cliffs and where huts or houses could be found.

A short preface to the guide was supplied by a great-grandson of the Reverend John Avery, Truro's first minister. He was John Avery, the society's secretary. Custom houses and insurance offices distributed the guide. It's difficult, however, to imagine how mariners would have this topographic information at hand or sufficiently memorized to be able to use it after surviving the ordeals of a raging storm at sea and shipwreck, usually in a blinding snowstorm. The third society leader with Truro connections was Benjamin Rich, a native of Truro and a shipmaster who became a Boston merchant and who was president of the Humane Society when it built the lifesaving huts.

However well-intentioned, the huts got little use, if any. There's no record of anyone taking shelter in the hut in North Truro, although it was there most of the 1800s when dozens of ships were wrecked. Thoreau was not impressed with what he saw on his visit in 1849. He peeked through a knothole and saw "some stones and some loose wads of wool on the floor, and an empty fireplace at the further end; but it *was not* supplied with matches, or straw, or hay, that we could see, nor 'accommodated with a bench,'" as Freeman had specified. Thoreau concluded that "it was not a *humane* house at all, but a sea-side box, now shut up."

Thoreau would chronicle more about pre-Civil War Truro than its lifesaving huts. He found much to write about the Atlantic Ocean shore, Highland Light and Truro's bare and windswept landscape. His interest, however, did not extend to commercial development, and he wrote little about Truro's brief period of commercial success—a fishing boom that also took the lives of many of its boys and young men.

PART III:
Boom Times, Hard Times

CHAPTER 11:
A FISHING BOOM,
BUT MANY LOST AT SEA

P amet Harbor–Freeman's "inlet or creek" of the 1790s–in just a few decades became a bustling fishing port with shipyards, stores, fish-processing sheds and three long wharves. More than sixty cod and mackerel boats worked out of Truro at the peak of the boom years, which ran from about 1830 to 1855. Vessels tied up and unloaded at wharves on both sides of the river. Carpenters sawed and hammered Truro timber to build the mackerel smacks and cod-fishing schooners. Hundreds of boys and men worked at Pamet Harbor or on its fishing vessels; men and women worked at the codfish flakes next to the wharves. The town was home to more people than ever before–slightly more than two thousand–a figure that would not be surpassed until the year 2000. Near the harbor, squat windmills turned in the wind to pump saltwater into shallow tanks under shed roofs to produce salt. A grist mill harnessed the tides to grind grain into flour. A lighthouse guided mariners seeking Pamet Harbor. Adding to the busy scene were the arrivals and departures of the packet boat, a schooner that carried freight packets and passengers to and from Boston.

Maneuvering under sail in the crowded, shallow harbor and its entrance must have been quite a challenge. The harbor entrance was a long, winding channel from the bay near Corn Hill to the wharves. Fishing boats had to enter or leave as close as possible to high tide. The harbor's strong tidal currents and brisk winds tested the seamanship of any sailor tacking between the shifting shoals of sand. Although the town petitioned Congress in 1833 for federal aid to deepen the harbor, there's no indication that any work was done. Town meeting voted to place buoys at the harbor entrance for the summer season, noting that they would have to be moved as the river channel changed.

Truro's economic boom, based primarily on its fishing fleet, also included the production of tons of salt from sea water and great quantities of wool from hundreds of sheep. New homes and commercial buildings went up everywhere, including a two-story building for civic and fraternal society meetings, which became the town hall that stands today, although in disrepair.

• • •

Before prosperity, however, came adversity. Cape Cod's fishermen had barely recovered from the hardships of the Revolutionary War when they had to cope with the nation's trade wars with England and France, wars both declared and undeclared. Trade embargoes were originally intended to punish the British, but American shipping interests suffered equally, if not more. Shebnah Rich noted that for Cape Cod the nation's trade embargo of 1808 was "a calamity . . . much referred to by the old people of our younger days . . . The ocean fisheries were abandoned; the dismantled vessels rotted at the grassy wharfs."

The embargo dispute and a desire to annex Canada led into the War of 1812 against England; and once again Truro, without adequate defenses, sought help from Boston against possibility of British raiding parties. The town asked the state for two field pieces and some small arms, but they did not arrive.

Once again, British warships controlled Provincetown Harbor. Writing after the war ended, Major James D. Graham, who was surveying Provincetown Harbor, reported that the British "kept a strong squadron almost constantly stationed here, enabling him [the British] not only to dictate the terms upon which its inhabitants were permitted to exist but also to cripple our commerce and to destroy the property of our citizens." And once again, the British fired cannonballs into Truro–but apparently without any hostile intent. Rich says that the *Majestic* anchored off Truro and "used the old mill that then stood on Mill Hill as a target during artillery practice" and that the townsfolk stayed clear of the old mill. One of the cannonballs reportedly was turned into andirons.

British warships controlled the seas off New England, interrupting shipping from Cape Cod ports. They captured American ships that dared to leave port, confiscated their cargoes and burned the vessels. Deyo's history states that "the *Spencer*, of fifty-two guns, held possession of Provincetown Harbor and was considered by the people of the Cape the 'Terror of the Bay.'"

Provincetown Harbor was still unfortified, and the poorly organized militias of Truro and Provincetown were in no position to repel the British Navy and Marines. British officers found they could come and go in Truro whenever they wished. Rich heard about their visits from his elders: "The officers often landed, visited the houses, were always very civil, and became well acquainted with a good many families. They purchased butter, milk, eggs, chickens and other supplies and secured small repairs as needed, paying for them quite liberally with British gold."

Meanwhile, behind the scenes of peaceful Truro, the men were making money by running the British blockade and attacking British shipping. Some fishermen took their catch under cover of night or fog to Sandwich, where they hauled boat and cargo overland to Buzzards Bay and then sailed on to New York City. Some engaged in privateering, outfitting their own ships or serving on others that preyed on British merchant vessels. "Considerable money was made privateering," says Rich, citing Captain Reuben Rich, who captured a British ship on his first day out, took her to Boston and collected seventeen thousand dollars from the sale of his interest.

The risks were considerable. Ten sailors from Truro were taken prisoner when their privateer was captured by the British. They spent the rest of the war in the English prison at Dartmoor. Just before the end of the war, Nathaniel Snow of Truro was captain of the brig *Reindeer*, manned mostly by Cape Cod sailors, that cruised off the coast of Spain, capturing and burning six British vessels. The War of 1812 ended in a stalemate, and when trade resumed, Truro was in a good position to share in the booming economy that followed.

· · ·

The greatest commercial prosperity and population growth in Truro's history began around 1830 and lasted for a quarter-century. Surprisingly, at the center of it was Pamet Harbor, which most observers had thought was no harbor at all. The first of three big wharves was Union Wharf, which was several hundred feet long. David Lombard started a mackerel-packing operation. Elisha Newcomb built the first flake-yard for drying codfish and sheds for fish packing, along with a house for himself.

At the fish-processing sheds, mackerel were packed in brine in barrels. The cod were split open, salted and dried on outdoor racks called flakes. Edward Augustus Kendall observed the process: "The making of fish is the employment of women. The fishermen throw out their cargoes upon the beach, and the women spread and turn the fish upon the flakes. The flakes are stands of ten or twelve yards in length, three or four in width and about two feet high. Branches of trees are spread on them; and the fish, being previously opened, is laid on the branches to lose their moisture." The smell, he says, was "most unpleasant."

The processed fish were loaded onto the packet boat *Post-boy* for shipment to Boston. The packet boat, which operated on a regular schedule subject to wind and tides, brought the mail and various goods back to Truro. Rich admired the *Post-boy* as "the finest specimen of naval architecture and of passenger accommodation in the Bay waters . . . Her cabin and furniture were finished in solid mahogany and bird's-eye [maple], and silk draperies."

Merchants built outfitting stores, a rigger shop, a hardware store and a variety store and stocked them with goods from Boston. Shipbuilding became a major industry; Deyo's history lists fifteen brigs and schooners built in the fourteen years between 1837 and 1851. Two sailmakers opened sail lofts. An entrepreneur dug a well at the foot of Tom's Hill to supply ships with fresh water.

Cod and mackerel fueled the economic boom. Men and boys began longer voyages to the major fishing grounds, particularly the Grand Banks and then Georges Bank. Like many other Cape Codders, they became professional, commercial fishermen. For most of the year, they were either at sea or were working on their gear. Although fishing was a seasonal occupation, almost all the men listed in the town's vital records in the 1840s were mariners.

Pamet Harbor was the home port for sixty-three vessels in the cod and mackerel fishing business in 1837, according to John Warner Barber, a Massachusetts historian writing just two years later. Shebnah Rich claimed that he saw forty-nine hauled out at Pamet Harbor one winter. A 1922 state survey of Cape Cod's economy reported: "It is said that in twenty-five years, from 1840 to 1865, 111 vessels, first and last, belonged to Truro, were sailed by Truro captains and manned by Truro crews." Thoreau was walking in North Truro one fine October day in 1849 when the mackerel fleet from the Outer Cape harbors sailed around Race Point and out to sea. He says he counted "about two hundred sail of mackerel fishers within one small arc of the horizon and a nearly equal number had disappeared southward."

The economic factors were all favorable. Cod, mackerel and herring were abundant. Fishing vessels small enough to use Pamet Harbor were still efficient and cost-effective. More than sixty vessels could find moorings, dock space or anchorages in Pamet Harbor. The markets in the East and Midwest were beginning to grow. Transportation to them was improving. As long as all these conditions remained favorable, Truro was well-positioned to share in the success of the New England fisheries.

Captains and crews on the fishing boats shared the risks, both personal and financial; but many of the crews seemed to be constantly in debt. Before going out on a fishing schooner, a crewman would go to Town Hall and have the clerk record his agreement to pay most or all of his earnings to the captain, the grocery store or a friend who would take care of the fisherman's family. The town clerk's books of the late 1800s are full of such records. Isaac Remick authorized Captain Daniel Atwood in 1871 to pay the Union Trading Company "all that I may earn with you the present fishing season in consideration of groceries furnished and to be furnished me and my family." Year after year, Luther P. Honey signed over all his earnings and that of his son, Willie, from fishing on the schooner *Mary Snow* in return for $150 from Joshua Knowles and Knowles's agreement to support Honey's family. The fishermen were constantly in debt to their captain, the company store or someone in town who would advance them money.

Many Truro sea captains began their careers as young boys. Benjamin Coan went to sea in 1833 at age nine and later was a captain for twenty years. Sylvester Atwood went to sea at age twelve and was a captain for eight years, then switched to weir fishing. Elisha Cobb followed the sea for fifty years, twenty-eight of them as captain. Richard Rich worked summers on fishing boats for nineteen years and then became a captain for eighteen years.

The demand for fishermen was such that boys as young as eleven often sailed with their fathers, brothers, uncles and cousins. With fair weather and the right captain, the voyages must have been fine adventures for the boys. Shebnah Rich, who worked on a mackerel boat off the Grand Banks when he was seventeen, wrote enthusiastically about the joys of sailing: "A larger fleet and finer maneuvering have never been seen than in a fleet of fishermen."

But when a ship foundered in a storm, boys and men drowned together, and Truro families mourned the loss of their loved ones and breadwinners.

. . .

"Lost at sea." "Washed overboard on homeward passage." "Fell from rigging." "Never heard from." The phrases appear again and again in records and on gravestones in the late 1700s and into the 1800s. Wives, mothers, sisters, small children were left waiting and hoping week after week, then month after month, for some word about the young men and boys. Eventually, for many, the only word was, "never heard from." Parents carried on without their sons; many of the young wives and mothers were widowed.

Over the years, almost three hundred boys and men from Truro died at sea. The Reverend Jude Damon listed eighty-one casualties from 1790 to 1825. And this was not yet the peak of the fishing business. The West Indies also claimed the lives of many Truro men; Damon recorded that twenty-eight died there, perhaps of tropical diseases, or on the voyages out or back. Four men, three named Rich, died in Havana. Rich continued the count of deaths at sea to 1880 and added more than two hundred names. The total of at least 285 deaths over the decades was an average of only three a year, but the deaths often came in major disasters that sometimes struck a family in a single, calamitous stroke of misfortune. In one storm in 1825, a Snow family lost three sons—Henry, John and Leonard—and a kinsman Reuben Snow.

The town's worst disaster occurred during the October Gale of 1841, which took fifty-seven lives. The gale struck the fishing fleet on Sunday, October 3, when the ships were at Georges Bank, about ninety miles east of Cape Cod. One of the few survivors was Joshua Knowles of Truro, master of the *Garnet*. He left a detailed record, printed by Rich. On Sunday night, the winds blew out the *Garnet*'s sails; the seas were breaking over the vessel. Knowles's crew of ten went below, except for his brother Zack. A tremendous sea broke over the vessel and almost rolled her over. Zack was washed overboard but caught the mainsheet and hauled himself on board. The foremast broke off and tangled rigging was all over the decks. "We were now a helpless wreck," said Knowles. The gale moderated on Monday. The weather was fine on Tuesday, and at sunset the crew flagged a passing merchant ship bound from Liverpool to New York with four hundred immigrants in steerage. Knowles was astonished to find that the captain was John Collins, "a Truro boy and formerly my nearest neighbor and a connection by marriage."

Seven other Truro boats were not so lucky. They foundered and all hands were lost. The seven captains were all under the age of thirty. The oldest fisherman was forty-one. Eight of the storm victims were named Paine–four of them brothers and great-great-grandsons of Thomas Paine. Eight were named Snow. Five were named Rich, three of them brothers. The youngest were a thirteen-year-old, two twelve-year-olds and one boy who was eleven. Three bodies of teenage boys were recovered when a capsized wreck drifted into Nauset Harbor. Search and rescue vessels found no survivors nor even any sign of the other vessels lost in the storm.

Truro had twenty-seven more widows as a result of the storm, making a total of 105 widows in town, many with children. Nearly all the husbands had been lost at sea, according to the *Yarmouth Register*'s account. Young women became wary of marrying fishermen. An elderly shipbuilder later affirmed that "the favor of young women and indeed of their parents in respect to marriage was extended much more freely to landsmen than to fishermen or sailors."

The report of the devastating disaster spread throughout New England and even to Washington D.C. Contributions poured into town. Boston sent two boatloads of provisions and clothing valued at eight hundred dollars. Benjamin Rich, a prominent Boston merchant and shipowner who was a native of Truro, collected more than four thousand dollars in cash for the families of the victims. Provincetown contributed $450, a Falmouth church thirty dollars. The Sandwich Amateur Band gave a benefit concert to raise a contribution. Daniel Webster, the famous orator and secretary of state in Washington, sent a modest but heartfelt contribution and recalled his visit to Truro several years earlier. A simple stone obelisk commemorating the disaster stands in the Congregational Church graveyard. The names of the storm victims are inscribed on the sides, and the epitaph ends, "and the mourners go about the streets."

Fishing and offshore whaling in small dories from Truro's beaches on Cape Cod Bay could also be perilous. Three young men of the Rich family drowned in the bay off South Truro when their skiff was swamped in November 1833. Two years later, two more Richs and three other men drowned when the *Bianca* capsized in heavy seas in the bay off Great Hollow just before they reached home. Four Truro boys under sixteen and the captain of their fishing boat drowned in the bay off Pond Landing in 1847.

In the worst of the local marine disasters, nine Truro fishermen and one from Wellfleet drowned in calm waters of Cape Cod Bay off South Truro, where they had anchored one morning in September 1844. People on shore saw the schooner *Commerce*, which had been out fishing for mackerel, swinging at anchor. When none of the crew appeared in town, several men boarded the *Commerce* but found no one.. Searching the shoreline, they found the schooner's boat washed ashore and intact except for a split in one of the hull planks. Over the next two weeks, the ten bodies washedup on the shore from Barnstable to Provincetown. LozienPeirce of South Truro, who reported the mishap for *Zion's Herald and Wesleyan Journal,* said that five wives were made widows and fourteen children fatherless. Among the victims were four men named Rich. Peirce surmised that since the captain's watch had stopped at four o'clock, the men must have been coming ashore in the pre-dawn darkness. Why they all drowned so close to shore was not explained.

Fishermen's shacks, not summer homes, lined the beach along the shore of Cape Cod Bay in the 1850s at the height of Truro's short-lived prosperity. Two chimneys suggest that some of the shacks contained try works for boiling oil from the carcasses of whales that grounded on the beach or were harpooned in the bay. The engraving is from *Gleason's Pictorial* of 1856. (Courtesy of Peabody Essex Museum, Salem, Mass.)

. . .

For a small fishing town with a shallow harbor, Truro produced a surprising number of captains who sailed deepwater ships on the seven seas. The Reverend James Freeman wrote in 1794 that Truro mariners shipped on vessels from other ports and that "many of the masters employed from Boston and other ports are natives of Truro." In the decades before the Civil War, Truro men commanded schooners, barks, brigantines and magnificent clipper ships that carried cargoes and passengers around the world. They were away from home so often and for so long, that records about who they were and where they sailed are not easy to find.

The historian Henry C. Kittredge interviewed descendants, ransacked attics and searched boxes of old papers in obscure corners of libraries in order to write *Shipmasters of Cape Cod* (1935). He regretted the lack of information about Truro captains in particular:

> Where are the records . . . of Captain Samuel Rider of Truro who wrote from Virginia that his 410-ton ship, Liverpool Packet, was too large and that he could have done better with a smaller vessel? Two other Truro captains, Nehemiah Harding and Jazzaniah Gross, were trading to European ports . . . but one may seek in vain for any account of their voyages. The same is true of two more Truro shipmasters, the brothers, Ephraim and Henry Snow. Captain Ephraim, trading to Liverpool and Spain, crossed the Atlantic fifty times in the years following 1807 in the schooner Ruth and the ships Mt. Vernon and Warren. His brother began foreign voyaging in the schooner Speedwell in 1811 and kept it up until about 1824. And what of their follow townsman, Captain Obadiah Rich . . . who could find his way between Boston and Archangel with no more elaborate reckoning than a few chalk marks on the cabin door?

Nevertheless, Kittredge and Shebnah Rich did manage to bring to light the names of many sea captains and some of their adventures and misfortunes. Truro in the nineteenth century was not only a fishing port and whalers' town but the hometown for no fewer than forty-five captains of long-voyage sailing vessels, including clipper ships.

Clipper ships were the queens of the ocean. In his maritime history of Massachusetts, Samuel Eliot Morison exclaimed that "never in these United States has the brain of man conceived or the hand of man fashioned so perfect a thing as the clipper ship." Kittredge called clipper ship captains "the aristocrats of an already aristocratic profession." At their design zenith, the ships were "extreme clippers." Faster and bigger than anything on the water, they were tricky to handle and required audacity and the ultimate in seamanship.

Three Truro sea captains commanded clipper ships. Levi Stevens was captain of the *Southern Cross* in 1851 when she beat the clipper *Buena Vista*, on the run from San Francisco to Calcutta. His ship made the voyage in fifty-six days, four days ahead of the *Buena Vista*. Another Truro captain of the *Southern Cross* was Elisha Paine; he died in Calcutta in 1858. Captain Atkins Hughes of North Truro commanded a later clipper ship of the same name. Upon his retirement, he became a leading investor in Truro's fish weirs and fish processing plant.

Many of the Truro men who were captains of merchant ships are known by the records that listed them as lost at sea or because Shebnah Rich knew many of them or their immediate survivors. The three Knowles brothers were early nineteenth-century ship captains, who died at sea, as did a seaman brother. Captain Paul Knowles was in command of a brig on a voyage from Spain to Boston when it foundered in a gale. Captain Caleb Knowles died on a passage from Senegal to Boston. Captain Isaiah Knowles died when a squall capsized his ship on his first voyage as captain, a voyage to the African coast. Another Truro captain who was lost at sea was twenty-six-year-old Samuel Mayo, commander of the

Malvina A., built in Truro, which foundered on its second voyage. Storms and shipwrecks were not the only dangers. Florida Indians reportedly killed Captain Shubael A. Thomas and his crew after they went aground; and pirates murdered Caleb Upham Grozier, captain of a brig, along with all but one of his crewmen in 1828.

Most of Truro's captains were only in their twenties and early thirties when they took command of fishing vessels. Many of them came from Truro's oldest families—Knowles, Snow, Paine, Stevens, Hopkins, Doane, Rich, Grozier, Cobb, Upham, Mayo, Lombard, Rich, Collins, Atkins. In time, captains who survived the dangers of seafaring changed careers or retired to a quiet life in Truro. Captain Freeman Atkins had a saltworks in Truro and was co-owner of the big grist mill on Town Hall Hill that was a landmark for seafarers.

Captain John Collins of Truro not only commanded the largest sailing vessels but was also closely involved in building the first transatlantic steamships. At eighteen, he was a seaman on an American privateer that was captured by the British during the War of 1812. After the war, he became master of merchant ships sailing from New York to Mexico and New Orleans. For several years, he was captain of the *Roscius*, one of the largest and finest merchant ships of her time. It was the *Roscius* that rescued the crew of the *Garnet* after the October Gale of 1841 that took fifty-seven lives. Captain Collins later became a partner of his nephew, Edward K. Collins, also of Truro, in a steamship line that would lead the world for a short few years.

Edward K. Collins was a businessman-hero. He left Truro at fifteen, went into the shipping business, and in the 1850s launched the first American fleet of transatlantic passenger steamships. Aided by a federal subsidy, the Collins line built and operated five ocean liners that competed successfully with Britain's Cunard Line. His paddle-wheel steamships could make the New York-Liverpool run in about eleven days, a day faster than the Cunard ships. The Collins line ships were praised for their speed, elegance and comfort and for giving America the lead in transatlantic transportation. Collins's ships were portrayed on postage stamps. He had a three-hundred-acre estate in Westchester County, north of New York City.

Then disaster struck. The Collins steamer *Arctic* collided with a French steamer, *Vesta*, and sank with the loss of more than three hundred lives. Collins's wife, daughter and son were among the victims. Scandal ensued, for not a single woman or child was among the eighty-six survivors who made it to shore in lifeboats. Two years later, another Collins vessel, the *Pacific*, left Liverpool with 240 passengers and was never heard from again. The next year, Collins lost the federal subsidy to Vanderbilt shipping interests. The Collins line had prospered for less than a decade before going out of business. Edward Collins died in 1878 in a modest house in Manhattan, left a small estate and was buried in an unmarked grave.

. . .

For a quarter-century before the Civil War, Truro enjoyed a spurt of prosperity and fame based primarily on its fishing fleet, some offshore whaling and the careers of its sea captains on the world's oceans. The economic boom, however, was not confined to Pamet Harbor and the fishing and shipping interests. A variety of industries blossomed in other parts of the town in a convergence of commercial endeavors that would never again be equaled.

CHAPTER 12:
SALT, SHEEP AND SUMMER
SOJOURNERS

The twenty-five years beginning around 1830 brought prosperity not just for the fishermen and their suppliers at Pamet Harbor but also for the rest of the town. Its population grew to be greater than at any other time in its history until the end of the twentieth century. The census of 1850 counted 2,051 residents; the census for the year 1999 counted only thirty-six more.

Construction boomed. Carpenters were kept busy building houses for the burgeoning population, stores for the businessmen, three lighthouses for mariners, six churches for the religious, grist mills to grind grain, evaporating tanks to make salt, and a community building that would become Town Hall.

Even shoemakers and haberdashers prospered. Truro cobblers made one thousand boots and shoes in 1837, according to a state report, although the business was short-lived. Hat-makers turned out Panama hats made of palm leaves, working in Union Hall before it became Town Hall, according to tradition. Much more substantial, along with its fishery, were two other Truro industries—salt manufacturing and sheep raising.

. . .

The production of salt from sea water on Cape Cod started during
the Revolutionary War when the British blockaded imports of salt.
In its peak year, 1837, Truro had thirty-nine saltworks that produced 17,490 bushels of salt, surpassing Wellfleet, Harwich and
Sandwich. Most saltworks operators in Truro had a dozen or more
evaporating tanks. One of the largest saltworks, extending over
several acres, was at Mill Pond, off Pamet Harbor. With the high
salinity of its shoreline water undiluted by rivers, Truro, along
with other Cape Cod towns, enjoyed success as a major producer
of salt until mid-century.

William P. Quinn tells in *The Saltworks of Historic Cape Cod*
how the saltworks operated by solar evaporation. The basic saltworks unit had three adjacent wooden tanks, each about ten feet
by sixteen feet and nine to twelve inches deep, topped by a wooden
roof on rollers. A windmill pumped salt water from Cape Cod Bay
into the highest tank, which was set on short posts. After most of
the water evaporated from the first tank, the strong brine was
drained into the next tank, the pickle room, where lime precipi-
tated. When solid crystals began to form, the liquid was drained
into the third tank, where the thick brine produced salt crystals in
quantity. The salt was then moved to a warehouse for final drying.
From sea water to salt took about three weeks.

The roofs were on rollers so that in good weather they could
be rolled back for evaporation by the sun. If a rainstorm struck
suddenly, neighbors would rush to help the workers roll the roofs
over the tanks. When all the roofs rolled at once, they reportedly
created a rumble that rivaled the thunder of a summer storm.

Eventually, Cape Cod's saltworks became uncompetitive.
Quinn lists the reasons: The state had ended its subsidy in 1834.
The federal government repealed its tariff on salt imports, which
had protected the local industry from lower prices. Storms dam-
aged the shed roofs and tanks, and the price increased for Maine
pine boards that were used to build and repair them. "Probably

A typical salt works with a windmill to pump salt water into the evaporating tanks. The peaked roofs could be rolled aside to expose the salt water to the sun. (From Simeon Deyo's *History of Cape Cod*, published in 1890.)

the chief reason for the decline," says Quinn, "was the increased competition from the salt springs in New York, Virginia and Kentucky."

Thoreau could have been writing about Truro when he described in 1849 the decline of the saltworks in Provincetown: "The turtle-like sheds of the salt works were crowded into every nook in the hills, immediately behind the town, and their now-idle windmills lined the shore . . . But [the men] were now, as elsewhere on the Cape, breaking up their saltworks and selling them for lumber." The recycled lumber struck strangers by its peculiar appearance. Frederick Freeman quotes an observer's wonder at "a sort of fancy-stained, rust spotted, regularly patterned boarding, which in admired disorder finally from its frequency comes to haunt the observer and demand explanation." The recycled boards were marked by rusty circles and streaks of rust left by the iron nails. Such boards can still be found today in a few old buildings.

. . .

Raising sheep for wool was a major occupation during the boom years, if only for a decade or so. In 1841, John Hayward devoted a third of his short article in the *New England Gazetteer* to Truro's success in producing wool: "No one would suppose that this was much of a wool growing place; and it is not so in regard to the quantity grown but much so as it regards its means. In 1837 the people of Truro sheared four hundred sheep of their own rearing. If the single county of Penobscot, in Maine, would produce as much wool in proportion to its territory and the quality of its soil as the town of Truro . . . the quantity would be sufficient to clothe all the inhabitants of the globe."

Hayward noted that the great flocks of sheep kept the hillsides and meadows cropped short. Although he also reported that Truro had to import almost all its fuel and most of its food, he concluded on a positive note: "There are but few towns in the state where the people are more flourishing and independent in their circumstances."

The shepherds' fortunes, however, soon plunged. A little more than a decade later, Thoreau would write: "A few years ago Truro was remarkable among the Cape towns for the number of sheep raised in it; but I was told that at this time only two men kept sheep in the town; and in 1855 a Truro boy ten years old told me that he had never seen one." The problem was the cost of fencing. Cedar rails had to be imported from Maine because Truro had no trees. Thoreau was told that sheep needed four rails, instead of the usual two, and the expense of the enclosure was the reason farmers no longer raised sheep.

. . .

Truro's Town Hall dates to 1848 when investors led by Barnabas Paine built a two-story building that they called Union Hall and rented to various groups. The Odd Fellows and the Sons of Temperance were among the social and civic groups that used it for meetings. Within two years, town meetings were moved there from the nearby Congregational meetinghouse. Union Hall was in the same architectural style as the meetinghouse and was almost as large.

On February 6, 1866, town meeting voted 67-49 to buy Union Hall from the original investors for no more than nine hundred dollars. Two years later, Union Hall became the Town Hall; the first town office consisted of a table and a bookcase on the first floor. The selectmen rented the second-floor auditorium and stage to a variety of groups, including the Truro Central Literary Institute, the Truro Benevolent Society, religious organizations, and anyone sponsoring "free lectures tending to promote the public good."

After the Civil War, part of Town Hall was briefly occupied by a shoe manufacturing business. In an effort to create jobs in its declining economy, town meeting voted in 1872 to subsidize the establishment of the Truro Cooperative Shoe Manufacturing Company and provide space for its operations in Town Hall. For a time, about eighteen cobblers were working in Town Hall; but the effort at small-town industrial development did not succeed. John B. Dyer, town clerk, said in his 1909 historical paper that in the company's first year "133 pairs were made complete in one day, but the inability to compete with the centralized industry brought ultimate failure to the business."

The building went through countless renovations, including a stubby addition that was attached at the rear. By the end of the twentieth century, plumbing and electrical systems needed upgrading. Paint was peeling, floors were sagging and the roof was leaking. The building did not meet standards for handicapped access. After 150 years, it was time for major renovations or a new Town Hall, and at the end of the century the town was considering its options.

. . .

Among the many construction projects during the boom years were three lighthouses. The federal government replaced Highland Light twice and built a smaller lighthouse at Pamet Harbor. The original, "wretchedly constructed" Highland Light, or Cape Cod Light, as it was known to mariners, was replaced in 1831. Unaccountably, the new lighthouse, the second of three Highland Lights, has been overlooked by Cape Cod historians. They generally have assumed that the first lighthouse, built in 1797, was replaced by today's lighthouse, which was built in 1857. The second lighthouse found a place in American literature in the writings of Thoreau. He stayed at the forgotten lighthouse and wrote about it in magazine articles and his book *Cape Cod*.

The second lighthouse was designed to be much more substantial than the first. It was made of brick instead of wood, and the walls at the base were more than three feet thick. The workmanship, however, again turned out to be shoddy, and the lamps in the lantern room were not always maintained as they should have been. In 1838, a government inspector arrived unannounced a few minutes before sundown. He reported that he "found the keeper (alarmed at the sight of the revenue cutter) stolen into his lantern to make a hasty rub-up . . . few of the lamps were trimmed. Such chimneys as had been touched were imperfectly cleaned. The reflectors had no appearance of being recently burnished, and the glass of the lantern was smoked."

Two years later, the top third of the tower was torn down and rebuilt by a contractor who said the wood was rotten and the masonry crumbling in the walls. He installed an iron staircase, whose hollow center-post ingeniously served as an air supply to the lantern room and a chimney flue out the roof. The lamp's new reflectors were plated with twenty-one ounces of pure silver. Upon completion of the work he had to defend its cost.

HIGHLAND LIGHT, TRURO, MASS.

The forgotten lighthouse, the second of three at Highland, which was built in 1831, is the lighthouse that Thoreau visited several times. The present lighthouse replaced it in 1857, the year after this engraving appeared in *Gleason's Pictorial*. (Courtesy of Peabody Essex Museum.)

In 1848, when Thoreau made his first visit to Truro he stayed overnight with the lighthouse keeper, James Small. James's son Mort, four years old at the time, would later recall that Thoreau appeared at their door one October day and asked to stay the night: "I thought him quite a wonderful man. I remember he was a man who required but little sleep; he would sit up until eleven o'clock or after and then be up the next morning at four. He would sit two or three hours on the edge of the cliffs watching the passing boats and the sea gulls." Thoreau gave the boy two lead pencils, probably of his own design and made in his family's factory.

At dusk, Thoreau climbed the circular staircase with the keeper to the lantern room with its fifteen lamps and reflectors. The keeper complained about the quality of the oil that was furnished. If the whale oil was not properly processed for winter use, it would congeal and burn poorly or not at all. Thoreau thought "perhaps a few lives might be saved if better oil were provided."

Shipwrecks were a major interest of Thoreau, and with some skepticism he noted that "notwithstanding that this lighthouse has . . . been erected, after almost every storm we read of one or more vessels wrecked here; and sometimes more than a dozen wrecks are visible from this point at one time." He found that "it would not do to speak of shipwrecks . . . for almost every family has lost some of its members at sea."

The experience of sleeping at a lighthouse impressed him: "The lighthouse lamps a few feet distant shone full into my chamber and made it as bright as day, so I knew exactly how the Highland Light bore all that night, and I was in no danger of being wrecked. . . . I thought, as I lay there, half awake and half asleep, looking upward through the window at the lights above my head, how many sleepless eyes from far out on the Ocean stream—mariners of all nations spinning their yarns through the various watches of the night—were directed toward my couch." In the next century, another nature writer, Henry Beston, author of *The Outermost House*, would stay with the lighthouse keeper and watch "the great spokes of light revolving as solemnly as a part of the universe."

While noting that the bluff on which the lighthouse stood "was fast wearing away," Thoreau also estimated that "generally it was not wearing away here at the rate of more than six feet annually." He allowed that he might have been wrong for lack of long-term data, and indeed coastal scientists today estimate the long-term erosion rate at two to three feet a year on average. "Erelong," Thoreau said, "the lighthouse must be moved." In less than a 150 years, it would be moved; but first it had to be replaced.

"They are now building another still on the same spot," wrote Thoreau in his journal for 1857 on his last visit to Highland Light. This was the third and present-day lighthouse. It was furnished with new optics from France, called a Fresnel lens, that concentrated the light in a powerful narrow beam, although the lamps continued to burn whale oil. A fog horn, installed in 1873, used compressed air blown across reeds to create the warning wail. Three coal-fired, piston engines compressed the air. For more than a century, the mournful sound of a fog horn at Highland Light could be heard throughout much of Truro on foggy days and nights.

. . .

As the maritime, salt and sheep-raising industries waned, tourism began to bring income to Truro homeowners who had rooms for boarders or houses for rent. The first vacationers arrived before the Civil War. In 1856, the *New England Gazetteer,* which claimed on its title page to offer descriptions of "fashionable resorts," recommended Truro as a seaside resort. Although Truro in the 1850s could not have been that fashionable, the author, John Hayward, wrote that Pamet Village "is very pleasant and flourishing, and is a fine location, and easy of access, for all those who wish to enjoy sea air and bathing, and marine scenery, in their greatest perfection, on terra firma."

Thoreau had also seen Truro as a seaside resort, and he may have inspired Hayward's recommendation. Shortly after Thoreau's overnight at Highland Light in October 1849, he returned to Boston and gave several public lectures on his visit to the Outer Cape. He might well have included a word on the attractions of Truro as a resort, for his book *Cape Cod* is based in part on his lectures and in it, he wrote: "The time must come when this coast will be a place of resort for those New-Englanders who really wish to visit the seaside." The tourist industry in Truro may have been launched by the public lectures of the naturalist Thoreau.

Thoreau and his companion, Ellery Channing, were among the earliest, if not the first, guests of the Small family. The family lodgings were the beginnings of Highland House, the first and most important resort in Truro. In a letter from Truro dated July 8, 1855, Thoreau invited a friend, Harrison Blake, to join him. Thoreau was staying at the keeper's house attached to the light-house, which he found much superior to the Provincetown hotel. He told Blake that "our host has another larger and very good house, within a quarter of a mile, unoccupied, where he says he can accommodate several more." The unoccupied house became Highland House. Blake did not join Thoreau in Truro, but vaca-tioners soon followed Thoreau to the Small family resort near the lighthouse.

The resort was a great success, even during the Civil War. On September 8, 1863, the *Barnstable Patriot* reported from High-land Light: "The season has been a successful one here, and greatly enjoyed by the crowds that have visited this delightful summer retreat. Squire [James] Small has been crowded to an overflow . . . In this age of enterprise it seems strange that there are not in-creased accommodations for the increasing numbers who desire to breathe the healthful and invigorating air of Provincetown and Truro . . . Large and small parties from Provincetown and Wellfleet come here every day and enliven the place with their great diver-sity of character." Before the end of the century, Mort Small would embark on an ambitious expansion program. The time would come, as Thoreau had predicted, that Truro would be a popular seaside resort.

. . .

Truro was a special place for Thoreau, and not only for its lighthouse. The young man in his thirties who would become the world famous author of *Walden* spent most of his time on Cape Cod in Truro, and a third of his book *Cape Cod* is about Truro. After his first visit of 1849, he returned the following June, probably staying a night or two at Highland Light. His longest stay, almost two weeks, was in July 1855; and his final visit was for three nights in June 1857. He read widely in the history of Cape Cod, including the early Plymouth Colony records and the writings of the Reverend James Freeman. He was well prepared; he was an acute observer of nature and human nature; and he drew conclusions, both humorous and philosophical, from his experience.

The ocean was the primary objective of Thoreau's rambles. He wanted "to get a better view than I had yet had of the ocean." He walked the ocean beach from Chatham to Race Point twice. On one of his walks, he spent a night with a Wellfleet oysterman, who lived at the Truro-Wellfleet boundary. Thoreau says he and Channing got up before sunrise: "We struck the beach again in the south part of Truro . . . We made no haste, since we wished to see the ocean at our leisure; and indeed that soft sand was no place in which to be in a hurry." Later, in his letter to Blake he wrote: "Come by all means, for it is the best place to see the ocean in these States."

He was greatly impressed with what he heard from the lighthouse keeper and townsfolk about how the shape and size of the Outer Cape was being changed by wind and wave. The Wellfleet oysterman had told him that a swamp inland from the Atlantic Ocean had disappeared twenty years earlier and that signs of it appeared recently on the beach. The cliff face was moving inland. "Another told us," says Thoreau, "that a log canoe known to have been buried many years before on the bay side at East Harbor in Truro, where the Cape is extremely narrow, appeared at length on the Atlantic side, the Cape having rolled over it; and an old woman said, 'Now you see, it is true what I told you, that the Cape is moving.'"

Thoreau walked across Truro to the bay but says nothing about the fishing port at Pamet Harbor or the thriving communities there and at Pond Village. He does describe the Pamet River, including a perceptive description of the effect of ocean washovers at the head of the Pamet River: "One who lives near its source told us that in high tides the sea leaked through, yet the wind and waves preserve intact the barrier between them, and thus the whole river is steadily driven westward, butt-end foremost, fountain-head, channel and lighthouse at the mouth, all together."

The lighthouse at the mouth of the Pamet River operated for only seven years, until1856 when the fishing fleet went into decline. It was located at the end of Tom's Hill, just upriver from the mouth of the Pamet, according to Walling's map of 1858. At that time, the river's mouth was near the south end of Corn Hill. The lighthouse was not a freestanding tower but projected above the center of the roof of the keeper's house. The lantern room was only thirty-one feet above the harbor waters, and the light was red. Although made of brick, the building no longer exists; and its exact site is unknown. Today, a small steel tower near the end of the south jetty holds a flashing light to mark the channel to Pamet Harbor.

Thoreau wrote very little about the people of Truro. Nature was his subject, and Truro's landscape struck him as "singularly bleak and barren-looking country . . . a kind of scenery which has been compared to a chopped sea." His principal metaphor for Truro's landscape, however, was the deck of a ship at sea: "To walk over it, makes on a stranger such an impression as being at sea . . . The almost universal bareness and smoothness of the landscape were as agreeable as novel, making it so much more like the deck of a vessel." As if he were on a ship at sea, he could look one way and see sailing vessels on the bay and turn around and see vessels on the ocean. Sometimes the mackerel fleet would be fishing under sail not far offshore, and Thoreau suggested that in "North Truro the women and girls might sit at their doors and see where their husbands and brothers are harvesting their mackerel fifteen or twenty miles off, on the sea, with hundreds of white harvest wagons, just as in the country the farmers' wives sometimes see their husbands working in a distant hillside field."

The impression of being at sea in Truro was reinforced, he noted, by "the make-shifts of fishermen ashore." Wells were equipped with a nautical block and tackle, instead of a windlass, to raise the bucket. Wood from wrecks went into the construction of houses, windmills and bridges. Nautical trim, including ships' nameplates, were nailed to some of the buildings. An old oar sometimes served as a fence rail.

At the end of *Cape Cod,* Thoreau offered advice for visitors to the Outer Cape. He recommended Highland Light for the view and October as the best time for a visit in order to avoid the summer fogs and to experience the storms off the ocean. His final words on the subject are often quoted: "A storm in the fall or winter is the time to visit it; a lighthouse or a fisherman's hut the true hotel. A man may stand there and put all America behind him."

. . .

Throughout the years of prosperity in the 1830s and 1840s, town meeting debated and voted regularly on plans and financing for roads, bridges, dikes and harbor improvements. Resources were also devoted to the poor. After years of paying households, and sometimes even relatives, to take care of the indigent elderly, the town voted first to buy a residence as a poorhouse and a few years later to build one.

Town meetings drew as many as two hundred men to debate and vote on measures to govern the town, more than many town

' WINDMILL NEAR HIGHLAND LIGHT, TRURO, MASS.

The boom and wheel were used to rotate the grain-grinding windmill so its vanes faced into the wind. The engraving is from *Gleason's Pictorial* of 1856. (Courtesy of Peabody Essex Musem, Salem, Mass.)

meetings drew in the twentieth century. The voters claimed Beach Point as town property in 1837 and sold it at auction for $828 foreight big lots. They sold the Old North Meetinghouse at auction and divided the $202 among twenty-six pew holders. They even sold sand from the beaches for ship ballast, after first noticing that "strangers" had been taking it without charge "thereby exposing the shores to waste by the working of the seas." The price was five dollars a ton for strangers, no charge for Truro men.

After several years of planning and debate, the first bridge from
Truro to Provincetown was built in 1855 from the end of Beach
Point across the East Harbor inlet. Before the bridge, travel by
land between the two towns meant circling East Harbor over trackless sand dunes along the Atlantic Ocean shore. Travelers invari-
ably complained of difficulty and danger. Of his trip in 1853,
W.H. Bartlett wrote: "During the blinding gales and snow-storms
of winter, it requires no small skill and intrepidity to pilot a four-
horse team, where road is none, over this intermixture of hill sand,
swamp and seaweed. The waves sometimes break fairly over the
narrow ridge, threatening to make a clear breach through, carry
coach and all out to sea and suddenly convert the extremity of the
Cape into an island."

Another traveler wrote that "our driver had driven stage [coach]
for a year over the route, and every day he had picked a new track,
often losing his way with the blinding and flying sand in a high
wind." Shebnah Rich says accidents were not uncommon: "In 1849,
during one of the high tides, the mail stage, while crowding the
bank, capsized, throwing a dozen passengers into the water, which
being quite deep, all were wet to the skin; some of the women
were dreadfully frightened, and one was in danger of being
drowned."

The bridge was sorely needed, but Truro apparently was reluctant to help pay for it. The previous June the *Yarmouth Register*
had complained about yet another delay: "We are sorry to learn
that the Town of Truro refused to do anything at its late meeting . . . The town will lose instead of gain by this neglect as they
cannot expect to employ others to do their own work for them so
well and cheaply as they can do it themselves."

The county and two towns reached agreement, however, and
work began. The nine-thousand dollar cost was shared by
Barnstable County, Provincetown and Truro. The *Register*'s correspondent in Provincetown hailed the "march of progress" that made
the trip to Provincetown "no longer a terror but a pleasure." He
also noted that Truro farmers bringing produce to Provincetown

seemed pleased with the shorter, easier route. The very next year, however, the bridge pilings were destroyed by the pounding of ice floes on a high tide. The county rebuilt the bridge, and Thoreau sat on the Truro end of it and watched great flocks of gulls. The vulnerable bridge, however, would soon be supplanted by a controversial dike.

The telegraph came to the Outer Cape, and in 1855 a telegraph station next to Highland Light began to alert Boston merchants to the arrival of ships. Thoreau visited the telegraph station in its first year and described the agent's work in a journal entry for June 20, 1857. In two books and a chart, the agent had the descriptions, names, owners, and identifying signals for more than 23,000 vessels, according to Thoreau. The agent claimed that with his telescope he could make out the name of a vessel seven miles away and a vessel's signals sometimes twenty miles away. The station also had signal flags of its own and, says Thoreau, the agent could carry on "a long conversation with a vessel on almost any subject. Mort Small, twelve years old at the time, would later become the longest-serving marine reporting agent.

. . .

In the pre-Civil War decades, Pamet Harbor and the hills and valleys on both sides of the Pamet River became the center of the town. The village of North Truro, also known as Pond Village, was eclipsed for a time. The small cluster of homes at East Harbor, one of the population centers in colonial times, stalled as the population shifted to the south. In the 1790s, Freeman had said that "the small village of East Harbor . . . is going to decay and probably will not long exist." A few decades later, only four or five houses remained, according to Alexander Young, who said that "an old gentleman, resident in the valley, told me on the spot in Aug. 1840 that he recollected when there were seventeen houses there." East Harbor never recovered as a village.

Truro families poured money into construction programs for

public school buildings and a private school, the Truro Academy, which opened in 1840 near Truro Center and operated for fourteen years. The principal speaker at the academy's dedication ceremonies was Horace Mann, head of Massachusetts public schools. Although he would become famous nationwide for his promotion of public schools supported by taxes, he agreed to help dedicate the privately financed Truro Academy. The academy's founder and first headmaster, Joshua H. Davis, later became head of the Somerville public schools, which were in Horace Mann's jurisdiction.

Almost a dozen public schools provided instruction for boys and girls from four to twenty-one years old. The historian Frederick Freeman wrote that in 1858 there were in Truro "seven school districts with as many neat and commodious school houses, six of which had double rooms . . . Until the year 1852 the school houses had been, under the old regime, built by districts, hence no mention of them in town records." Classes were also held in four homes, making a total of eleven neighborhood schools. Women were taking over the role of educators from the ministry-educated schoolmasters; seven of the eleven teachers were women in 1858.

Secure in their jobs, Truro's townsfolk became more social and indulged in religious fervor and civic self-improvement. Camp meetings on the Outer Cape, including one in Truro, combined religious experience with social get-togethers. Town meetings combined civic duty with social get-togethers. Book lovers founded the Truro Library Association. They joined together in societies dedicated to self-improvement, civic betterment and brotherhood. These societies included lyceums, literary societies, and fraternal organizations such as the Cadets, the Sons of Temperance and the Independent Order of Odd Fellows.

Debating societies flourished. The Truro Lyceum, formed in 1833, shifted to North Truro seven years later and became the North Truro Literary Society, then the Lyceum again, then the Philomathesian Society and finally, just before the Civil War, the North Truro Debating and Literary Society. Their discussion topics suggest not only the burning issues of the day but the members' keen sense of community: "Which is most conducive to happiness, celibacy or matrimony? Is intemperance or gunpowder the most injurious to the community?" Town issues included: "Have palm leaf hats been a benefit to this community? Are vessels employed in mackerel fishing entitled to bounty?" And as the Civil War approached: "Resolved that the dissolution of the union will be more beneficial to the North than the South." A few were whimsical: "Resolved that tight lacing [of corsets] has been more injurious to the community than the use of tobacco." About the same time the women of the South Truro Methodist Episcopal Church organized a Ladies Literary Sewing Society. Men could join but "without the right of suffrage."

The camp meetings were organized by the Methodists, who made Truro one of their first targets for evangelical proselytizing. They would transform religious life in Truro, luring worshipers from the century-old Congregational church.

CHAPTER 13:
THE QUICK AND THE DEAD

T ruro built six churches between 1826 and 1851, more than in all the rest of its history. The burst of ecclesiastical construction was the result of the town's sudden prosperity combined with the arrival of charismatic Methodist ministers who converted many of the townsfolk.

Before the Methodists arrived, Truro's churchgoers were members of only one church, the Congregational, the church of the Pilgrims; and their ministers served for life. The first three generations of townsfolk had only three ministers–Avery, Upham and Damon. That changed at the end of the 1700s when Methodist preachers arrived on the Outer Cape. They were fiery orators, performers in the pulpit who exhorted the faithful to repent and be saved. If a meetinghouse was not handy, they would preach out-of-doors. They brought to Truro an evangelical form of Christianity, as well as the temperance movement against alcoholic drinks.

Unlike the Congregational pastors, the Methodist preachers were generally not from Harvard's divinity school; often they had little education and less theological training. They were itinerant preachers who came to town for one, two or three years and then moved on while the town recruited a new minister with new and different sermons. Sometimes, Truro natives who felt divine inspiration and who had a gift of oratory would be authorized to exhort the faithful. Shebnah Rich, who lived through much of it, says the Methodist evangelizing "turned the community upside down religiously."

. . .

The first Methodist preachers to reach Cape Cod arrived in Provincetown, but they met determined opposition there. When the preacher and his flock prepared to build a meetinghouse, the traditionalists seized their lumber and burned it, along with an effigy of the preacher. The Provincetown Methodists, plus several from Truro and Wellfleet, looked for another building site on the Outer Cape and selected a stand of oak trees on a hilltop in South Truro. Almost a century later, Rich analyzed Methodist records and concluded that South Truro was the site of the first Methodist church on Cape Cod and only the second in New England. The simple meetinghouse was built about 1794, not near a village but about half a mile from a main road, Old County Road, in South Truro. It was the town's first new church in seventy-five years, and the preacher was Joseph Snelling.

Truro suddenly found itself in the vanguard of the latest and the most successful wave of evangelical Christianity in New England. The new preachers, full of zeal if not highly educated, quickly won converts in Truro. Kittredge attributes the success of the evangelical preachers on Cape Cod to their "sensational appeal to the emotions," while "the old Congregational clergy had to content itself with ministering to the staid and cautious." George Pickering, one of the earliest preachers, said that "in the winter season, when they were all at home, our meetinghouse was filled to overflowing. Our singing was excellent, for many of them sang with the spirit and understanding also." Hymn singing became popular; in 1797 town meeting authorized forty dollars for a singing school.

The Methodist preachers were renowned, too, for their common touch. Not for them the theological sermonizing of the Harvard graduates. They knew their audience–tough, plain-spoken, individualistic men and women who were citizens of a new nation dedicated to expansion, prosperity and a religion that promised joyous salvation to those who repented.

In later years, Shebnah Rich especially appreciated the Truro men who became exhorters in the pulpit. One of the most eloquent was Ephraim Doane Rich, about fifty years old: "He would stand against the rail of the little altar, with one hand in his pocket and with the other force home his rugged reasoning and vivid personal experience with an energy and eloquence that swept like a torrent. . . . Sometimes when wrought upon with his theme, his heart on fire, his face aglow, his tall frame bent, his long arm outstretched, his impetuous utterance fairly breaking through his pent-up prison-house, the Spirit rested like cloven tongues upon the audience." Although Rich praised the preaching style of several exhorters, including an unnamed woman, some were not to his liking. He said that Thomas Dodge, a former sea captain, "could make more noise in the pulpit with less religion and spoil more Bibles than any man I have ever heard."

Evangelistic fervor in Truro probably peaked in the summer of 1826 when the town was host to a Methodist camp meeting that drew many hundreds of worshipers. They lived in tents on a hill overlooking the Pamet valley, sang hymns, gathered to pray in groups and listened several times a day to sermons by some of the best of New England's fiery preachers. Camp meetings in America combined religious devotion with a big picnic. They may have been the first occasion in Truro's history when the townsfolk got together and had a really good time.

After its one summer in Truro, the Methodist camp meeting moved to North Eastham, where as many as five thousand people reportedly gathered from Cape Cod and from as far away as Boston. (It's doubtful that Truro might have accommodated anywhere near that many.) By the mid-1800s, Cape Cod's camp meetings had settled not far from the railroad station in Yarmouth, where Truro's Methodists had cottages and tent sites for many years. At the end of the century, Isaiah Snow of Truro owned and operated a dining tent, ice cream parlor, store and cottages there.

· · ·

In the same year as Truro's camp meeting and in the following year, carpenters built two more churches–a church for Methodist Episcopal worshipers and a new meetinghouse for the Congregationalists. The Methodist Episcopal church was built by a newly organized society in 1826 on a hill north of the Pamet River. Its site is marked by a stone in the Methodist Cemetery on Snow Field Road. Shebnah Rich reported that originally it was a plain, barn-like structure about forty feet square "with a two-storey pulpit with red doors." More than three dozen different ministers served the church, usually for a year or two, sometimes three, in its early decades. After a century as a church and a town landmark, it was sold in 1925 to Caleb Arnold Slade, a painter, who moved it to the bank of the Pamet River and made it into a residence and studio that is still there.

The Congregational meetinghouse, built in 1827, is Truro's oldest public building in continuous use. Its floodlighted steeple, along with that of the nearby Town Hall, is a beacon for residents and visitors approaching Truro Center from the south on Route 6. As landmarks, both buildings were even more conspicuous when Truro's hills were treeless pastures and farmland. In old photographs, they stand out starkly on the top of the barren ridge north of the Pamet River.

The Reverend Jude Damon was the Congregational minister when the new meetinghouse was built, but he died less than a year later. He had served as minister for forty-two years and was the last of the purely Congregational ministers. His successor was a Methodist, and members of both denominations worshiped together. In the 1950s, the building was extensively refurbished and restored; and electricity was installed. Today, it is known as the First Congregational Parish of Truro, has about thirty members and offers services on Sunday during the summer months.

Truro's churchgoers in the early 1800s had four places of worship: the long-established Congregational meetinghouse of 1721 on the Hill of Storms, the evangelical Methodist meetinghouse of 1794 in South Truro, the combined Methodist Episcopal church north of the Pamet River and the newly built Congregational meetinghouse on Town Hall Hill. Within twenty-five years, the South Truro edifice would be replaced twice, the Christian Union Church would be built in North Truro, an Adventist church would meet in South Truro for a few years, and construction of a Universalist Church building would be started but then abandoned after a destructive storm. Religion in all its proliferating forms had caught the imagination of the people of Truro.

The South Truro meetinghouse of the Methodists was replaced in 1831 and again twenty years later, as Truro's population grew to its historic high. The 1851 building, enlarged and remodeled with an imposing façade and tall steeple, stood on the west side of Old County Road for just over a century. Upwards of five hundred worshipers crowded into the pews; and on busy Sundays benches were brought in for the children. After the Civil War, however, the town's population and the church's membership began falling rapidly. By the end of the century, there were only twenty-eight members, and by the end of the 1920s the building was boarded up. Preservation efforts began in the 1930s, and in 1936 the Truro Neighborhood Association took ownership. But on March 21, 1940, it caught fire during a lightning storm and burned.

The Christian Union church, located on Route 6A in the village of North Truro, was built in 1840 by churchgoers in the northern part of town. By that time, there were only a few worshipers left to maintain the old Congregational meetinghouse on the Hill of Storms, and it was torn down the same year. Weatherbeaten and almost a 120 years old, it had fallen into disrepair. The remaining Congregationalists from the old meetinghouse and Methodists in the northern part of town united to form the Union Church and build what is known today as the Christian Union church. As a result of this realignment of congregations, both the new Congregational church on Town Hall Hill and the Christian Union church in North Truro can trace their lineage to the original Congregational church of colonial times.

In the 1870s, the Christian Union Church was raised so that meeting rooms could be constructed on the ground floor. The interior walls and ceiling are finished in hammered tin, and an ancient chandelier, which once provided gaslight, still hangs from the ceiling. The church has about sixty members today and is non-denominational.

Two Roman Catholic churches were built by Portuguese immigrants who brought the faith with them from Europe. Many Portuguese families were buying homes in Truro by the 1870s, and a priest from Provincetown said Mass in one of their homes for years. In 1895, Provincetown's energetic priest, the Reverend Manuel C. Terra, led the effort to build a church in Truro. For two hundred dollars, he bought an old school building near Mill Pond that had been converted into a roller skating rink. It was "flaked," that is, taken apart, and moved to the corner of Route 6A and Town Hall Road. Father Terra and his Truro flock dedicated Sacred Heart Roman Catholic Church in January 1896. In *Catholicism on Cape Cod* (1984), Harold A. Whelan says "Terra became a legend in his time, both loved and feared by his parishioners. His sermons were usually in Portuguese and were dogmatic and emotionally charged. His sermons and his stern behavior earned him the title "Holy Terra." The church flourished for a century until it was closed in 1997. The second Catholic church was built in 1915 on Pond Road in the village of North Truro. By the end of the century, it, too, had lost parishioners and was used for Sunday Mass only during the summer months .

. . .

The oldest graveyard in Truro is the Old North Cemetery on the Hill of Storms. The graveyard was probably started in 1704, when the Congregational meetinghouse was built there; but the oldest grave marker still existing is dated 1713. It marks the grave of Hannah Paine, the wife of Thomas Paine. The graveyard was Truro's only burial ground for almost a century. Graveyards also surrounded five of the six churches built in the 1800s, sober reminders for Sunday worshipers of their mortality.

The next graveyard to be laid out was at the site of the first Methodist meetinghouse in South Truro. It is now called Pine Grove Cemetery. The oldest gravestone there is for James Paine, who died in 1799. More than a third of its graves hold the remains of members of the Rich family.

The graveyard around the Congregational Church on Town Hall hill is the site of the obelisk commemorating the death of fifty-seven Truro boys and men in the October Gale of 1841. Next to it is Snow Cemetery, the first on Cape Cod to have natural landscaping and noteworthy for artists buried there. Begun before the Civil War as a private burial ground, it was taken over by the town in 1995. Truro and Provincetown artists of the twentieth century, believed to have appreciated the natural landscape, chose it for their burial ground. Well-known artists and literary figures interred in Snow Cemetery include Hans Hofmann, Charles Hawthorne, Gerrit Beneker, Katharine Dos Passos and Susan Glaspell. Hofmann designed his own monument—a tall, granite slab that includes the signature that he put to his paintings.

The Roman Catholics laid out their own cemetery next to the Methodist Episcopal cemetery three years before they built their first church in 1895. Truro's newest cemetery, New South, was laid out in 1992 on land the town took for unpaid taxes.

Some families had private burial plots on their own property before it became illegal. The oldest family plot dates to 1776 and is, according to Rich, the grave of a smallpox victim, Thomas Ridley, Jr. Two other remote graves hold the bodies of men who also may have died of smallpox. Some families buried smallpox victims as quickly as possible, and perhaps secretly, to avoid the stigma and the risk of contagion. Seven family or private burial grounds have been located; all are untended and overgrown. The most recent marker is in the Ball family plot, located in woods on a hilltop not far from the Atlantic Ocean. The only headstone in the plot marks the grave of "Sheldon Wm Ball, 1856-1923."

CHAPTER 14:
ECONOMIC DECLINE,
THE CIVIL WAR AND A
CONTROVERSIAL DIKE

The decline of the off-shore fishing industry in Truro started before the Civil War. Bigger harbors in New England were already sending out bigger and safer ships capable of hauling in bigger and more profitable catches farther from their home ports. Truro's fishing fleet was rapidly shrinking and would never recover. The town had lost scores of its most able-bodied men in storms and shipwrecks. Almost 150 men went off to fight in the Civil War. Pamet Harbor was silting in, and an attempt to improve it with pilings failed. Deyo's history of Cape Cod noted that by 1860 "the sand had so choked it that the industries clustered there were discontinued." The Union Company store at the harbor went bankrupt as had the Truro Marine Insurance Company, ruined by the loss of eight vessels and their crews in the October Gale of 1841. The Pamet Harbor lighthouse was abandoned. At the same time, the extensive saltworks became uncompetitive, and raising sheep had only a short-lived success.

The situation was much the same in other fishing towns. R. B. Forbes of Boston visited many New England ports and reported seeing "hundreds of vessels laying idle. . . . At this moment I have in view from my yacht a hundred sail, more or less, in Provincetown, Wellfleet and Truro laid up for want of work to do." Kittredge says of Cape Cod that "after the Civil War the whole drift of Cape enterprise set shoreward, and fishing took the form of tending traps [called weirs] instead of sailing to the Banks." Without weir fishing, Truro's decline would have been even steeper.

For more than a century, Truro men and boys had been going to sea on whalers, fishing vessels and merchant ships to face death far from home. In 1861, when the Civil War broke out, Truro men went off to war to face death on battlefields, in prisons and in army hospitals. Scores of Truro's young men left their boats and took up arms. The Civil War brought out the patriotism on all Cape Cod as President Lincoln issued calls for volunteers to go to war to preserve the Union. Kittredge says Cape Cod towns responded with an enthusiasm that was surprising for maritime communities Almost all the towns exceeded their quotas for volunteers, although enlistment bonuses paid by the towns undoubtedly helped recruiting efforts. In the summer of 1862, Truro town meeting voted allowances for its volunteers and for families that needed assistance while their men were at war.

During the four years of the war, Truro supplied more than its quota of recruits. According to Deyo, "Truro furnished 144 men for the war– an excess of fourteen over all demands." Shebnah Rich indicates that 124 volunteered early in the war, although some may not have served. At least seven died. Rich gives short sketches of them, based on interviews with their survivors. The first on record was Edward Winslow, who died in Washington D.C. on October 12, 1862. Town meeting voted to bring home his remains and pay a death benefit of one hundred dollars to his widow.

Although Rich is the best authority on Truro during what the North called "the War of the Rebellion," he was not living in the town during those years. He turned forty during the war and was living with his family in St. Louis. Writing less than eighteen years after the war, he says of his experience only that "being in another part of the country where armies met, and my own house often threatened, I knew little in particular that was going on in the North and have been obliged to gain information at great expense of time and labor from best seeming sources."

Rich recorded the military careers of forty-one men. Elkanah Paine Jr. probably saw more fighting than most; he was in all the battles in Virginia, including Gettysburg. "Was shot once in his knapsack," reported Rich, "had the breech of his gun shattered by a ball, and another carried away a piece of his nose. Sergeant Paine's regiment went in with two hundred and eighty men, came out with eighty." Two Truro men, John C. Rider and Benjamin Keith Lombard, died at the notoriously unsanitary prison at Andersonville, Georgia.

Truro mariners served on Union vessels, many of them new, steam-powered, propellor-driven ships that were blockading the South. The blockade tried to cover more than three thousand miles of coast, and its success was crucial to victory for the North. Samuel Eliot Morison, the naval historian, called sailors patrolling the blockade unsung heroes of the war: "Few officers and still fewer sailors who kept this ceaseless vigil became known to fame." Rich identifies fourteen Truro seamen who served on the blockade; five became acting masters of gunboats.

At home, the townsfolk of Truro again felt the threat of enemy raids. Morison observed that Confederate gunboats "raised havoc among fishing vessels in the Gulf of Maine" north of Cape Cod. One of them entered Portland harbor and captured a Union vessel. Deyo's history stated that "the exposure of this extreme portion of the Cape induced the government to erect earthworks, which were garrisoned by a company of volunteers." When the war ended in 1865, survivors began arriving home in the spring and summer. Some of them, however, having seen other parts of the country, undoubtedly sought their fortunes off-Cape. Truro was no longer the booming fishing port of pre-Civil War days. The town's population had already started to decline before the war. By 1880, it would be only 1,017, half its pre-Civil War peak. Rich wrote in the early 1880s that "over one hundred families from Truro now reside in Somerville," the Boston suburb.

The attractions off-Cape were the excitement, career opportunities and financial rewards of the big cities' burgeoning growth. The nation's population nearly trebled, the value of manufactures grew sixfold and the postwar expansion led to a shift of population from country to city, especially in the East. The shift had a dramatic impact on Truro. Pamet Harbor was moribund. Stores closed. Fishing boats rotted on the shoreline. The churches must have been half empty. Farms were abandoned. "There are many empty houses in Truro," said a state report in 1897. For more than half a century, Truro would be a quiet town of a dwindling number of families, despite the coming of the railroad, the development of weir fishing, the arrival of the first vacationers and, right after the Civil War, the controversial decision to build a dike across the East Harbor inlet, the largest public works project in the town's history before construction of the railroad and in the twentieth century Route 6.

. . .

Blowing sand, silting sand and ocean washovers at Truro's East Harbor combined to generate a storm of controversy after the Civil War. At high tide, the shallow lagoon of East Harbor covered about a thousand acres across the north end of Truro from Cape Cod Bay to the sand dune along the Atlantic Ocean. All that separated East Harbor from Provincetown Harbor was Beach Point, a low, narrow, peninsula of sand almost two miles long. Twice a day, nine-foot tides poured through the inlet connecting the two harbors. At low tide, East Harbor was nearly dry. The Pilgrims had found shelter for their shallop in East Harbor, and later on, fishermen would sail in on flood tides and beach their boats on the inside of sandy Beach Point. It was never, however, a dependable anchorage for ships of any size.

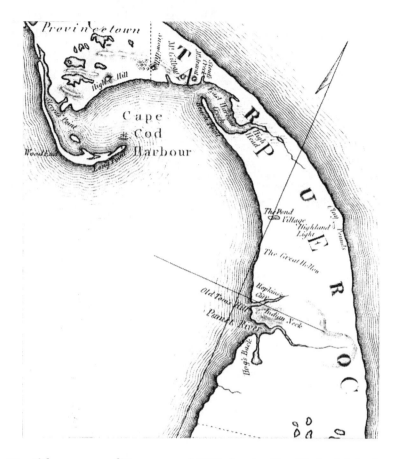

Detail from a map of Truro around 1835 showing East Harbor's inlet (top center) at the end of the Beach Point sand spit. Until it was closed by the controversial dike in 1868, the inlet connected East Harbor to "Cape Cod Harbor," later called Provincetown Harbor. Also shown is the wide mouth of the Pamet River before the narrow channel and rock jetties were built in the twentieth century. Corn Hill, seemingly designated "Hopkins Cliff" on this map, is just north of the river mouth. (From Alexander Young's *Chronicles of the Pilgrim Fathers from 1602 to 1625*, published in 1841, based on charts and maps of the 1830s.)

At issue in the mid-1860s was whether silting sand in Provincetown Harbor near the East Harbor inlet threatened harbor navigation, where the sand was coming from and what, if anything, should be done about it. In addition, some saw a potential catastrophe if Atlantic storm waves at the other end of East Harbor broke through and carried even more sand through East Harbor and into Provincetown Harbor. Shoaling sand was shrinking the northeast corner of Provincetown Harbor near the East Harbor inlet and supposedly making it difficult for big sailing ships to tack into anchorages and the docks. Whether this was a real problem for navigation, however, is not certain for there are no recorded complaints by sea captains.

As early as 1714, Boston merchants had recognized the importance of Provincetown Harbor. The provincial legislature passed an act noting that the harbor was "very useful and commodious for fishing and the safety of shipping both inward and outward bound" but was "in danger of being damnifyed, if not made wholly unserviceable" by wind-blown sand. Throughout the rest of the century, the legislature in Boston repeatedly passed laws to control grazing on the fragile sand dunes and marshes around the harbor, but with little effect. Winds blew sand from the denuded landscape into the harbor.

Truro's concern was that the blowing sand, if allowed to continue, would bury some of its hay-producing salt marshes at East Harbor. In 1825, at the request of the town's selectmen, the Massachusetts legislature ordered a study, the first of eight over the next twenty-eight years. Two commissioners, Zabdiel Sampson and Nymphas Marston, however, identified what they saw as a more serious problem—silting sand from East Harbor that "will greatly endanger, if not wholly destroy" Provincetown Harbor. They recommended planting beach grass to catch wind-blown sand, imposing severe penalties against cutting brush and grazing animals, and building brush fences to catch blowing sand and build up the narrow barrier beach dune at the far end of East Harbor that separates it from ocean storm waves. Truro's concerns about its salt-hay marshes got little attention.

A dike across the East Harbor inlet, which was on the boundary between the two towns, was proposed for the first time by the State Senate Committee on Mercantile Affairs and Insurance, which noted that Provincetown Harbor "is of priceless value to the commercial world." This time it was the Provincetown selectmen who asked for the study; and at hearings in Provincetown, seven Provincetown men testified that sand coming through the East Harbor inlet was the problem. No one from Truro testified. This would be the Provincetown position from then on, and a dike across the inlet would be the solution. The committee also recommended a dike at "the wading place," about halfway from the inlet to the far end of East Harbor, in case the ocean broke through. The Civil War interrupted further studies and debate for four years.

Throughout the 1700s and well into the 1800s, East Harbor also presented a second problem: It was a barrier to travelers by land to Provincetown. Its upper tidal creek reached southeast almost to the Atlantic Ocean, so that stage coaches and wagons had to travel across the trackless sand dunes. It was a perilous trip, especially in bad weather. When big storm waves broke through the ocean beach and into East Harbor, travel by land to Provincetown was impossible.

The earliest washover on record was during the winter of 1761-62, and a half-century later people were still talking about it. Timothy Dwight, the former Yale College president, was in Truro in the 1820s and heard that "the sea broke over the beach which connects Truro with Provincetown . . . and swept the body of it away for some distance." Beach grass was planted in the break, probably the first time beach grass was used to stabilize sand dunes, a relatively benign and inexpensive remedy that would continue into the twentieth century. In 1853, W. H. Bartlett was greatly impressed by the perils of the trip, "where road is none." At least once, a stage coach tipped over, spilling its passengers into the water.

The overwashes contributed to the urgency to do something, but the primary rationale for a dike was the perceived danger of shoaling in Provincetown Harbor. The issue was the subject of dinner table conversation at Highland Light. A guest at the lighthouse keeper's table in 1855 wrote about her visit in an article for the *Barnstable Patriot*: "We sat chatting about the probability of Provincetown one day becoming an island, and of its harbor being destroyed for want of a little care to prevent the sea breaking through in one particular part–a circumstance which Captain Small [the lighthouse keeper] considers by no means improbable–and of Beach Point being gradually washed away."

. . .

Six months after the Civil War, harbor studies resumed and the debate intensified. In October 1865, James Small, Mort's father, wrote a long letter to *The Barnstable Patriot* complaining that a fact-finding visit by legislators from Boston was monopolized by Provincetown men. Small argued strenuously against the need for a dike. The shoaling sand, he wrote, was not coming from East Harbor but from along Beach Point. A dike would, in fact, foster more shoaling. "Instead of the dike saving the Harbor," he wrote, "it will hasten its destruction, in my humble opinion."

His view drew an equally long and impassioned rebuttal from "Stonewall," also of North Truro. "To any person living in this vicinity," he wrote to the *Patriot*, "the theory seems so entirely absurd as to be undeserving a moment's notice." Stonewall (identity unknown) argued that the ebb tides from East Harbor were the problem and urged construction of a dike.

In November, the U.S. Corps of Engineers made its first study and submitted its recommendations. Colonel James D. Graham, who had drawn the first detailed map of Provincetown Harbor and environs, recommended a dike across the East Harbor inlet and fifty-foot jetties all along Beach Point. He said it would be a "catastrophe" if ocean storms created an opening in the barrier beach dune separating the Atlantic from East Harbor.

For the next two years, federal engineers, surveyors, hydrologists and generals of the U.S. Corps of Engineers made surveys and reports, and state legislators held hearings. Experts disagreed on where the sand was coming from. They differed on whether storm waves would cut a permanent channel from the Atlantic Ocean to East Harbor, thus severing the only land link to Provincetown. They differed on whether such a break would seriously threaten Provincetown Harbor with more silting and what to do about it. Their conflicting recommendations included planting more grass, allowing blowing sand to fill up East Harbor, building a dike across the inlet, building a dike at "the wading place" on the tidal creek, building both, and building bulkheads and groins along Beach Point since dikes would not solve the problem.

While the debate over the dike raged on, General H. W. Benham of the U.S. Corps of Engineers built a bulkhead along Beach Point with groins projecting into Provincetown Harbor. He saw no need for a dike, and his map of Beach Point refers to "bulkheads for the preservation of Provincetown Harbor." Like James Small, he held that alongshore currents were carrying sand into the corner of Provincetown Harbor and that the groins would slow the shoaling. His wooden bulkhead stretched three-quarters of a mile along Beach Point and was studded with almost a hundred groins reaching up to thirty feet into the water. Remnants of it still survive.

General Benham and others considered Beach Point itself to be in danger of storm-driven waves from Cape Cod Bay. Even at its highest point, the sand spit was no more than ten feet above high tide; at its narrowest it was only twenty feet across. The great storm of 1851 inundated a half-mile of Beach Point. Ten years later, the Truro selectmen advised the county that not only the bridge across the inlet but the road along Beach Point was in such unstable condition that it was too costly for the town to maintain.

General Benham's work on Beach Point did not deter those who, for whatever reason, wanted a dike at East Harbor. A state commission proceeded rapidly in early 1868 to authorize $150,000 for a dike At the last minute, however, there came another voice of outraged opposition. Representative Francis W. Bird, an outspoken and independent legislator, produced a six-thousand-word, blistering attack on backers of the measure for rushing it through "in such hot haste." He called it an "alarming assault upon the treasury of this Commonwealth." He analyzed the engineering studies and concluded that "there is not a particle of proof that the sand comes from East Harbor." He noted that the federal government had studied the situation and recommended against a dike. He said it was "absurd" to think the federal government would reimburse the state after the state completed the work.

Three times he noted that James Gifford of *Provincetown* (his emphasis) was one of three men, then only two, on the state commission recommending the dike. Gifford was an innkeeper and businessman. "Why," Bird asked, "are the friends of this scheme pushing it so persistently and so zealously? Is there a cat under this meal?" He suspected that legislators were trading favors and noted that Paul Hill, the other commissioner, had expertise in railroads but not dikes. A dike, he said sarcastically, "when built by the state, would furnish an excellent road-bed for the track of the Cape Cod Railroad, when extended to Provincetown." The railroad had reached Orleans three years earlier and Provincetown was the logical extension of the line. Bird was convinced that an unnecessary dike was to be built at taxpayer expense for the benefit of the railroad. He deplored the lack of public hearings.

Without delay, the House scheduled hearings for March 26 to April 3. Three U.S. Corps of Engineers were among the witnesses. General Benham, who had recently finished the bulkheads and groins along Beach Point, maintained that the offending sand had been coming from Beach Point and farther south. Another general testified that he was not sure where the sand was coming from. A third general thought the sand was coming from East Harbor, but earlier he had agreed to defer building a dike to see how the shoaling progressed.

Supporting the Provincetown and railroad interests was a U.S. Coast Survey engineer and three fishermen from Provincetown, Truro and Wellfleet. Henry L. Whiting, the engineer, blamed sand from East Harbor. To test his theory, he and his men marked some potatoes and threw them in the water off Truro. "And then we spent three days looking for them," he testified. But he record ends there. The three fishermen, expert witnesses who were supposed to know ocean currents, all testified that they thought the current along Beach Point ran south toward Wellfleet and thus could not be the source of the silting sand. In fact, it runs north toward the shoaling spot in the corner of Provincetown Harbor near the inlet to East Harbor. .

Three months later, on June 26, 1868, work began on the dike across the East Harbor inlet "without a day's delay," according James Gifford of Provincetown and two other legislators who formed a new State Commission of the Provincetown Dike. Four steam-engine pile drivers, each with a crew of eight, worked ten hours a day. Six thousand tons of stone went into the foundation. Workmen filled thirteen thousand sand bags with sand from nearby hills. On a typical day, seventy men and fifteen horses worked on the project. When finished the following summer, it was more than a quarter-mile long, 250 feet wide at its base and 75 feet wide at the top, which was planted with beach grass. The project came in under budget at $132,000–still a multi-million dollar public works project in 1990 dollars. In addition, a much smaller dike was built across East Harbor Creek at the wading place.

Although the ostensible purpose of the big dike was to stop shoaling, Provincetown now had a solid, all-weather, land link to the rest of the Commonwealth. The dike also protected the wooden bridge from tidal currents and ice floes. Four years later, in 1873, just as Representative Bird had anticipated, the railroad laid its tracks across the state-built dike. James Gifford and the other Provincetown merchants must have been gratified. Two decades after that, a roadway over the dike replaced the bridge; and in the

1950s the dike was widened to carry the four-lane Route 6 highway.

Contrary to arguments by proponents of dike construction, the dike did not stop the shoaling in the corner of Provincetown Harbor. As James Small of North Truro had argued, it was the alongshore currents coming mainly from the south that had carried the sand to the shoaling spot; and the shoaling there continued to shrink the harbor after the dike was completed. Disregarding their earlier rationale, Gifford and his two fellow commissioners finally recognized the effect of the alongshore currents. "Already," they wrote in a report, "the currents along shore appear to be bearing the sand which they transport up against the dike and along Beach Point, in a natural process of repair." What there was to repair they did not explain. Forgotten was the effect on navigation in Provincetown Harbor. Forgotten, too, was any hope of reimbursement by the federal government. The state's taxpayers paid for the dike to carry the railroad tracks to Provincetown.

The continuing shoaling, combined with wind-driven sand, created new land in the controversial corner of Provincetown Harbor. In mid-twentieth century, motels and cottage colonies were built where nine-foot tides once poured through the East Harbor inlet. Property owners there have seen their lots increase in size, while those on the southern third of Beach Point have watched their beaches shrink and high tides reach toward their doorsteps. Their beach sand is being carried on alongshore currents to the shoaling spot. Several of them have built new bulkheads and brought in sand to replenish the beach.

At the south end of Beach Point, the land link to Provincetown is still fragile. Storm waves have flooded parts of the two-lane road, and the sea level is rising. A rare combination of wind and tide–gale force winds from the southwest extending over two or more high tides–could cause major damage to dozens of motels and cottage colonies. Such a storm would also put at risk Provincetown's telephone lines, electric power lines, the four-lane highway and the water main that supplies Provincetown with water from Truro well fields. Despite all the fill, asphalt paving and construction, Beach Point is still a sand spit, although it may be decades or even a century before a series of damaging storms might once again generate calls for action by the U.S. Corps of Engineers and the Commonwealth of Massachusetts.

Just three years after the dikes were built, Truro landowners sought to restore drainage flows into and out of the landlocked lagoon. The first were the Proprietors of the Eastern Harbor Meadows, who got permission to drain their meadows cut off by the smaller dike across East Harbor's creek, which had been designed to protect East Harbor from flooding if the ocean broke through the barrier beach dune. Despite professed fears that a catastrophic breakthrough was imminent, the last recorded major overwash there was in 1854, fourteen years before the dikes were built.

Over the years, East Harbor, isolated from tidal flows, became a big, stagnant, freshwater, slightly brackish lagoon. As it lost its salinity, it gained a new name, Pilgrim Lake. Coastal geologist Stephen Leatherman describes the lake as "a very rich organic broth" with "colossal blooms of blue-green algae" in the summer, which made it unsuitable for swimming or boating. It was stocked with carp, perch and alewives from time to time, presumably to eat mosquito larvae. The carp grew as big as fifteen pounds.

In 1958, an old culvert under Beach Point that drained a cranberry bog was expanded to control the water level of the stagnant lake and thus reduce the breeding of mosquitoes that pestered tourists on Beach Point. The state installed a much larger drain pipe, about five feet in diameter and 750 feet long, and added an adjustable spillway and double tide gates. The effectiveness of the tide gates and the waterway's impact, if any on Pilgrim Lake, were undetermined at the end of the century.

In the late twentieth century, sand was rapidly filling the lake, which was only three to five feet deep, shallow enough to walk across, and less than half its size when the dike was built. Giant

Beach Point with its motels and cottages, and no longer a point, lies between Provincetown Harbor on the left and Pilgrim Lake, formerly East Harbor. The inlet from Provincetown Harbor to East Harbor was at the top left where the Route 6 mid-Cape highway turns. The "walking dunes" and the Atlantic Ocean are at the top.(Photo courtesy of the *Provincetown Banner*.)

sand dunes were slowly rolling into it from the north and east. Strong northeast winds built up these "walking dunes" and pushedthem forward, shaping them like a boomerang. Coastal geologists estimated that the walking dunes, the blowing sand and other sediments were depositing about an inch a year on the bottom. Atthat rate, Pilgrim Lake will disappear within this century, perhaps as soon as 2025. In the 1990s, the Cape Cod National Seashore was considering a study of the potential impact of Pilgrim Lake's being re-connected to Provincetown Harbor to restore its salinity.

. . .

No doubt inspired by the flurry of dike-building at East Harbor, Truro town meeting voted in 1869 to build a solid dike the next time Wilder's bridge over the Pamet River at Truro Center needed repair. The solid dike not only replaced the bridge but also stopped the tidal flows up the Pamet River from Truro Center to the ocean. The isolated half, sitting at the top of the freshwater lens, gradually became a freshwater habitat. A few years later, town meeting voted to put a culvert through the dike to drain the upper Pamet meadows. A one-way clapper valve kept saltwater flood tides from flowing back through it. In 1998, the U.S. Army Corps of Engineers investigated the pros and cons of replacing the small culvert with a much larger one that could restore saltwater tidal flow the full length of the Pamet. The estimated cost was one million dollars and nothing was done.

Dikes have had a major impact on Truro's environment. The dike-builders of the nineteenth century probably never considered the effect that isolating wetlands would have on wildlife and the fisheries. The saltwater wetlands of East Harbor, among the largest on Cape Cod to be destroyed in the nineteenth century, were important nurseries for the fishery at a time when fish stocks in Cape Cod Bay were declining.

Smaller dikes that held back salt water were built throughout Truro for a variety of reasons, primarily transportation. A railroad embankment near Pamet Harbor stopped tidal flows into Mill Pond until a storm in 1978 broke through the dike, which was not rebuilt so that Mill Pond could revert to a tidal lagoon. The railroad embankment also cut across the mouth of the Little Pamet River, changing it into a fresh-water marsh. Smaller dikes converted portions of salt-water marshes to vegetable gardens, cranberry bogs and hay fields. Environmentalist Mark Robinson observed in his study of the Pamet River that "the long-term effects are profound and are still being felt." More pressure was put on saltwater wetlands and coastal banks in the late twentieth century by the increased demand for summer homes on the water and the limited number of waterfront sites.

East Harbor before it was closed by the dike, the short-lived harbor at Pond Village and Pamet Harbor—all on the west-facing shoreline of Cape Cod Bay—were protected from the Atlantic Ocean storms from the east. By contrast, the Atlantic shoreline, which bulges to the northeast, bears the full brunt of the strongest northeast gales; and it was along that shoreline that many ships have come to a violent end, often with great loss of life.

CHAPTER 15:
SHIPWRECKS, MOONCUSSERS
AND LIFE-SAVERS

A northeast gale with rain, sleet and snow was blowing hard the night of December 5, 1893. The *Jason*, a three-masted square rigger, never should have tried to round the tip of Cape Cod. She didn't make it past Truro but struck a sand bar just north of Ballston Beach. Pounded by the waves on the outer bar, she broke in two; and twenty-four men were lost in one of the worst shipwrecks on Cape Cod.

Bound for Boston with a cargo of jute from Calcutta, the *Jason* was first sighted south of Truro by lifesaving crews stationed along the Atlantic shore. The wind must have been more from the east than from the north, for she was working her way north just off shore, beating close to the wind, when she went aground after sunset about a half mile north of the Pamet River Life-Saving Station. Lifesaving crews from both the Pamet and Highland stations raced to the scene and fired a line to the stricken ship, but by then the ship's crew had all been washed overboard. The keeper of Highland Light reported laconically in his log: "A terrible night and the worst wreck ever known on this coast."

The lone survivor, Samuel J. Evans, said that the captain had ordered lifeboats launched, but the breaking waves destroyed them. Evans put on a life jacket and, with the rest of the crew, climbed into the rigging to escape the waves crashing across the deck. Later, he told a reporter for the *Yarmouth Advocate* how the waves swept him and his shipmates from the rigging, banged him against the side of the ship several times and then carried him to shore. Evans later posed for a photograph of himself wearing his life preserver over a suit. He returned to England, shipped out on another sailing vessel and reportedly died when he fell out of his bunk.

Twenty bodies of the twenty-four lost in the wreck of the *Jason* were eventually recovered. They were buried in a mass grave in a Wellfleet cemetery. The common grave had no marker for almost a century. Then, in the bicentennial year of the United States, Wellfleet and the Rich family erected a monument; and the British ambassador sent a message of appreciation to Wellfleet. The museum of the Truro Historical Society has capstan bars from the *Jason* and a model of the ship made by Dan Sanders, a Truro summer resident.

The wreck of the *Jason* was one of the three in Truro that took the most lives. Twenty-one men were lost in the wreck of the British warship *Somerset* during the Revolutionary War; and eighteen men, including two would-be rescuers from Truro, drowned in the wreck of the *Josepha*.

The *Josepha* was driven onto a sandbar near Highland Light during a three-day northeast gale in April 1852. The shouting from the wreckage inspired Jonathan Collins and Daniel Cassity to try to row out to the ship despite the warnings that the seas were too high. Both drowned trying to row through the heavy surf. Cassity, twenty-three, was the last of three Truro brothers who drowned at sea. He had just been married to a young woman who had also lost her father and her only brother to the sea. Collins, forty-seven, left a wife and three children. Eighteen years earlier, at the same spot, Elisha Paine of Truro reportedly had perished during rescue operations after an unnamed Prussian brig went aground.

The worst shipwreck off the coast of Truro was the wreck of the *Jason* on a winter night in 1893. The ship broke in two under the onslaught of the pounding waves. Twenty-four men lost their lives. (From the H. K. Cummings collection courtesy of Snow Library, Orleans MA.)

The keeper of Highland Light, Enoch S. Hamilton, described the wreck of the *Josepha* in a letter to "P. Greely Esqr" that he sent through the British consul:

> Heavy seas struck her on the starboard side, carrying away the masts. . . . The deck then gave away from the stern to the foremast. Then the main and the mizzenmast went overboard. . . . The men at this time were up in the fore rigging. When the foremast gave away two of them were washed overboard and the remainder clung to the starboard side of the vessel. [On] the third or fourth sea she broke apart altogether. Fourteen men were washed off. The two remaining ones were providentially nearer the stern and after regaining their hold by endeavoring to make themselves fast to this place of [the] wreck, they were, however, washed off two or three times, but were fortunate enough to regain their hold. . . . Then a heavy sea cleared the rigging. They [the two sailors] came directly ashore nearly opposite the light [of fires] on the beach.

While the wrecks of the *Jason*, the *Somerset* and the *Josepha* produced the greatest number of fatalities, they were only three of at least a hundred recorded shipwrecks in the history of Truro. The roster will never be complete, especially for the 1600s and 1700s. No one compiled accurate records. John Perry Fish searched newspapers, diaries and government records for his book *Unfinished Voyages* (1989) on shipwrecks in the Northeast from the 1600s to 1956; and for Truro alone he found sixty-five wrecks not previously mentioned in history books. Nevertheless, even his methodical search missed the *Unity* in 1732. In his 1930 history of Cape Cod, Henry C. Kittredge estimated that a thousand ships had been wrecked on the outer shores of Wellfleet and Truro, an average of about three a year since 1600, which seems possible although unverifiable. So many wrecks lie on the bottom off the Atlantic coastline of Cape Cod that salvagers and treasure hunters have dragged the bottom in hopes of snagging an anchor chain and anchor.

Mariners have always considered the outer shore of Cape Cod one of the most dangerous coastlines in the nation, one of the "graveyards of the Atlantic." The danger is not in rock ledges but in constantly shifting sandbars up to a mile offshore. The most notorious are the Peaked Hill Bars stretching northwest from Truro's boundary with Provincetown. With the port of Boston at one end of Cape Cod and the approaches to the port of New York at the other, ship traffic was heavy. The keeper at Highland Light counted 1,200 vessels in eleven days during the summer of 1853. To escape shipwreck, mariners had to stay well clear of the outlying sandbars, especially during the powerful northeast storms.

. . .

The earliest recorded shipwreck on Cape Cod may well have been in Truro. The wreck of an unnamed French vessel in 1616 or 1617 is mentioned by William Bradford and by the adventurer Thomas Dermer, who explored the New England coast in 1619. Dermer wrote in a letter that he had "redeemed" two French survivors of a shipwreck three years earlier "at the northeast of Cape Cod," which is roughly where Truro is located. In his annals for 1620-21 in *Of Plymouth Plantation,* Bradford also mentions the shipwreck, adding that after the crew got ashore they were attacked by Indians, who killed most of them but kept some of them as prisoners.

The first shipwreck firmly on record in Truro, which has been overlooked by historians, occurred more than a century later. The *Boston Weekly News-Letter* of March 16-23, 1732, reported: "The schooner *Unity* of about 100 tons, Peter Latimore commander, who sailed from New London harbor the 24th of February last, having on board a very valuable cargo of molasses, pork, beef, cheese, etc., bound for this place, did in the night between the 2nd and 3rd instant, run on the breakers near Truro, on the back of the cape, and in about two hours time the vessel stove to pieces; the men got safe to shore but saved very little of the cargo."

Records from the 1700s have yielded the wrecks of only four ships in Truro, a small fraction of what must have been a much greater number. The two recorded wrecks in addition to the *Unity* and the *Somerset* were those of the *Union* and the *Rachel*, both with great loss of life. The *Union*, from London, went aground off North Truro in a blizzard in 1755. Kittredge says "all hands perished, either by drowning or by freezing to death on the beach." The *Rachel* went aground just south of Highland Light in 1798, the same year the lighthouse first went into service. The crew of five perished, and their bodies were buried in Old North Cemetery. A rough stone marked the grave until a grandson of the thirty-two-year-old captain visited Truro eighty years later and erected a marble tombstone. The *Rachel* was one of seven vessels wrecked on Cape Cod in a gale that produced one of New England's heaviest snowfalls. The *Salem Gazette* reported that the seven ships had all "gone to pieces," and that "twenty-five dead bodies have been picked up and buried."

The nineteenth century, "the century of sail," was also the century of shipwrecks. Truro experienced more than sixty on its coastline, more than half the total during its recorded history– plus the grounding of two ocean liners and a U.S. Navy warship.

For the first half of the century, John Perry Fish is the sole compiler of all but one Truro shipwreck (the *Protector* in 1804). In his list are the following: the schooners *Active* in 1808, *Hannah Jane* in 1829 and *Francis* and *Hazard* in 1831; the brigs *Splendid* in 1832 and *Amelia Charlotte* and the sloop *Napoleon* in 1833; the schooners *Catherine* in 1835 and *Arms* in 1836; the brigs *Cumberland* and *Osceola* in 1844; the schooner *Boston Packet* in 1846; the bark *Cactus* and brig *Baltic* in 1847; the square-rigged *Clara* in 1848; the schooner *Athalia* and brig *Hayward* in 1850; and in 1851 the schooners *Haven, Marianne, Eagle* and one unidentified by name. In addition, the disastrous storm of December 15-16, 1839, wrecked or sank forty-three ships in the Northeast, including twelve on the Outer Cape, of which four were in Truro waters: the sloop *Harvard* and three brigs, the *Carrabassett*, the *Lucy Ann*, and one unidentified.

Not all groundings ended in terrible disasters. The ocean liner *Cambria* from Liverpool, went aground in 1846 at the Truro-Wellfleet boundary. While awaiting rescue, some of the passengers had a great time sightseeing on shore. Thoreau's Wellfleet oysterman, the source of much of the author's local lore, told of "English passengers who roamed over his grounds . . . and also of the pranks which the ladies played with his scoop-net in the ponds." The ponds must have been those by the ocean along Truro's boundary with Wellfleet. Eighty-one years later, another ocean liner would be grounded on Truro's beach. The 250-foot *Ozark* collided in fog with a fishing trawler in 1927, and the captain ran her ashore to keep her from sinking, according to William P. Quinn, author of books on maritime disasters. The fishing trawler, cut in two, sank and three men were lost. Tugs pulled the *Ozark* off Truro's beach and took her to Boston for repairs.

No records of any shipwrecks in Truro from 1851 to 1871 have been found. Ships continued to be wrecked at about the same rate in the Northeast, including the Outer Cape, but none has been reported for Truro. Possibly, mariners were spared shipwreck on Truro's shores. More likely, records were not kept or have been lost.

The strange gap of twenty years for Truro ended in 1872 with reports of five shipwrecks. Two occurred on the day after Christmas, when the square-rigged *Peruvian* and the three-masted bark *Francis* went aground in a fierce snowstorm with gale force winds. Both were carrying cargoes from Calcutta. The *Peruvian* smashed into the Peaked Hill Bar almost a mile from the Truro-Provincetown beach and quickly broke apart. Mort Small, the marine observer at Highland Light, recalled how Charles H. Vannah, captain of the *Peruvian*, had promised his sweetheart in New Hampshire that this would be his last trip and that they would be married after he reached home port. No one survived the wreck.

The iron-hulled *Francis* went aground a few hundred yards off the North Truro shore, and her remains could be seen at low tide more than a century later. She was carrying tin and sugar, which would later result in an unusual salvage scheme by Truro men. The lifesaving station had been designated for Highland, and Edwin P. Worthen was named captain, but the station was not yet manned nor supplied with boats and rescue equipment. Worthen recruited volunteers, who rushed to bring a whaleboat from the bayside to the scene of the wreck.

Isaac M. ("Mort") Small, marine reporting agent at Highland, owner of a resort there and town chronicler, described the scene in one of booklets. Worthen's men dragged the boat the length of the frozen pond in Pond Village and then loaded it onto a set of wheels hitched to a pair of horses for the rest of the trip across the Cape. They had to shovel through snow drifts so the horses could get through. The whaleboat brought the *Francis's* crew safely ashore, but the ship's captain, who had been ill for several weeks, died four days later at Small's Highland House and was buried in Old North Cemetery. Worthen went on to be captain of the Highland Life-Saving Station for more than three decades.

Salvage operations by the owner of the *Francis* began a few days later, and about twenty-five men were hired to unload the cargo of sugar. Some of the bags broke, spilling sugar on deck. The foreman said that at the end of the day they could fill their lunch pails with the loose sugar. Each day, wrote Small, "the size of these lunch pails and baskets increased amazingly. . . . so that the boat in her last trip to shore was in danger of being swamped with the great weight of lunch baskets." Before the foreman put an end to it, the men had stocked up a year's supply of sugar.

Also wrecked in 1872 were the *General Marion*, the *Superior* and the ill-fated *Clara Belle*, whose crew of seven abandoned ship. Whether to abandon ship or stay with a grounded hulk in the pounding surf was often a difficult decision. The crew of the *Clara Belle* made the wrong decision. The two-masted schooner, loaded with coal, had struck a sand bar two miles north of Highland

Light. The men left their ship in a small boat, but it overturned almost immediately. One sailor, John Silva, came ashore holding a piece of wreckage and wandered the rest of the night looking for shelter from the snow and cold. His story was told by Mort Small: "A farmer going out to his stable in the early morning found this unfortunate, frozen and exhausted sailor standing in the highway a short distance from the Highland House, so dazed by his terrible night of torture that he could not speak or move. He was carried into the farm house and the writer was one of those who helped to revive him."

Small and others hurried to the beach through snowdrifts to look for survivors. They found the *Clara Belle* high and dry on Truro's beach: "We walked on board dry-footed and passed down the cabin stairs. There in the cabin stove burned a nice cheerful fire and all was dry and warm. The haste of Captain Amesbury and his crew to leave the strong vessel for a little frail skiff had cost them their lives." A rising tide must have lifted the ship off the outer bar. The wind drove her ashore at high tide, the falling tide leaving her on the beach.

The bark *Giovanni* struck a sand bar off North Truro in a March gale and snowstorm of 1875, three years after the U.S. Life-Saving Service had build a station in Truro. Small, who was on the scene, told in detail how two lifesaving crews had to watch from shore as fourteen men were swept away by the roaring surf. Launching a lifeboat "would have foolhardy in the extreme," he says, "and would only have added to the death roll the lives of the life-savers, without accomplishing the saving of a single life." It was not unusual for lifesaving crews to judge the seas too rough to permit them to reach a wreck. Ironically, these were precisely the times when mariners were most in need of rescue. Only one sailor made it to shore from the *Giovanni*.

The year 1876 saw four major shipwrecks. An early snowstorm, apparently with hurricane force gusts, drove the brig *H.A. Frost* onto a sand bar a mile south of Highland Light. Waves breaking on the hulk swept five men to their deaths. Small was on the scene at daybreak: "There we saw the last member of the crew clinging to a piece of wreckage and being swept towards the shore with every on-rushing sea. We formed a life chain by holding hands, one remaining firm on the beach, while the others pushed through the surf to reach the sailor who was struggling to reach the shore. Soon, the outermost man grabbed him by the collar, and the chain [of men] and the sailor were pulled to safety."

The rescued sailor liked Truro so well that he went to live with a farmer at High Head.

During the same storm another brig, the *Cementhia Hopkins*, was wrecked two miles north of Highland Light. She, too, had a crew of six, of which only one survived. Two schooners, the *Cherub* and the *Idabella* (or *Isabella*), were also wrecked in Truro in that year. The *Idabella* went aground and broke up off Ballston Beach. Again, the ship carried a crew of six, but this time five were saved, apparently by the newly organized lifesaving crew at the Pamet River station, for J.W. Dalton includes it in his list of wrecks in *The Life Savers of Cape Cod* (1902).

Although the backside of Cape Cod must have had an alarming reputation by the end of nineteenth century, sailing ships continued to pile up on the sand bars. The year 1878 was particularly disastrous. Twelve men were reported lost on January 3 in wrecks off Ballston Beach of the *Miles Standish, Addie P. Avery* and the *Pow-wow*, which was a Provincetown fishing boat with five men aboard. A week later came the wreck of the schooner *Edna Harwood*.

In 1885, the schooner *Mary Doane* was wrecked, and the following year the schooner *Lookout* and the brig *Emily T. Sheldon* were lost. In 1887, the schooner *Carrie W.* sprang a leak, began to sink and was driven ashore; and the following year the barge *American Lloyds*, being towed by a tug, sprang a leak and sank. In the same year, the *Plymouth Rock* struck the outer bar off High Head in a southeasterly gale and went to pieces in the heavy surf. The High Head life-saving crew rescued the crew of six. In 1890, the schooner *Belle A. Nauss* went aground in fog and eventually went to pieces. In 1892, two barks, the *Active* and the *Kate Harding*, were wrecked. The crews from the Highland and High Head life-saving stations used their breeches buoy to bring ashore the crew of ten on the *Kate Harding*, which was aground on an outer sand bar in "a fierce gale and dangerous sea." The following year occurred the disastrous wreck of the *Jason* in a storm so severe that the lifesaving crews from Pamet River and Highland could not launch their boats into the pounding surf.

Three schooners were lost in 1896: the *Fortuna II*, *Silver Dart* and *Carrie Walker*, the last at sea off Truro. In 1898, the lifesaving crew at High Head saw the wreck of a small schooner, the *Red Rover*, and a month later the grounding in fog of a naval warship, the *U.S.S. San Francisco*. She was floated off the bar at the next high tide.

. . .

Despite the dreadful loss of life in the wreck of the *Jason* in 1893, enterprising Truro men rushed to the wreck to exercise their traditional skills as mooncussers. The town was notorious for the speed and boldness of its mooncussers, who salvaged for their own use whatever cargo and miscellaneous wreckage seemed to be free for the taking from shipwrecks. Several Truro men figure prominently in Kittredge's *Mooncussers of Cape Cod* (1937), including "old" John Thompson, storekeeper William Morton Small and E. Hayes Small, farmer and assistant lighthouse keeper. .

E. Hayes Small began a long career as a mooncusser at the age of thirteen, when he joined Thompson and William Morton Small, who were salvaging bales of jute washed onto the beach from the wreck of the *Jason*. Later on, Small used his farm horses and ropes to haul timber and other useful goods up the coastal bank from shipwrecks. He and his eight horses were often called upon to assist mooncussers (and sometimes shipowners) in salvage operations in neighboring towns. He built the floors and walls of his stable with pine planks from a Provincetown wreck and was hired by the owner of a wreck in Wellfleet to haul the ship's engine to the top of the ocean bluff. In Truro, he salvaged a thick hawser that he cut in pieces and sold as junk, and in his most notable feat hauled the deck-house from the hull of a wrecked schooner-barge to the top of the ocean bluff.

Strictly speaking, mooncussing is probably a misnomer when applied to marine salvage. It originally described robbers in England who used lanterns to mislead travelers on dark nights and lure them into an ambush. The robbers were said to curse the moon because it provided light for travelers and thwarted the robbers' scheme. Seafaring legend has it that coastal mooncussers set up lights on shore that lured ships to their destruction on moonless nights. Over the years, perhaps unfairly, townsfolk who took advantage of shipwrecks, whether or not they occurred at night, came to be called mooncussers, too.

The legality and ethics of mooncussing were often in dispute. The government sometimes considered mooncussers thieves. The mooncussers no doubt thought of themselves as expert beachcombers, quicker to reach wreckage, better organized and harder working. In their view, they were simply exercising traditional rights of salvage when a vessel was wrecked or abandoned.

Despite the title of his book, Kittredge was ambivalent about the term "mooncussers" and preferred to call them "wreckers," although this did not lessen his admiration for their boldness and ingenuity. "No generation of Cape men," he wrote, "showed any hesitation in stripping a vessel clean once her crew were either drowned—and so past help—or safe in a lifesaving station or a Truro kitchen."

Whatever the term—beachcomber, wrecker, mooncusser or thief—Truro had a reputation for being more aggressive than most. Kittredge quoted a Provincetown mariners' adage: "Don't get ashore on the backside of Truro; there's women there waiting for you with a brick in a stocking." The two towns were rivals in salvaging wreckage near their boundary, prompting another observation by Kittredge's that "any Truroer worthy of the name is convinced he is a better man on the beach than any Provincetowner, or for that matter than any man from any other town on the Cape." After the wreck of the *Somerset* during the Revolutionary War, mooncussers from Truro and Provincetown contended with the Boston revolutionaries for the salvage rights to the wrecked ship and its contents. Their dispute went to a Massachusetts maritime court, which split the proceeds from the sale of the contents three ways among the province, men from Provincetown and men from Truro. The Truro mooncussers won by far the greatest part of the proceeds.

On rare occasions, Truro men got credit, whether deserved or not, for responsible salvage operations on behalf of the owner of the wreck or its cargo. After the wreck of the *Union* in 1755, according to Kittredge, "a rich cargo was spread along the highwater mark for miles. Men of Truro and Provincetown built two shanties on the beach and put into them for safekeeping everything they could find that had come out of the *Union*, exercising, according to the report, 'great care and diligence' in the matter. The goods were shipped to Boston, and the incident was closed." He mentions no payment to men for their work, but nothing in his account suggests any other reason for such diligence and restraint.

. . .

So many sailing ships were wrecked along the nation's coastlines in the nineteenth century, and so many men were lost in the disasters that the federal government, after several false starts, established the U.S. Life-Saving Service in 1872 to build lifesaving stations and man them with full-time, professional crews of surfmen. The stations gradually replaced the Humane Society huts and volunteers. Three of the new stations were built in Truro—more than in any other Cape Cod town even though Truro's ocean coastline is only eleven miles long.

The lifesaving stations were two-story buildings with lookout towers for daytime observations. Most had a stable for the horses that pulled the wagon with the lifeboats and other lifesaving gear to the scene of a wreck. Stations were manned round-the-clock except for one or two months in the summer, when storms were infrequent. During the day, the crews maintained their equipment and practiced working with the lifeboat and other equipment, especially the breeches buoy, a device to haul seamen ashore from a stranded ship on a line fired to the ship by a cannon.

At night, men patrolled the beach or dune top north and south to a halfway house, where they met the patrol from the next station. If a patrolman saw a wreck, he fired a flare to let the ship know they had been seen and to alert the lifesaving crews. The twelve stations on Cape Cod were linked by telephone lines so that a station could alert others to a ship headed their way in a storm, as happened during the ordeal of the *Jason*, beating north from Nauset to her grave off Truro.

Truro did not lose any of its surfmen, but the captain and two men from the Peaked Hill station in Provincetown were drowned while rescuing sailors from the wreck of the *C.E. Trumbull* in 1880. The captain's body was found on the beach by men from the Highland station in Truro, where the captain's son was one of the surfmen.

The lifesaving stations continued to be manned into the 1920s and 1930s, but the need for them was rapidly diminishing. After the Cape Cod Canal opened in 1914, many ships no longer had to round the Outer Cape with its dangerous shoals. At the start of World War I, the U.S. Coast Guard took over the lifesaving stations and personnel. The High Head station was closed in the early 1920s, and by mid-century Coast Guard had phased out its operations on Truro's Atlantic coastline.

. . .

Ship sinkings and disasters at sea far beyond Truro's sand bars sometimes left their debris—and the victims' bodies—on the town's beaches. The worst disaster in the offshore waters was the sinking of the coastal steamer *Portland* in a storm with hurricane force

The Highland Lifesaving Station, located on the Atlantic coast a mile north of Highland Light, was one of three lifesaving stations built in Truro in the 1870s and 1880s. The rescue crew lived at the station, except in the summer when severe storms were rare.

winds during Thanksgiving weekend of 1898. Almost two hundred men, women and children were lost; there were no survivors. The *Portland* was on her way from Boston to Portland,
Maine, when mountainous waves smashed her and sent her to
the bottom. She probably went down about twenty-five miles
northeast of Truro, according to John Perry Fish. Within a few
hours, Truro's ocean beach was covered with wreckage. Many
bodies of the victims, debris from the superstructure and furniture from the ship's cabins and salons came ashore up and down
the Cape Cod backside. In *Cape Cod Annals* Marise Fawcett describes the wreckage:

> Windows, paneling, doors, bunks, furniture, mattresses,
> upholstery, light fixtures, washstand tops, life preservers, all
> in a ghastly jumble, with cargo that included whiskey, wine,
> casks of lard, varnish, piano parts, crates of vegetables, cases
> of tobacco and cigars—plus, of all macabre things, a sizable
> shipment of coffins. An observer said the beach looked like
> a cemetery that had been washed open. Human nature
> being what it is, Cape Codders reacted to this tragic wind-
> fall in time-honored fashion, which is to say they began to
> cart it home by the wagon load the instant the storm abated.

The Portland Gale, as it came to be called, destroyed more than a
hundred ships on the New England coast and took more than four
hundred lives on land and sea. Seven large sailing vessels were demolished in Provincetown Harbor, reputedly one of the safest in
all New England. The steamship *Pentagoet* went down off Truro.
The deep snowfall paralyzed the East Coast and disrupted communications. News of the disaster did not reach Boston and Portland for almost three days. In Truro, storm tides washed through
the low-lying roads, and Union Wharf was destroyed. Waves on
the high tide washed out thousands of feet of railroad track. Buildings were blown down, including a roller skating rink that Mort
Small had built four years earlier.

Occasionally, bodies washed up on Truro beaches from distant wrecks. Thoreau reported that in 1849 on his first visit to Truro he heard about two bodies that he assumed came from a wreck he had seen before he arrived on Cape Cod: "An inhabitant of Truro told me that a fortnight ago, after the *St. John* was wrecked at Cohasset, he found two bodies on the shore at the Clay Pounds [at Highland Light]. They were those of a man and a corpulent woman. The man had thick boots on, though his head was off, but 'it was alongside.' It took the finder some weeks to get over the sight." In September 1865, four bodies washed ashore, but nothing in the records suggests where they came from. No shipwreck was reported off Cape Cod that year. The deaths appear in the records the following April when the state legislature approved payment of $61.25 to Truro for the expense of burying the bodies.

Early town records include affidavits by men who claimed ownership of small boats and other goods that were washed ashore. In February 1727, Moses Paine "with some others took up a ferry boat on the backside of said Truro." Richard and Benjamin Collins found two barrels of rum on the backside in March 1765. Later in the same year Elisha and Elkanah Paine found a long boat with an iron pot and a sounding lead and line.

Another disaster in offshore waters took no lives but littered Truro's beaches with dead fish. S. Osborne ("Ossie") Ball told the story to Edward Rowe Snow when Snow was hiking on the Outer Cape and stopped to interview Ball. Just after the turn of the century, the *Longfellow*, carrying a load of explosives, sprang a leak and sank four miles off Ballston Heights, where Ball had a summer home. Lifesavers rescued the crew. A few months later, said Ball, "there was a terrific explosion off the Ballston Beach. For a moment we wondered what it was, and then we all realized what had happened. The *Longfellow* had been pulled off the ledge by the gale and had blown up in some inexplicable way. We went down to the shore shortly afterwards and found dead fish piled up two and a half feet high! The earthquake seismographs all recorded the explosion." In his account, William P. Quinn said there were two explosions, "the first at 7:45 p.m. and the second at 8 p.m. The beach was littered with dead fish, killed by the two blasts."

. . .

After the turn of the last century, huge "barges" began to go aground in storms and be wrecked on Truro's shoreline, sometimes with fatalities. The barges, old sailing ships towed by tugboats, carried captains and several men even though they were being towed. Most still had their sails. Coal was usually their cargo. The lives of these men were at great risk should their barge break loose from the tug in a storm.

A snowstorm with gale force winds in February 1907 took the lives of six sailors on barges off Truro. A tug was towing the schooner-barges *Alaska* and *Girard* off North Truro when the towline snapped and both drifted toward the outer bar. Both dropped anchors just outside the breakers, but they failed to hold and both struck the bar. The *Alaska* sank quickly and the four men aboard were never seen again. The *Girard* stayed afloat and dragged over the outer bar. The lifesaving crew from the Highland station brought two of the crew to shore in the breeches buoy. Two other men died at the wreck. Kittredge noted of the *Girard*: "Her planking and timbers were spread along the beach for miles, and a ton and a half of anchors and many fathoms of chain were left offshore for someone to pick up." Two weeks earlier, men from the Pamet River station had rescued six sailors from the schooner-barge *Woodbury*, which had also lost its tow line in a storm.

Another schooner-barge, the *Oakland*, was being towed in a string of three in 1913 when a gale caught them off Truro. The tow line broke. Two of the barges raised sail and managed to escape to the south. The *Oakland*, too close to the breakers, dropped anchor just outside. The tugboat took off two members of the crew, but two stayed with the barge. Mort Small watched the ship "pitching and rolling in the heavy seas . . . expecting every moment to see her drag to the bar and be pounded to pieces." While he watched from shore, the two men on the barge appeared with suitcases, which they put into their dory. They launched the dory but lasted only fifteen minutes. "Then came a great overpowering wave," says Small, "that swept the boat to its crest and sent it a hundred feet away [from the barge], hurling the men into the rushing waves and turning the boat bottom up. For a brief moment the heads of the men appeared above the wild sea, then dropped from sight."

Three big barges were beached high and dry near Highland Light during a northeast gale in 1915, resulting in a romance, a new shoreline dwelling and a nautical clubhouse for the golf links. Again, Mort Small tells the story. The barges–the *Manheim*, the *Tunnel Ridge* and the *Coleraine*–had originally sailed as three-masted schooners. They were being towed from Maine to Philadelphia, apparently without cargo. The captain of the tugboat cut them loose when the northeast wind drove all four vessels toward Truro's beaches. The tug made it safely to Provincetown Harbor. Two of the barges went aground right away, and the Highland Coast Guard crew brought their crews to shore. The captain of the *Manheim* dropped anchor outside the breakers, but the two anchors dragged and the Coast Guard brought him and his four crewmen ashore in the breeches buoy.

Overnight the northeast wind and the rising tide put all three vessels well up on the Truro beach. "One might walk dry-footed entirely around them," wrote Small. Only the *Manheim* escaped serious damage. Its captain and two or three men lived for a year on the beached wreck. Their waterfront home was closer to the Atlantic Ocean than anyone could ever hope to build, although they may not have been inclined to appreciate the scenic beauty of their site. The ship was re-floated a year later to the day. Meanwhile, one of the men found romance in Truro. He met, wooed and won the former wife of Ralph Mayo. The other two barges were burned, but not before E. Hayes Small, another of Mort's many relatives, took apart the two-story deckhouse of the *Coleraine*, hauled the parts to the top of the cliff and put them together to make a three-room cottage. Later, the cottage became a nautical clubhouse for Highland Golf Links.

Despite powerful engines, radios, new navigation equipment, improved weather forecasting and the beacon of Highland Light, ships continued to go aground on the Truro beach well into the twentieth century, although with fewer casualties. Besides the tug-towed barges, they included the sloop *Wanda* and schooner *General Sheridan* in 1900; the *William Marshall*, which had been abandoned at sea, in 1906; the *Julia Costa* in 1908; the *Ox, Quonnapowitt* and *Oakland* in 1913; the *Fuller Palmer* and *Terranova* in 1914; the *Azorian* and *Briganza* in 1916; the *Sintram* in 1921; and three in 1927—the steamship *Tracy,* schooner *Avalon* and diesel-engine powered *Surge.* John Perry Fish lists eleven from 1930 to 1953, the last year on his list: the *Progress* and the *Flora L. Oliver* in 1930; *Grace and Evelyn, John Mantia* and *Carrie Roderick* in 1932; *Osceala* and *Lulu L* in 1942; *Venture* in 1949; *Nancy F* in 1951; and *Marietta & Mary* and *Little Nancy* in 1953.

With the development of tugs with powerful engines, ships that grounded or went ashore without damage could often be pulled off the sand at high tide. One of the earliest was the schooner *Charles A. Campbell,* which went aground in thick fog in 1895. Tugs pulled her off a few days later. In 1927, the *Elsie G. Silva,* a two-masted fishing schooner with a crew of twenty, was re-floated after going aground near Ballston Beach. In 1940, the trawler *Palestine* came ashore at Long Nook, reportedly because of a faulty compass. At about the same location two years later, another fishing boat, the *Teresa Dan,* was stranded. In 1991, a fifty-one-foot fishing boat, the *Brasil,* with two crewmen, lost its steering and came ashore north of Ballston Beach near high tide. Waves smashed the deckhouse, but the principal concern was the possibility of a fuel spill. A thousand gallons of diesel fuel were removed. Eleven days later, the boat was towed to a shipyard. In 1999, the seventy-two-foot *Marlu* ran ashore south of Ballston Beach at 3 a.m. after the helmsman fell asleep. A tug re-floated her two days later.

CHAPTER 16:
RAILROAD TRACKS,
FISH WEIRS AND THE
PORTUGUESE

At mid-day on July 23, 1873, Truro townsfolk gathered at Pamet Harbor for the official opening of the final section of railroad track from Boston to Provincetown. Some brought American flags, and all were eager to see the first passenger trains arrive in Truro. First came an excursion special with thirteen cars filled with railroad buffs and sightseers. The second train, which followed an hour later, was the official inaugural special. Among its passengers were railroad executives, business leaders, the mayor of Boston and other government and civic leaders. As the trains chugged through Truro, the ground shook and the wooden trestle over the Pamet River trembled. The *Barnstable Patriot* reported that a crowd of people at Pamet Harbor were "displaying the stars and stripes, waving handkerchiefs and giving cheers." But the two trains swept through without stopping: "Owing to the utter impossibility of taking on another passenger, no stop was made between Wellfleet and Provincetown."

In Provincetown, the inaugural train was welcomed by booming cannon, a brass band, a banquet and the inevitable speeches by politicians. Truro had no opportunity for welcoming ceremonies. Its citizens, who must have wondered what impact the coming of the railroad would have on the town, returned to their work and their homes. Within ninety years, the railroad would be gone, replaced by automobiles and trucks.

The railroad tracks had reached Wellfleet two and half years earlier. From there, a fleet of stage coaches took passengers the rest of the way to Truro and Provincetown. The stretch of railroad from Wellfleet to Provincetown was the last to be built on Cape Cod. Robert H. Farson writes in *Cape Cod Railroads* that "the final distance seemed tantalizingly close." First, however, the fourteen miles of rights-of-way, roadbed and rails had to be financed by loans from individuals and the towns. Presumably, it would have been considered a good investment, both for the interest on the bonds and the increased business for the towns. Provincetown taxpayers were expected to fund almost half the $200,000 bond issue, and town meeting voted to do it. Farson says that the town of Truro was expected to come up with $25,000. The Truro town meeting, however, seemed less than enthusiastic. It voted to invest $13,600 of town funds and to set up a citizens committee to consider further investments. In the end, individuals bought the rest of the railroad bond issue, and construction began.

The final, single-track stretch was built in eight months. Work crews began at both ends. Schooners brought iron rails and wooden ties to a railroad pier in Provincetown. Freight trains brought the rails and ties Wellfleet. The right-of-way along the Truro bayshore crossed several saltwater marshes, but in the 1870s there were no environmentalists to question the damage to the marshes. Workmen shoveled sand from nearby hills for fill, which was loaded onto horse-drawn wagons. Hundreds of loads must have been needed to build the roadbed across the wide marshes at Bound Brook on both sides of the Wellfleet-Truro boundary and across the marshes on both sides of Pamet Harbor. Some in Truro worried about the trestle curtailing the tidal flow in the Pamet River since its buttresses and pilings would dam and slow the ten-foot tides.

At Great Hollow, instead of erecting a trestle, workmen hauled tons of sand to build an embankment fifty-five feet high that carried the rails across the deep, narrow valley. The embankment has since been removed. Another was built across the hollow at the end of the pond in Pond Village. It's still there. At the north end of town, the tracks ran along Beach Point and over the dike damming East Harbor.

The crew that started in Provincetown met the crew that started in Wellfleet somewhere in Truro, where they spiked the last pair of rails to the ties. The final stretch of Cape Cod's railroad was finished four years after two crews building the transcontinental railroad had met in Utah, where they celebrated with a symbolic gold spike. If there was any celebration in Truro, it went unrecorded.

Truro had more railroad stations per mile than most towns. The four stations at South Truro, Pamet Harbor, Corn Hill and North Truro were only a few miles from each other along the fourteen miles of track. The Corn Hill railroad station, small and unattended, was a flag stop used mainly by summer visitors. Pamet Harbor, a booming fishing port twenty-five years earlier, had become a stop on the railroad, with a small station, maintenance shed and freight siding. Trains stopped four to six times a day. With all the station stops and grade crossings, train whistles sounded across Truro many times during the day.

Residents and visitors could use the train as a town trolley. For a few pennies, they could take the train to visit friends and relatives or conduct business in another part of town. Farson heard about a vegetable farmer and a clam digger who would take the morning train from Truro to Wellfleet, sell their produce and return on the evening train. Trains would also stop, or slow down, for privileged passengers. Warren Chamberlain told Leona Rust Egan, a Provincetown author, that when he and his grandparents arrived in Truro to spend the summer near Great Hollow, the train would slow and almost stop near their cottage so they could all hop off, dragging suitcases, groceries and two cats, before the train picked up speed and pulled away.

The railroad was a mixed blessing. It did provide some full-time jobs and was a boon for the weir fishermen. The fish packing sheds on the bayshore were close by the railroad, and a fish freezing plant was built between the tracks and the shore. Iced and frozen fish could be loaded easily onto freight cars. In addition, Truro's dwindling number of merchants and travelers could depend on the train getting them to Boston in only five hours, compared to two days by stage coach and a day by schooner, depending on wind and weather. Vacationers could arrive by train in relative comfort.

Still, the railroad did not transform Truro. The town's population continued to decline, dropping by half during the forty years after the railroad's arrival. The train made it easier for Truro's young people to move to the cities. Most of the vacationers, tourists and day-trippers arriving on the Outer Cape by train stayed on until they reached Provincetown, a colorful, bustling seaport and soon to be a bohemian art colony. In contrast to Truro, Provincetown's population was growing rapidly and by 1900 was five times that of Truro. Three U.S. presidents—Ulysses S. Grant, Grover Cleveland and William H. Taft—rode the train to Provincetown, but they didn't stop in Truro. Anthony L. Marshall devoted a chapter of *Truro, Cape Cod, As I Knew It* (1974) to the railroad in the early 1900s but said nothing about any benefits to the town. Instead, he dwelt on storm washouts and blizzards, the railroad's operation and maintenance, which he admired, and the many brush fires started by burning coals spewed from locomotive smokestacks.

Year-round passenger service continued well into the twentieth century, although with fewer and fewer passengers. Automobiles and buses gradually replaced trains. The railroad ended regular passenger service in 1938. Freight trains continued on an irregular schedule into the 1950s but finally gave way to over-the-road trucks. The handsome railroad stations stood abandoned for years. The South Truro station was moved back from the railroad right-of-way and remodeled as a cottage. The other stations were torn down.

One day in early September 1960, Tom Kane, town clerk and newspaper columnist, noticed a strange-looking work train on the long abandoned tracks in North Truro. It was a diesel locomotive with a flatcar and two gondolas. As the train moved slowly south, workmen yanked the spikes out of the ties, and a winch pulled up the steel rails. Eighty-seven years after the railroad had come to Truro, the work train was carrying off the rails on which it was riding. "Thus ends the era of the iron horse for the Lower Cape," wrote Kane. "History in reverse, we'd seen, and it left us a mite sad." Today, some sections of the roadbed are used as footpaths or rough roadways. Other sections have been bought by abutters or are part of housing developments, and the possibility of a hiking trail or bicycle path from one end of town to the other has been lost.

. . .

Faced with the decline of deep-sea fishing, some of Truro's fishermen and retired sea captains switched to weir fishing in the 1870s, and their success provided jobs and a cash crop. Key to their success was the railroad and refrigerated freight cars.

Marshall described fish weirs in his memoir. They were a complex of netting attached to long poles driven into the sandy bottom of the shallow, offshore waters of Cape Cod Bay. The largest net hung vertically on poles that stretched hundreds of feet into the bay. The rows of pole tops sticking out of the water would puzzle visitors who did not know about weir fishing. At the weir's shoreward end, circular netting trapped fish encountering the long, vertical net, which reached from the bottom to the surface. Turned aside by the net, the fish followed it and swam through a narrow opening into the trap, where they milled around. Fishing boats entered the trap, which had a bottom to it, and closed the gate to the trap. The men then hauled up the basket-shaped net hanging beneath their boats and lifted the fish into the boats with dip nets. Deyo's history lists twelve weirs, each 2,500 feet long, off Truro around 1890.

Edmund Wilson went out with weir fishermen at a "delicate and barren Truro dawn" in 1932 and described the scene:

> The fins and tails of a shark, shiny and black, cruising
> around inside [the net] . . . fight with the shark, hooked
> and hauled up and stabbed . . . the mackerel, silver and
> vibrating like the glass beads of a chandelier–the starfish
> and hermit crabs and sea crabs and spider crabs clinging
> onto the net as it is pulled up, the whiting of the second
> catch, gaping up as their heads are brought out of the
> water . . . the goosefish of the fourth catch, muddy, amor-
> phous, ugly, lying on their bellies in the boat, automati-
> cally chewing at mackerel, which would slip down their
> throats as they lay there . . . butter fish like thin silver
> coins, brown hake dripping long pink tentacles–a bonita,
> a few bluebacks, with beautiful metallic sections along
> their backs. The fishermen were nine weeks behind in
> their pay–"the help are carrying the company"–mack-
> erel worth only three-fourths of a cent a pound.

Each weir had a fish house on shore, where the fish were sorted, gutted, cleaned, iced and packed in barrels for shipment by the next train to Boston. The arrival of the railroad was a major factor in the success of weir fishing, for the obvious route for the railroad was along the bayshore. Ice came from Truro's ponds and was stored in ice houses insulated with salt-marsh hay. Ice houses and fish houses were numerous on both sides of the railroad tracks along the bayshore. The fish houses also provided shelter for mending nets and for sleeping quarters.

Almost all the weir fishermen were Portuguese immigrants or second-generation Portuguese, many from the Cape Verde Islands. As Truro's population declined and its young people moved off-Cape, the Portuguese acquired their homes, some of which had been left vacant. The work of weir fishermen was to set the poles and netting in March, repair the weirs after storms, and haul in the fish until November when they dismantled the whole structure and stored it for the winter. Weir fishing was hard work, all of

Weir fishing flourished in Cape Cod Bay in the late nineteenth and early twentieth centuries. The fish were caught in nets hung vertically on poles driven into the sandy bottom. Shown here at low tide is part of a typical fish weir, set close to shore. Horse-drawn wagons carried the fish to shore for processing.(From the H K. Cummings collection courtesy of Snow Library, Orleans MA.)

it manual labor until the coming of the gasoline engine for boat motors, pumps, winches and pile drivers. Besides working on the weirs, the Portuguese ran small farms, and both men and women gained a reputation as industrious and thrifty.

One weir could yield 250 barrels of mackerel in a single catch, sometimes much more. "Some wonderful catches are reported from these weirs," according to Deyo's history—forty tons of pollock from one weir in one morning in 1887 and on another occasion 330 barrels of mackerel. "These weirs give employment to seven persons each, and the salting and packing houses, and boats, with the necessary appendages for the business, give a more active appearance to the shore than any other part of the town." Marshall reported that one weir crew caught thirty-eight tuna, averaging five hundred pounds each in their nets.

Weir fishermen prospered for the last two decades of 1800s and well into the 1900s, although the catch varied from year to year. In a profile of Truro in 1897, the state labor bureau reported that in the previous two or three years the catch was disappointing. "Whether this means the fish weirs are destroying the fisheries remains to be seen," the bureau reported, "but the question is troubling the fishermen of the Cape exceedingly. To put a stop to this mode of fishing, however, means interference with the employment of a large number of fishermen." The fisheries were not destroyed, but fish stocks generally diminished over the next half-century until weir fishing was no longer profitable. A contributing cause to the decline may have been the destruction of wetlands, the nursery for many species of fish. Farmers had built dikes against the salt water to create freshwater meadows and vegetable gardens. The railroad, seeking a direct route across low land and marshes, had also destroyed many acres of wetlands.

· · ·

Weir fishing led to the construction of three fish processing factories—a fish-freezing factory that was commonly called a cold storage plant, a fish canning factory, which operated for several years around the turn of the century; and after World War I the East Harbor Fertilizer Co., which processed so-called trash fish that were not popular with American fish-eaters. The fertilizer factory, located at the south end of East Harbor next to the railroad, had an aerial tramway over Route 6A and out into Provincetown Harbor, where boats unloaded their catch on two piers. According to town records, steam engines powered the grinders, cookers, digesters and driers. Like the canning factory, the fertilizer factory failed after a few years and was torn down.

The cold storage plant was built, according to the *Barnstable Patriot*, "largely through the investment and influence of Captain Hughes." Atkins Hughes, retired at fifty-two as captain of the *Southern Cross* and became a major investor in fish weirs and the fish processing plant. The plant, one of fourteen on Cape Cod at the height of weir fishing, was built in 1893 between the pond of Pond Village and Cape Cod Bay. Marshall says it was "a clapboarded affair of good size, painted white and it was situated close to the railroad tracks . . . It could handle three thousand barrels of fish at a time." The fish were brought ashore from the weirs in horse-drawn wagons that went into the bay where it was not too deep for the horses and not too shallow for the weir boats bringing in the catch. A cable car replaced the horse-drawn wagons in 1935. It ran on a cable from the top floor of the plant more than a hundred yards to a tower in the bay. Fishermen transferred their fish from their boats to the cable car, and workers in the plant hauled it in to be quick frozen and put into cold storage to await shipment.

The cold storage plant froze and packed fish caught in weirs offshore in Cape Cod Bay. The fishermen kept their nets and gear in the buildings along the shore. Poles to hold the nets are piled in the right foreground; a railroad car is at the far right. (Photo from a 1908 postcard by Mort Small in the collection of Noel W. Beyle.)

The plant in Truro burned down in 1914, but Captain Hughes, now eighty-six, insisted that it be rebuilt, and within a week investors began to organize the work. The new plant had twice the capacity. As many as thirty-two men worked there in two shifts during the fishing season. The large frame building, open to visitors in the 1930s, was a tourist attraction and a subject for painters. The WPA *Guide to Massachusetts* considered it of equal importance with Highland Light as one of Truro's sights: "The freezer is able to freeze everything–except the smell of fish. In the storage rooms, tiers of horizontal frosted pipes hold trays of mackerel, whiting and herring taken in the weirs a few hundred yards offshore. A temperature of five degrees below zero is maintained, and 30,000 pounds of fish have been shipped in one day." Along with Highland Light, the cold storage plant was a favorite subject of artists and writers. Edward Hopper painted it.

The plant probably would have gone under during the Depression, except for the return of John C. Worthington from his adventures in the West and in Latin America. Worthington had summered in Truro as a boy in the early 1900s and had gone out to the weirs with the fishermen, lending a hand and learning about weir fishing. Then he went off to work on railroads, ranches, copper mines and oil fields. He became an oil drilling engineer in the Southwest and in Mexico. He also became a commercial pilot and something of a daredevil; he once flew a plane under the George Washington Bridge spanning the Hudson River.

In 1932, he returned to Truro and took an interest in the cold storage plant. Although business had fallen off and the plant had closed, he found investors and acted as the chief engineer while at the same time working as a pilot and flying salesman for the Monsanto chemical company. For three decades, he was active in plant operations and management. By 1967, however, fish stocks in the bay were depleted and competition was growing. Ten years later, the abandoned plant was torn down as a safety hazard. The location is now a public beach called Cold Storage Beach.

A leading citizen of Truro, Worthington, served on many boards and committees and was a strong advocate for the proposed national park on the Outer Cape. Born at the turn of the twentieth century, he died at age ninety-three. When the Federal Aviation Administration wanted to dedicate in 1996 a new, powerful radar to a Truro aviator, the obvious choice for the selectmen's recommendation was Worthington, who had flown military transports during World War II in addition to his early barnstorming flights and his years as a commercial pilot.

Shortly after Worthington and his family arrived in Truro, his wife, Ada, a tall, imposing woman known as "Tiny," started Cape Cod Fishnet Industries in North Truro. In the midst of the Depression, her cottage industry quickly went international. Using standard fishnet that she dyed, she designed curtains, dresses, handbags and hats that were featured in fashion magazines. About fifty women made the fishnet apparel that was sold from coast to coast. When the major manufacturers began to copy her styles in the 1940s, she converted her business in North Truro into a boutique where she sold her fishnet creations and marine artifacts. At her death in 1989, her obituary noted that she was probably Truro's most famous businesswoman. Her gift shop, which was in an old schoolhouse in the center of North Truro, later became a small, summertime art gallery.

For most of the twentieth century, the tops of scores of fish-weir poles were a prominent sight from Truro's bayshore. As the fish disappeared and markets shifted, however, the weir companies went out of business; in the 1970s only four remained. They were at Beach Point and were operated mostly by men from Provincetown. Two of the old fishing shacks still remain; one has been fixed up as a summer cottage. The tower for the cable car was removed in 1999.

. . .

Truro's population was about 50 percent Portuguese for several decades at the end of the nineteenth century and beginning of the twentieth. Anthony Marshall, who was himself of Portuguese descent, wrote that the Portuguese were "a very large percentage of the town's population" and that the men who worked the fish weirs were "nearly one hundred percent of Portuguese extraction." In 1908, when he was a pupil in the Wilder school, more than 80 percent of the thirty-eight pupils were of Portuguese ancestry. (All instruction was in English.) During his youth, he recalled, "the Portuguese language could be heard spoken in all parts of town." Provincetown, too, was almost half Portuguese, and the foreign-born families brought with them a European lifestyle that artists and writers would find attractive. Still, the Portuguese did not arrive fast enough to prevent the population decline. From 1865 to 1895 Truro's population dropped almost 44 percent to 815, much faster than Cape Cod's 20 percent decline, while Provincetown gained 31 percent.

The Portuguese in Truro seem to have come primarily from the Azores, islands lying nine hundred miles west of Portugal, and to some extent from the Cape Verde Islands, four hundred miles west of Africa. Both were Portuguese colonies that were also ports of call for merchant ships from New England. The "Western Islanders," as they were called, were part of a sizable influx of Portuguese to southeastern New England. They were hard-working fishermen and skilled farmers, and Provincetown and Truro offered good opportunities to go into the fishing business. In Truro, they also began working on farms and cranberry bogs and buying farm property. The state report on Cape Cod characterized the Western Islander as being "frugal, industrious [and] takes readily to gardening." They enriched the town with their customs, festivals, costumes, language and cuisine. Marshall, who grew up on Portuguese cooking, describes a dozen ethnic dishes brought to Truro, some of which are still served in homes and restaurants today.

Descendants of the Portuguese immigrants are numerous in Truro. Some families have kept their Portuguese surnames, including Duarte, Dutra, Lopes, Silva, Souza, Vieira, Madruga, Cabral, Cadose and Mayo. Many others Anglicized their names, changing Rosa to Rose, Mauricio to Morris, Perreira to Perry, Nunes to

Noons. Second generation Portuguese who stayed in Truro and their children became leading citizens, and some became town officials. They prospered and filled the places left by the sons and daughters of long-established families who had left town to make their fortunes elsewhere in America. Without the Portuguese, Truro in the first half of the twentieth century would have fallen even further into economic and social decline.

· · ·

With the population decline came a reduction in the number of schools to three. Marshall was a pupil in the two-room Wilder School on Depot Road. The school had about forty pupils in nine grade levels. One of the two teachers was Betsy Holsberry, whose tenure as a teacher went back to pre-Civil War days. A plaque to her memory is at Holsberry Square. School buildings were often moved and recycled for other uses. The Wilder school became a post office and then a real estate office and a seamstress shop. The Long Nook school was moved and became a gift shop next to the Whitman House restaurant. The North Truro School at Pond Road became the home of the Cape Cod Fishnet Industries and then an art gallery.

Truro has always been too small for a high school. In the early twentieth century, a few of Truro's children went to high school in Wellfleet or Provincetown. They either found their own transportation or boarded with a family when school was in session. The first school bus, a sisteen-passenger Studebaker, began operations in 1916, carrying students to Provincetown High School. By the 1930s, cars and buses made it possible to centralize the town's elementary schools in one building. Truro's voters, however, were not very enthusiastic about spending $21,000 for a central school. In a town meeting on March 25, 1935, voters first defeated the measure, which required a two-thirds vote. On reconsideration, the measure passed by the thinnest possible margin, 98 to 49. About eighty pupils went to the new school, which was completed in 1936. Since then, the building has been renovated and expanded twice.

. . .

Life in Truro in the first two decades of the twentieth century is fondly recalled by Anthony L. Marshall, who grew up on his parents' farm and left town when he was eighteen years old to begin a career in the electric power industry. He was in his late sixties and early seventies when he wrote his memoir, a valuable primary source of homely details about everyday life in Truro. Marshall was struck by the changes in the half-century since his youth. Pine, oak and locust trees covered much of the farm land and open pastures he had known as a boy. Back then "quite a few windmills dotted the landscape;" small vegetable gardens, orchards and cranberry bogs were everywhere along the roads.

His father owned several of the many cranberry bogs around town, and Marshall described how they were cultivated and harvested. One of the largest bogs was at the head of the Pamet River, off North Pamet Road. Cultivation of the bog began in the 1880s; in 1953 it produced a peak harvest of 166 barrels. In 1963, it became part of the Cape Cod National Seashore, which built a boardwalk across it and tried to restore it as a demonstration bog. The bog house, where the berries were cleaned and packed, was built around 1830 in South Truro and moved to the bog at the turn of the century. In 1998, the national seashore restored it.

The automobile, which would doom the railroad and transform Truro, began to appear on Truro roads just after the turn of the century. A newspaper reported the sighting of an automobile at Highland House in 1903 and three or four a day there in 1906. Marshall, who devotes a chapter to automobiles, recalls that it was around 1910 when the first Truro people began buying automobiles and the town began tarring main roads. Marshall's uncle, Manuel ("M. J.") Marshall, the town blacksmith, opened the first gasoline station around 1915. The telephone arrived in Truro long

before electricity; in January 1900, the selectmen authorized the
telephone company to erect poles and wires in Truro. Although
several homes had gasoline generators, electricity from central power
plants did not arrive in Truro until the 1930s, according to
Marshall.

Besides the cold storage plant and, briefly, the fish fertilizer
factory, Truro had a different and more genteel enterprise, the Bayberry Candle Place. Albert Perry Bingham, who visited Truro in
1915, described it:

> There is a small factory far out on the Cape, at North Truro
> station, which is more in harmony with the environment.
> Here are made jellies of beach plum and wild grape, baskets
> of cat-tail flags, and trays and table mats our of beach grass.
> But the main product here is bayberry wax. The gray, round
> berries, the size of shot, are brought here in autumn, in
> October and November, for making bayberry balm, bay-
> berry cold cream and bayberry Christmas novelties, most of
> all the bayberry candle.

The factory operated into the 1930s. As fishing became less profitable, small factories such as Bayberry, which operated into the
1930s, and Tiny Worthington's Cape Cod Fishnet Industries provided employment opportunities.

In the first years of the twentieth century, and despite a slug-
gish economy, the townspeople organized two celebrations–for the
two-hundreth anniversary of Pamet gaining township status and
for the dedication of the town's first library. A day-long celebration on July 16, 1909, marked the town's two centuries. Church
bells pealed from seven to eight in the morning. Truro played
Wellfleet in baseball. No one could miss the decorations–flags and
bunting hung from a wire stretched taut from the steeple of Town
Hall to the steeple of the Congregational church. After speeches in
the church, a band played for dancing on the second floor of Town
Hall. Among the speakers was John B. Dyer, a descendant of one

of the earliest settlers and town clerk for forty-five years. He delivered a lengthy address on the history of Truro.

. . .

Another celebrated event was the dedication of the town's first public library building. On a sunny Saturday afternoon in August 1912, the townspeople gathered at Truro Center for to dedicate Cobb Memorial Library. The library was financed by Elisha W. Cobb, fifty-six years old and a native of South Truro. As a young man, he had left the Cobb family farm and made his fortune as cofounder of a leather goods company in Winchester and Boston. His gift of the library building was probably inspired by the philanthropy of Andrew Carnegie, the steel tycoon, who helped found public libraries in thousands of towns and cities. Anthony Marshall, ten years old at the time, recalled Cobb's presentation of the library to the town in memory of his parents. The first librarian in the new building was Laurena Ryder, who had been running the library from her nearby home.

Elisha Cobb not only funded the first library, he also provided for its maintenance and some of its books. In his will, he left the town ten thousand dollars in trust for upkeep and repairs and for book purchases. After his death, his daughter, Nelle C. Magee, became the family benefactor. She donated a clock tower for the library and chimes for Town Hall, gifts noted on a plaque at the library. In the 1930s, she and her husband, Richard Magee, a volunteer fireman, donated firefighting apparatus and an ambulance. The town gave them a book of thanks signed by almost everyone and which included paintings by local artists. Edward Hopper contributed a watercolor of the Magee's barn.

Until Cobb Memorial Library was built, Truro's libraries for almost two centuries had been solely in the homes of book-minded people like the Reverend John Avery. The first library collection for dues-paying members was launched in 1840, when Truro was enjoying its greatest commercial prosperity. Twenty-eight

booklovers got together and formed the Truro Library Association. By the end of the 1800s, they had three collections in
homes in South Truro, Truro Center and North Truro.

The "Truro Town Library" was founded in 1894 when the
town received 174 books from the Commonwealth. The collection grew rapidly to 2,400 volumes, which filled the principal librarian's pantry. Soon, a state library inspector would report that "the walls are lined with books from floor to ceiling
and some of the books are piled on the floor and on chairs."
North Truro had its own, smaller collection in the corner of a
dry goods store. "There is some friction between the two libraries," reported the state official but without elaborating.

Cobb Memorial Library centralized the collection and removed the friction. Less than a decade later, however, book
borrowers in North Truro still felt the need for a library in
their own neighborhood. Land was donated, and the money
for the building came from the proceeds of a Pilgrim Pageant
celebrating the tricentennial of the Pilgrims' landing on Cape
Cod in 1620. The new branch, called Pilgrim Library, was a
tiny, wooden structure located at the corner of the North Truro
village crossroads. It proved to be too small for its nearly three
thousand books, and the second Pilgrim Library was built in
1961 south of the village. The first building became an office
for the public works department.

Truro's population more than doubled in the decades since
construction of the first library buildings, and in 1999 a new
library building opened in North Truro. Just as individuals
paid for subscription libraries of the 1800s and Elisha Cobb
built the first public library, individuals contributed more than
a quarter of the cost of the new public library at the end of the
century. Cobb library was closed.

. . .

While the railroad did not change Truro much and weir fishing began to decline, another trend, which Thoreau had predicted, would have the biggest impact on Truro in the twentieth century—the arrival of tourists, vacationers, artists, writers, and summer people who bought and built vacation homes. And the pioneer in Truro's leisure-time industry was the multi-faceted Mort Small.

PART IV:

*Twentieth Century Truro, A
Seaside Town for Summer People*

CHAPTER 17:
MORT SMALL, THE
OUTSPOKEN INNKEEPER

At the start of the twentieth century, Isaac Morton Small, known as Mort, was the owner, manager and genial host of a much-expanded Highland House. Fifty-five years old, he had been running the summer resort since he was twenty, and he had made it into the largest and most successful in Truro. His ocean-side resort prefigured the character of Truro in the twentieth century–a rural, seaside, summer vacation community.

A large addition to Highland House in 1876 had more than doubled its size, and in 1898 Small built the nine-room Millstone cottage next door on the site of his father's gristmill. It was the first of eight cottages to be built over three decades bearing names such as "Beacon," "Haven" and "Pilgrim." The resort also had a bowling alley and pool room. A large building for roller skating and dancing was destroyed by a storm in 1898.

Mort Small's son, Willard, laid out a nine-hole golf course, more properly a golf "links," in 1898 that is one of the ten oldest in the United States. The year 1892 is often given as the date, but 1898 is more likely the correct year. Larry Lowenthal, who wrote comprehensive histories of Highland Light and Highland House for the National Park Service, cites a newspaper item in August 1898 reporting that "fine golf links have been laid out near the Highland House and will be for the use of the guests of the house next season."

The name "links" describes a windswept, seaside layout on sandy ground with coarse grass; it evokes the origins of golf played on links in Scotland. Almost every hole at Highland has a view of the ocean and the lighthouse. A painting of the ninth hole illustrated the publisher's letter in a 1974 issue of *Sports Illustrated,* which carried paintings of the best short par-3 holes in the country. Truro's did not make the list of the best but appeared as the publisher's whimsical footnote because Walter ("Bing") Bingham of Truro, a senior editor and Highland Links golfer, worked with the artist on the magazine story.

In 1907, Mort Small built a new and larger Highland House with fifteen guest rooms, kitchen and dining room. His wife, Lillian, was the chef and also his partner in running the resort, which could accommodate more than a hundred guests. Lowenthal says that Small "led his town into modern times, guiding and inspiring its transition to an economy based largely on tourism." Small's brochure for the 1909 season promoted the resort as "a quiet, health-giving spot . . . where the demands of fashion are not exacting and where the ocean air . . . is undefiled with any malarial conditions. . . . a Mecca of rest for the tired pilgrim from the noisy city" with surf bathing, perfect drainage, pure drinking water and no annoying odors.

Highland House drew a faithful clientele, some of them from Boston, New York and other large cities, who stayed for several weeks or months and returned year after year. They were the first of Truro's summer people in significant numbers. One day in August 1919, several got together in the parlor of Highland House to discuss the possibility of a pageant the following summer to celebrate the three hundredth anniversary of the Pilgrims' landing in

Isaac M. ("Mort") Small (1845-1934) was the most prominent businessman and civic leader in Truro during his long lifetime. He and his wife Lillian operated the Highland House resort. His last booklet, *True Stories of Cape Cod*, published the year he died, included his obituary from the Boston *Globe* and these portraits.

the New World and their exploration of Truro. Mrs. H.B. Sharman had prepared a paper proposing the celebration. Her idea found favor, and several committees were formed, mostly of summer sojourners, as they called themselves, plus members of the Small clan. Mort Small was named honorary chairman, and Arthur Small and Mrs. Hayes Small led the committees on refreshments, a specialty of Highland House, and casting, which required recruiting scores of local people. J.H. McKinley, another summer sojourner, was tercentenary president and fund raiser.

For a small town, the pageant was a formidable undertaking. Dressed in Pilgrim and Indian costumes, more than 150 men, women and children acted in a dozen scenes. Their open-air theater was the hillside south of Pond Village pond, the site of the Pilgrims' encampment. On the afternoon of August 25, 1920, "a beautiful summer day," a crowd estimated at more than 2,500 people gathered on the hillside, along with newsreel cameramen from five companies and reporters from all the Boston newspapers. In its own report, the pageant committee wrote that "automobiles grouped upon the crests of the surrounding hills, the many fluttering flags and the many colored costumes of the actors presented a never-to-be forgotten picture." Mort Small welcomed the audience: "Could the *Mayflower* Pilgrims who trod these hills and valleys three hundred years ago in search of a suitable habitation look down upon this scene today it would certainly be a revelation." The elaborate pageant began with Indian life on Cape Cod, depicted the Pilgrims' expeditions in Truro and closed with a re-enactment of the first Thanksgiving Day feast.

. . .

Besides running the Highland House resort, Mort Small was a farmer, the marine reporting agent for the Boston Chamber of Commerce, an elected public official who held many positions and the author of five booklets on the Outer Cape. He lived eighty-eight years, his adult years spanning the Civil War and World War I.

His grandfather, Isaac Small, sold the land for the first lighthouse and was the first keeper. His father, James, a farmer, was elected to the state legislature nine times and left a "political biography" in manuscript. James Small was also for a time the light-house keeper, but his wife, Jerusha, did most of the work. Mort Small says that before he could walk his mother took him with her to the top of the lighthouse when she tended the lantern. Although he lived all his life at Highland, he never took on the job of lighthouse keeper.

Mort Small expanded his seaside resort in 1907 with a new Highland House for summer vacationers. The building now houses the collections of the Truro Historical Society. (Photo from a postcard by Small in the collection of Noel W. Beyle.)

Mort Small's hard-working mother was the subject of an admiring profile in the *Barnstable Patriot* in 1855 by "Mrs. Margery Daw," who stayed at the Small's summer boarding house: "There was never, I do believe, in this working world a busier woman than my hostess . . . One morning I happened to go up the iron-winding staircase into the lantern, and there she was trimming the lamps; one evening I paid a similar visit, and there she was, lighting them. All mariners, as they pass Highland Light ought to bless Mrs. Small. Go out into the little porch when you will, and you will find her up to her elbows in flour, or feathers. Step into the little yard and ten to one she is feeding the turkeys. Wander in the green space outside, and you will find her chopping fire wood . . . Stroll down to the barn, and if you do not see her in the cornfield doing something or other useful you will find her busy there milking the cows in company with her brisk little boy [Mort] . . . and not the least, [she] cooks to admiration."

After schooling in Truro, Mort Small attended private schools for a year or two off-Cape and at eighteen became the marine reporting agent at Highland, a position he would hold until his death. With all his interests and occupations, Mort Small was not peering through his telescope every hour of every day. His daughter, also Lillian, became expert on the telegraph key and was, he says, "thoroughly familiar with marine reporting and was my always reliable and competent assistant." When she married and left home, a cousin by marriage, Olive M. Williams, who had come to live with the Smalls, became the assistant marine reporting agent. "She handles the key and knows the ships like a veteran," said Small in 1922. She was his assistant for thirty-four years; and it's likely that she and Small's daughter before her did at least as much marine reporting as he did, if not more. Katharine Crosby saw Williams at work in the 1920s and wrote in *Blue-Water Men and Other Cape Codders* that "she was on duty all day long, every day in the year."

Mort Small was elected to office for the first time when he was only twenty-one, and then it was to three offices at the same time— as a selectman, a member of the board of assessors and one of the overseers of the poor. The other assessors named him chairman, and he apparently did most of the work. "As I was at that time trying to run Highland House, one may imagine the strenuous work mapped out for me. After one year of this, I threw it up and devoted my time to the hotel and farm."

He returned to town politics in his thirties and for decades served in all the important town offices. He was a selectman for twenty-six years, chairman of the board of assessors for twenty-three years and chairman of the school committee for sixteen years. In 1901 and 1908, the voters of the Outer Cape elected him their representative to the state legislature in Boston, where he and his wife lived during the two sessions. He recalled that he voted for women's suffrage and opposed controls on weir fishing advocated by conservationists. As a director and the secretary of Truro's fish-freezing plant at Cold Storage Beach for more than twenty years, he had a special interest in weir fishing.

Small's five booklets are collections of anecdotes, shipwreck accounts, jokes, personal reminiscences, descriptions of Truro, autobiographical notes and articles he had written for newspapers. His first was *Highland Light: This Book Tells You All About It* in 1891. This was followed by three in the 1920s and finally *True Stories of Cape Cod*, published in 1934, the year he died. Small was also the Outer Cape correspondent for the *Boston Globe*, the Associated Press and Cape Cod newspapers. More of a raconteur than a historian, Small's dates and facts sometimes do not square with the records. He even gives different dates for his first marriage. Nevertheless, his first-hand accounts of shipwrecks and events in town, which often sound like stories he might tell to entertain his guests, provide a vivid picture of Truro during his lifetime.

Never shy about expressing his opinions, Mort Small felt obliged to instruct his guests how to behave and have a pleasant stay at his resort. His brochure for the 1912-15 years offered the following advice:

> DON'T wear heavy clothing or fashionable silks at the sea-shore. Wear comfortable clothes and you will be correspondingly happy.
>
> DON'T try to beat the hotel keeper and don't think he is trying to beat you; he is just as anxious to have your vacation a pleasant one as you are to enjoy it.
>
> DON'T go to a mountain or seashore resort on a hot midsummer day, dusty, weary and hungry and immediately rush out over the country in an effort to see how miserable you can make yourself. Rest, dine and spend at least a day in taking in the situation.
>
> DON'T blame the heat and the cold and every evil under the sun on the hotel keeper.
>
> DON'T be selfish, there are other people in the world besides ourselves.
>
> DON'T engage rooms at a summer hotel and at the last moment write that you cannot come, hotel managers are only human.
>
> DON'T in departing leave any of your things.
>
> DON'T expect free rides to and from the station to meet friends or see them off.
>
> DON'T be exclusive.
>
> DON'T fuss.
>
> DON'T arrive at a strange hotel after dark if you can avoid it.
>
> DON'T go to a summer hotel in mid-August for a week's stay and expect to find the best rooms in the house awaiting you.

His writings about town affairs also reveal a man of emphatic opinions. When stone breakwaters at the mouth of Pamet Harbor failed to keep a channel open, he wrote: "If there ever was a more scandalous and foolish expenditure of public funds, we have not been able to discover [it]." When someone put up signs identifying the main road through Truro as "The King's Highway." He said the signs were "manifestly misleading . . . a farce." The King's Highway was the sand track around the head of the Pamet and past Highland House. Others shared his opinion, for town meeting voted to protest to a board of public utilities that the signs were "both untrue and misleading."

Small also disputed the traditional location of the Pilgrims' spring, where they got their first drink of water in America. "Let us see how absurd the claim is," he wrote, and went on to describe a more accessible spring several hundred yards away where he and his father had watered their oxen.

Erosion of the ocean cliffs was a regular topic of speculation, and Small was firmly of two minds. In 1891 and again in 1926, he said the lighthouse would be in danger of falling over the cliff in thirty years. (In fact, it took more than twice as long.) But in 1934, he said the erosion was "very little," and caused mostly by rain not the ocean, high tide being far from the base of the cliff at that time. "We may feel quite sure," he said, "that . . . the path of the Coast Guard patrol [along the top of the cliff] will be over the same route they are traveling today." Erosion, however, would sweep away the path.

Mort Small was alert and energetic to the end. Katharine Crosby recalled that when she met him he had just celebrated his eightieth birthday by making a hole-in-one on his golf links. His last booklet was at the printer when he died in 1934, six weeks before his eighty-ninth birthday. It opens with his obituary from the *Boston Globe*, which called him the "Sentinel of Highlands." As the sentinel of the Highlands and keen observer of life in Truro, he had seen steamships give way to sailing vessels in the shipping lanes, electricity replace whale oil in the lighthouse, and tourism succeed the fishing fleet and weir fishing. During his lifetime, Truro's population dropped from more than two thousand to fewer than five hundred. Taking shape, however, was a new Truro of re-

tirees from off-Cape and increasing numbers of tourists and owners of summer homes, including famous artists and writers.

Small outlived his two wives and his two sons by his first wife,
Sarah. Their daughter Lillian inherited half the Highland House
resort (two grand-daughters shared the other half) and Cliff House,
which Small had built north of the lighthouse in 1880 as his home
and marine reporting station. Olive Williams succeeded him as
the official marine reporting agent; and he had made special provision for her in his will, leaving her his largest cash bequest, seven
hundred dollars, and directing that she could live the rest of her
life at Cliff House and receive twenty-dollars a month plus room
and board as long as she was the marine reporting agent.

Lillian Small and the two granddaughters ran Highland House
until 1942 when it closed because of World War II. Harold J.
Conklin of Paterson, New Jersey, bought it in 1947. An avid golfer,
he rebuilt the golf course. Finally, in 1964 the National Park Service acquired it for the Cape Cod National Seashore. The park
service granted the town the concession to operate the golf course
and the Truro Historical Society permission to use Highland House
as a museum.

Mort Small's Highland House typified resorts of the era. In
his history of Highland House with Regina Binder, Lowenthal
says, "The development and decline of the resort offers a clear
picture of the characteristic progression of tourism on Cape Cod."
Modes of transportation determined the progression—from the
horse-and-buggy days of the Small family's farmhouse as boarding
house to the railroad-based tourism of the Highland House and
its cottages to the time of the automobile, which greatly expanded
the choices of seasonal visitors and increased the competition for
"the increasingly anachronistic Highland House operation." Today, Highland House is a museum housing the collections of the
Truro Historical Society.

. . .

Mort Small and his family, although the first and most successful, were not the only entrepreneurs to develop summer resorts in Truro. Around the turn of the previous century, others in town began to offer board and room for summer visitors. A Cape Cod business directory in 1901 listed three hotels for Truro—Highland House, the Ballston Beach Cottages and Central House, which advertised itself as a first class livery—and boarding houses owned by W. H. Hart in North Truro and B. E. Corlew near Pamet Harbor. The directory also listed six grocers, six milkmen and a physician but only one real estate broker.

The first to follow Mort Small's initiative was Sheldon W. Ball of New York City, who bought a thousand acres on the ocean in 1889 and built the Ballston Beach Bungalows colony. A few years later, Lorenzo Dow Baker of Wellfleet, who made his fortune introducing bananas to America, built a cottage colony on Corn Hill overlooking Cape Cod Bay as an adjunct to his large hotel at Wellfleet Harbor. Burton S. Hart operated the Whitman House in North Truro. Around 1915, Will Rich, Shebnah's son, built a dozen cottages on the wind-swept ocean dune heights at the end of Long Nook Road. When Herbert W. Stranger, Sr., bought the colony in 1939, the wind had ruined two of the cottages. All were taken down when the Cape Cod National Seashore acquired the property. Other enterprising homeowners took in boarders and expanded their properties. Entrepreneurs from out of town also thought Truro could be a summer resort. The March 1897 report of the state bureau of statistics of labor noted that "during the last two or three years an attempt had been made by a New York syndicate, with partial success, to develop this town as a summer resort." The syndicate has not been identified.

Sheldon Ball and his son, S. Osborne ("Ossie") Ball, ran the Ballston Beach Bungalows for more than half a century. Their advertising in New York City newspapers aimed at attracting well-to-do families who would rent for the full season, even though the cottages were not luxurious. The appeal was their location—a remote, unspoiled stretch of Atlantic Ocean beach. Ossie Ball would tell anyone who complained about his prices that they were paying for the beach and the ocean view and that the cottages were free. Although the cottages were quite primitive, the resort did have a clubhouse and a bowling alley. Golfers could play at the nine-hole course of the Pamet River Golf Club laid out on both banks of the Pamet River near Ballston Beach. The golf course no longer exists.

Northeast storms battered the colony almost every year and ocean waves ate away at the beach dunes, undermining foundations. A storm in 1913 lifted a roof from the clubhouse and sent it sailing into the headwaters of the Pamet River. *Yankee* magazine reported in a profile of Ossie Ball that in 1932 one of cottages was swept out to sea "and all the porches of the front-row shacks were ripped off." Two years later, another storm wrecked the porches again. The cottages were moved back several times. Today, one of the Ball cottages survives, having been moved back from the ocean, remodeled and raised on pilings, but where all the others originally sat is under water.

Sheldon Ball and his wife Lucy also built a big summer home on a bluff overlooking the Atlantic Ocean. It was one of the first oceanfront homes on the Outer Cape. He collapsed and died while walking on Ballston Beach in 1923 and was buried in a family plot on a hilltop behind his home. His is the only headstone in the plot.

His son, Ossie, was described as "an amiable but eccentric lawyer" by E.J. Kahn Jr. in *About the New Yorker and Me*. Ossie Ball lived in Provincetown and had his law office there; but, according to Kahn, he "used to handle the care-taking chores himself for the old wooden summer bungalows . . . which, though arguably tumbledown, were much prized by the seasonal tenants who occupied them." Ball regularly flew a large assortment of flags that most people were at a loss to identify. In 1972, his friends and former tenants erected a flagpole as a memorial to him at the

The Ballston Beach Bungalows resort, established by Sheldon Ball in 1889, was built beside the Pamet lifesaving station, the building in the center with the cupola. The long, low structure was a bowling alley, the two-story building the community center and dining hall. Storm waves and constant erosion undermined nearly all the buildings shown in the photograph from the early 1900s. Some were destroyed; others were moved. (Photo from a postcard in the collection of Noel W. Beyle.)

old Coast Guard station. A plaque carries the inscription: "He made a way of life for them all, young and old." The Cape Cod National Seashore acquired the Ball properties, and the Ball house on the bluff, abandoned for decades, was torn down in 1986.

. . .

Summer cottages occupied by their owners began to appear in the late 1800s. The Cape Cod business directory of 1901, which also listed residences, identified twenty-nine summer homes. A few of the owners came from as far away as Chicago. Anthony Marshall wrote that in the first two decades of the twentieth century there were already "a sizable number of summer homes" in Truro. By the 1990s, summer homes would outnumber year-round residences two to one.

Around 1900, Beach Point, the long sand spit facing Provincetown Harbor, was divided into more than two hundred tiny lots on both sides of the road to Provincetown. Mort Small counted more than forty cottages there in the mid-1920s. Their numbers increased steadily over the decades, as did the number of motels. By the 1990s, more than two hundred motels and cottage colony units lined the water's edge, some of them so close to high tide that storm waves undermined their seawalls, which had to be replaced. The most prominent cottage colony was the row of twenty-two identical white-clapboard cottages of the Days family, which were built in the 1930s. Beach Point is by far the town's highest density commercial area, looking more like an extension of Provincetown than mostly rural Truro.

An ambitious but ill-fated summer-home development project was launched at High Head in 1911 by E.E. Phillips of Provincetown. He offered to sell tiny lots on seventy acres overlooking Provincetown Harbor and Pilgrim Lake. He called it Pilgrim Heights and offered building lots as small as fifty feet by a hundred feet. He promised electricity, telephone service, water from the new Truro-Provincetown water main, a flag stop on the nearby railroad and an automobile and driver for visits to Provincetown. The deeds carried restrictions for the good of the community: "No intoxicating liquors are to be sold; no house costing less than $800 will be allowed to be built; no outside unsanitary buildings [outhouses] will be allowed." Farm animals were to be kept out of sight behind the barns. At least two mansard-roofed houses of "cement art block" were built, but Phillips ran into trouble or was ahead of his time, for the ambitious project stalled. Finally, in the early 1950s, the state purchased most of land and created Pilgrim Springs State Park, which later became part of the Cape Cod National Seashore. Despite the failure of the Pilgrim Heights project, the purchase and construction of vacation homes in many parts of Truro continued through the twentieth century, interrupted only by the two world wars.

· · ·

World War I was raging in Europe in March 1917 when Eugene O'Neill and a friend were arrested on suspicion of spying for the Germans at the U.S. government radio station near Highland Light. The United States was just a few days away from entering the war, and everyone was on the alert. In their biography *O'Neill,* Arthur and Barbara Gelb wrote that the arrest was "at the instigation of the chief of the United States radio station in North Truro, who had somehow persuaded himself that O'Neill and [Harold] De Polo were German spies." The two men, both outspoken pacifists, were held for several hours in the Provincetown jail. "Rumors were rife," reported the Provincetown *Advocate,* that the men drew revolvers when arrested and that they had in their possession plans of the radio station and Provincetown Harbor. The rumors proved false.

O'Neill, twenty-eight years old and at the start of his career as America's greatest playwright, later recalled the episode: "I was the victim of war hysteria. Somebody over at the wireless station watched us and decided we were German spies. We were having dinner in a

[Provincetown] hotel in town one evening when some Secret Service men [actually the town constable] pounced on us at the point of a revolver and carried us to the lockup in the basement of the town hall. They wouldn't even let us see a lawyer." O'Neill and his friend were able to explain why they were walking near the radio tower, and the holding charge of vagrancy was dropped.

Once again, Truro was experiencing the threat of wartime hostilities on its shoreline. Enemy submarines lurked off its Atlantic coast; one U-boat surfaced off Orleans, tried to sink a tugboat and its barges and lobbed shells onto the Orleans shore. A British ship was torpedoed about a hundred miles at sea, and three lifeboats with survivors came ashore at Ballston Beach. U.S. Marines were stationed at Highland to guard the radio station. The Marines also helped organize Truro's home guard. Anthony Marshall, just old enough at sixteen to join the home guard, recalled that drills were held regularly at town hall.

On Armistice Day, Marshall was at the railroad station when he learned that the war was over. He and a friend ran up the tracks and across fields to the Old South Meetinghouse where they "everlastingly rang that bell" to celebrate the end of the war. The names of thirty-five veterans are inscribed on a plaque at Cobb Library. Marshall notes that for some reason the plaque does not carry the name of Louis Morris, the only serviceman from Truro, he says, who was killed in action.

After the war ended, enemy submarines off Truro's Atlantic coast were replaced by power boats engaged in rum-running. Prohibition went into effect in 1920, and Truro probably had its share of smuggling, but records of it are scarce. In *Time and the Town: A Provincetown Chronicle* (1942) Mary Heaton Vorse tells of one episode at Long Nook Beach: "Lonely roads like Long Nook made good landing places for liquor. Harriet McGinnis came back from a picnic there with stories of seeing a lantern on the high bluff and an answering wink at sea. They saw them come in, landing the stuff and presently a truck went whizzing down the Cape, perhaps to be hijacked." The Coast Guard was supposed to stop the smuggling from ships, but Vorse says bootlegging was everywhere on the Outer Cape: "We had plenty of bootlegging in Provincetown."

. . .

In the late 1920s, Truro became an unlikely center of aeronautical record-setting feats by German and American aviators. The Treaty of Versailles had limited the number of airplanes Germany could have after the war, and several Germans pilots turned to motorless aircraft. According to *Hang Gliding* magazine, J. C. Penney Jr., of the Penney retail stores, who summered on Cape Cod and had seen gliders in Germany, funded German pilots to come to the Cape and teach Americans. Corn Hill appeared to be a good launching spot for gliders, or sailplanes, which could soar on the updrafts of the prevailing westerly winds that struck the high bayshore cliffs. Three Germans began flying sailplanes there in 1928.

Their soaring school drew scores of fledgling pilots. Tom Kane, town clerk and columnist, was much impressed. "Gadzooks," he wrote, "what a glamorous group of men. . . . the officers wore monocles, and carried swagger sticks, and sported highly polished leather puttees . . . [they] made inroads into the cocktail party set and swept every available female from the local dating lists." He watched them launch their sailplanes at the cliff edge with "a big rubber cable . . . Visualize a slingshot, if you will."

On a windy day in July, Peter Hesselbach of Darmstadt, Germany, flew fifty-five minutes to break Orville Wright's American soaring record, set in 1911. A few days later, he broke his own record with a four-hour flight. The following year, Ralph S. Barnaby, a Navy lieutenant, became the first American to beat Orville Wright's record. Barnaby launched from Corn Hill and stayed up fifteen minutes, six seconds. The National Soaring Museum dedicated a plaque at the foot of Corn Hill to commemorate Barnaby's flight. To this day, it is not unusual to see hang gliders soaring on the updrafts along the bayshore beaches and ocean cliffs. Since 1974, the Seascape Motel on the bayshore north of Corn Hill has been host to the annual Halloween Fly-In, which draws dozens of hang gliders to Truro.

. . .

A monumental mystery and myth were left for the town to ponder by Henry M. Aldrich, a Boston lawyer. The monument is a seventy-foot, granite tower in the Cape Cod National Seashore just south of Highland Light. It's known as the Jenny Lind Tower. No road leads to it, and no plaque tells why it is there. Originally, the tower was part of the Fitchburg railroad station in Boston. When the station was demolished in 1927, Aldrich, whose family was connected with the railroad, had the tower taken apart stone by stone and rebuilt on land he had bought from Mort Small. Small says that it took five men more than two months to complete the work. Aldrich had nearly a hundred acres fronting on the ocean, and he built five cottages there but left no word on the purpose of the round, hollow tower.

The myth is that Jenny Lind, the "Swedish Nightingale," sang from this same tower at the Fitchburg railroad station for admirers who could not get into her oversold concert and that Aldrich was much taken with the superstar soprano. In fact, she did give a concert in 1850 in the auditorium that was part of the railroad station. Her fans crashed the gates, and she had to cut short her performance. Newspaper reports of the incident, however, said nothing about her singing from the tower to the public in the street below. And Henry Aldrich, her supposed admirer, was not born until seventeen years after her concert.

In *A Pilgrim Returns to Cape Cod* (1946), Edward Rowe Snow embellished the myth that had entered into local lore. He hiked through thick undergrowth to the Jenny Lind tower where he "tried to imagine the singer's voice as it had echoed in that same tower Columbus Day night in 1850." Aldrich, he wrote, noticed the demolition work in 1927 and "decided that it was a definite shame that one of the towers could not be saved for posterity."

Snow did not give the source for his information. "There are those who like to believe," he continued, that one of the Aldrich family group was captivated by Jenny Lind's voice and that this influenced him to move the tower to his land in Truro. Snow undercut his speculations, however, by stating that Aldrich's son, Samuel Nelson Aldrich, told him that Jenny Lind's performance in no way motivated his father to move the tower.

Nevertheless, local lore has prevailed, and Aldrich's tower became the Jenny Lind tower, a problematical and inaccessible tourist attraction. In 1968, Tom Kane added further embellishments. In a newspaper column, included in his book *My Pamet*, he wrote that "Aldrich, so rumor has it, had carried the torch for her" and that Truro folks still insist that on certain moonlit nights they hear singing coming from the Jenny Lind tower.

. . .

By 1930, Truro's population had declined steadily from its peak of 2,051 before the Civil War to a low in 1930–only a few hundred more than were living in Pamet when it became Truro in 1709. The turnaround began in 1935 with an increase of forty-five people. A few artists began to buy homes in Truro; a few more summer vacationers began to retire in Truro; and no doubt fewer natives were leaving town during the Depression. From then on, the population increased steadily.

Although few in number, the summer people wanted to preserve the charm and traditions of small-town Truro, and in August 1931 they and some town residents formed the Truro Neighborhood Association "to beautify Truro and preserve its natural charm." One of the first items of business was to help get rid of junked automobiles. In her short history of the organization, Past President Joyce Edinberg observed that "in the main, it appears that for its first few years, the TNA's prime concern was getting rid of the garbage, trash and other eyesores." Soon, the organization had more than a hundred members. It took ownership of the abandoned South Truro Meetinghouse and planned to renovate it, but the building burned down. The organization also campaigned against the nude beach south of Ballston Beach that drew huge, unruly crowds and against plans in 1990 for a small amusement park on Route 6.

Before the 1930s, there was no fire department; and before the 1950s no police department. Firefighting was "a matter of men, shovels, brooms, pump cans and perspiration," in the words of Tom Kane, who says that Richard ("Dick") Magee was the father of the first organized fire department. Magee had married Nelle Cobb, daughter of Elisha Cobb, who gave the town Cobb Library. A dedicated firefighter, Magee even had his own fire engine, a pre-1920 model. Over the years, he bought firefighting equipment for the town, as well as the town's first ambulance. After a major forest fire in South Truro in 1927 that burned for several days out of control, town meeting supported Magee's volunteer efforts by voting six thousand dollars for two pumpers. Police protection was provided by the county sheriff's deputies until 1949, when town meeting authorized three thousand dollars for a police department. The first police chief was Harold Berrio of Wellfleet, who had been town constable.

Twenty years later, Berrio had a gruesome and sensational murder case on his hands. The dismembered bodies of four young women were found in shallow graves not far from Pine Grove Cemetery, itself deep in the woods. Antone Costa, twenty-four, a carpenter-handyman and the divorced father of three children, was arrested soon after. He was living in Provincetown, where he was involved with drugs and where he had met at least two of his victims. Calm and seemingly gentle at his trial in 1970, he argued that he was a recovering drug addict. He was convicted and sentenced to life in prison. Four years later, he hanged himself in his jail cell. Kurt Vonnegut, the novelist, wrote about the murders for *Life* magazine, and in 1981 crime-writer Leo Damore published *In His Garden: The Anatomy of a Murder*.

In the 1930s and 1940s, Truro had a medical research laboratory–the marine experimental station of the Lankenau Hospital Research Institute of Philadelphia. The station was a summer program staffed largely by volunteers in three small buildings near the bayshore. Investigators studied the growth of cells in marine invertebrates found in the exceptionally clean water of Cape Cod Bay off Truro. Their work led to a series of scientific seminars, the first of which was held at the elementary school. All was not lab work, however. A report on the laboratory noted that "several romances which developed along Cape Cod Bay and the Pamet River culminated in happy marriages."

In the two decades between World War I and World War II, only five hundred to six hundred people lived in the town year-round. Most of them worked family farms. Some worked at Mort Small's Highland House or other summer lodgings. Some of the men worked at the fish weirs, which were, however, on the decline; women could sew fishnet apparel for Tiny Worthington. No one was building new houses, and some of the older ones were left vacant. No one found Truro particularly attractive except for a growing number of authors and artists who appreciated its rural tranquility and who would make Truro a mostly undiscovered artists' colony.

CHAPTER 18:
TRURO'S AUTHORS, ARTISTS
AND COMPOSERS

An extraordinary number of eminent authors, artists and composers have lived in Truro or sojourned in the town for varying periods of time. Winners of Nobel prizes, Pulitzer prizes, National Book Awards and PEN/Faulker awards and the nation's poet laureate have been among the authors who sought out Truro. They include Eugene O'Neill, Edna St. Vincent Millay, Margaret Sanger, John Dos Passos, Susan Glaspell, Edmund Wilson, Mary McCarthy, Robert Nathan, Gilbert Seldes, Dwight Macdonald, John Berryman, E.J. Kahn, Jr., William Gibson, Norman Mailer, Paul Brodeur, Annie Dillard and Robert Pinsky.

The most prominent artists were Edward Hopper and Ben Shahn; the most prominent photographer was Walker Evans and the most prominent composer Elliott Carter. The town's many authors, artists and composers–and the list will never be complete–have had different reasons for living or sojourning in Truro. Some were born in town, some became residents, some have come regularly to summer homes, some have rented or stayed in friends' cottages.

A short list of Truro authors should also include the two who wrote about Truro after brief but intense visits—William Bradford, considered one of the great prose stylists of the colonial era, and Henry David Thoreau, who achieved world-wide renown as a writer on nature and civil disobedience. More recently, no authors have been more closely associated with Truro than Shebnah Rich, Anthony L. Marshall and Thomas A. Kane, who each wrote a book about its history, its people and their memories of it; and Isaac M. ("Mort") Small, chronicler of Truro and its shipwrecks in his five booklets.

. . .

Shebnah Rich wrote the first book-length history of the town. *Truro—Cape Cod or Land Marks and Sea Marks* was published in 1883, with a second printing the following year. He includes the first transcriptions of early Town of Truro records, lengthy accounts of religion and town ministers and dozens of genealogical notes as well as an account of life in Truro in the mid-nineteenth century.

Born in 1824, the youngest of three sons of Belinda (Higgins) Rich and Shebnah Rich, Truro mariner and farmer, he left town as a young man to make his career in Boston as a merchant, probably in the dry goods and clothing business. There's no record he attended college or even high school, but his book shows all the signs of a well-educated writer. He married a hometown girl, Delia Knowles, in Boston when he was twenty-three years old.

He had a lifelong interest in the fishing industry. When he was seventeen, he went out with the mackerel fleet and later in life published his lecture on the mackerel fishery. During the Civil War he moved his family to St. Louis, where he had gone to start a wholesale fish business. He was also associated with a mission school there. After the Civil War, according to a family genealogist, he returned to Boston, became superintendent of the Grocers' Packing Company and traveled to Paris and other European cities on business. In 1872, he and a distant cousin organized a reunion of the Rich family, one of the earliest and most prolific families on the Outer Cape.

Twelve years after his book was published, he was living in Salem, Massachusetts, where his wife died. He then moved to Waltham, Massachusetts, where he died in 1907 at the age of eighty-three. He is buried in Pine Grove Cemetery in Truro, where a third of the seven hundred burials are Rich family members. His five children had no children of their own, and so his line died out. The house where he was born, which he remodeled and used as his summer home for many years, still stands.

Anthony L. Marshall also left Truro as a young man. He was eighteen when he went to Rhode Island, where he made a career in the electrical power industry. He took correspondence courses, and at some point he attended an engineering school in Boston. Like Shebnah Rich, he seems to have been self-educated, for one of his hobbies was foreign languages. His father was a farmer and carpenter of Portuguese ancestry, and Anthony grew up on a sizable farm off Depot Road. Marshall published his memoir, *Truro, Cape Cod, As I Knew It*, more than half a century after he left Truro, but he had a remarkable memory for the geography of the town and what it was like to grow up in Truro in the first two decades of the twentieth century.

No one has written about Truro with greater affection than Tom Kane, and he was not a native. Kane arrived as a young boy and grew to know the town intimately. A schoolteacher for thirty years, he also served for forty years in the combined elective offices of town clerk, treasurer and tax collector. On the side, he clerked in a liquor store, drove the Lower Cape ambulance, cut the grass in the graveyards and played the trombone in the Lower Cape Concert Band. His weekly newspaper column, under the byline "Town Father," ran for forty-three years–from the 1940s through the 1980s–in the Provincetown *Advocate* and later also in the *Cape Codder*. Just before his death in 1989, he put together selections for his memoir, *My Pamet: Cape Cod Chronicle*. It's full of gossip, reminiscences, droll anecdotes, tall tales and descriptions of the weather and foliage in the Pamet valley, where he lived. He knew almost everybody in Truro; his book's index lists almost nine hundred names.

Kane's anecdotes capture forever the town characters: Horace ("Snowie") Snow, "purveyor of petrol, wit, bon vivant, artist and raconteur;" Richard A. ("Dick") Magee, another "raconteur par excellence," gourmet, genial host, enthusiastic firefighter, and fellow Irishman; and especially Phat Francis. Kane allowed that "no complete history of Truro will ever be written without some mention of one of Pamet's most colorful characters, Anthony Robert ("Phat") Francis, onetime postmaster, general storekeeper, perennial political candidate, collector of automobiles, raconteur, newspaper correspondent and dog fancier." A rather large man who never married, Phat Francis, with his packs of unlicensed dogs, seems not to have cared that he was a figure of fun in town. After he died, the town gave his name to the short sand road where he lived.

Kane's consistent output had other writers in awe. E.J. Kahn, Jr., wondered "how a young upstart writer like this [could] go on writing every week when we professional writers struggle for a month to do it. Now it's more than forty years he has been writing, while we're still sweating. I think it is one of the most remarkable feats of non-stop writing that I know of." Kane said writing the columns was "automatic, like going to the bathroom, although I hope the results are a little better."

. . .

Eugene O'Neill will always be associated primarily with Provincetown and the Provincetown Players, but his first summer home on Cape Cod, if it can be called a home, was in North Truro. It was the hull of an abandoned wreck on the beach. Arthur and Barbara Gelb wrote in their biography *O'Neill* that in 1916 O'Neill and a friend from Greenwich Village chose the isolated wreck to get away from the close-knit bohemian group in Provincetown and because it was cheap. In fact, it cost nothing; the two men were summer squatters. While O'Neill was living in the wreck, the first production of any of his plays was staged by the Provincetown Players. *Bound East for Cardiff* marked the debut of twenty-eight-year-old O'Neill, who would go on to become one of America's greatest playwrights with works such as *Long Day's Journey Into Night*. Four of his plays won Pulitzer prizes, and in 1936 he was awarded the Nobel prize for literature.

In 1919, O'Neill asked a Provincetown friend to find an inexpensive and isolated cottage in Truro for the summer. When he and his wife, Agnes, arrived, however, his friend had a surprise for them. O'Neill's father had bought for them the Peaked Hill Life-Saving Station, which had been abandoned by the Coast Guard and converted to an elegant summer cottage. Isolated in the sand dunes just north of the Truro boundary and so close to the encroaching Atlantic that it would fall into the ocean ten years later, it was the perfect summer workshop for O'Neill, who was a marathon swimmer and who had already put the sea and ships into his plays.

Susan Glaspell, a writer who had a summer place on Higgins Hollow Road for many years, is generally credited with bringing O'Neill and the Provincetown Players together. She and George Cram ("Jig") Cook had visited Provincetown in 1912. Even before there were many automobiles, they found it a bustling, noisy town. Married the next year, they looked for a quiet summer place instead of Provincetown. In *The Road to the Temple* (1927) about her life with Cook, she wrote: "In summer, motors jam the narrow winding street which faithfully followed the line of the sea, and never meant to be a highway. Having been much tormented the summer before by horns and people, we bought an abandoned farmhouse a little way up the Cape, near Truro. 'The peace of God is in this valley,' Jig said one twilight as he turned off the Ford, after a trip to Provincetown." Almost a century later, not much has changed on Higgins Hollow Road.

Glaspell is neglected today, but in her day she was a successful novelist and playwright who won a Pulitzer Prize in 1931 for her Broadway play *Alison's House*. In a newspaper interview she said she did most of her work in Truro: "We have a farmhouse on Cape Cod, ten miles from Provincetown, away from everything. There I've built myself a little shack 10 by 12, among the pines, a good fifteen minutes walk over the hill from the farmhouse. It's just pine boards–not even painted. There's nothing in it except a table and a chair, not even a sofa or book. Nobody comes there with me but my dog, and if I don't work I just feel silly."

Jig Cook, a playwright, scholar of Greek theater and professor-turned-bohemian, was the impresario behind the founding of the Provincetown Players. When the Provincetown Players moved to New York, he talked about starting the Truro Players in the abandoned house he and Glaspell owned next door on Higgins Hollow Road.

After Cook's death, Glaspell met Norman Matson, also a novelist and playwright, and they began living together in Greenwich Village, Provincetown and her summer place in Truro. Glaspell was a regular in the summer literary crowd of Provincetown and Truro in the first half of the century. Among her friends were literary critic Edmund Wilson, poet Edna St. Vincent Millay, novelist John Dos Passos and the revolutionary John Reed.

It was Reed who had persuaded O'Neill to go to Provincetown for the summer of 1916. A radical revolutionary, Reed was one of the nation's most famous foreign correspondents. He and Louise Bryant bought two houses near the Pamet River, but apparently never stayed there. Outer Cape historian Clive Driver of Truro and Provincetown researched the purchases and found that Reed sold one of the houses to Margaret Sanger, but kept the other and evidently planned to use it as a summer home. Reed, however, was indicted for sedition during World War I, fled the country and died of typhus in Russia at the age of thirty three.

Margaret Sanger, the crusader for birth control and author of a dozen books, was with Reed when he first looked at the Pamet River properties. They both wanted to get away from the Provincetown crowds. "The place became littered with easels and smocks," she wrote. She and her children spent several summers in Truro. Clive Driver determined that in 1923 she sold her property to C. Arnold Slade, an artist, who built a cottage colony known as Sladeville on the bank of the Pamet River. Years later, Sanger, who traveled widely, wrote in her autobiography that the town "still seems to me to be one of the most beautiful spots in the world." A measure of her devotion to the Truro cottage is that her daughter's ashes are buried near it.

John Dos Passos, prolific author of socio-political novels and travel books, and his wife, Katharine ("Katy") Dos Passos, also a writer, owned a summer place in South Truro during the 1930s, the decade when he wrote his trilogy, *U.S.A.* The first volume was entitled *The 42ⁿᵈ Parallel,* which is the line of latitude that runs through Truro. Edmund Wilson didn't think much of the location of the Dos Passos cottage. He likened it to one of those "places where people would drive old cars into the yard and leave them." Wilson was critical, too, of Dos Passos's books, but the two summer neighbors on the Outer Cape remained friends for many years. Dos Passos, who traveled the world gathering material for his books, considered Provincetown his home.

Katy Dos Passos and a Wellfleet friend, Edith Shay, collaborated on *Down Cape Cod* and *The Private Adventure of Captain Shaw.* Years later, Edith Shay and her husband, Frank, a bookseller who had briefly owned a house in the Pamet valley, compiled and contributed to *Sand in Their Shoes: A Cape Cod Reader.* Katy Dos Passos was killed in an automobile accident just off-Cape in 1947; her husband, who was driving, lost an eye. Her burial in Truro was arranged by Phyllis Duganne, a writer, and her husband, Eben Given, a painter. Edmund Wilson was much affected by Katy Dos Passos's death and wrote about the funeral scene in his journal, *The Forties*: "The Given plot is just on the edge of a hill, and just below it is a big grove of unusually tall pine—beyond is Pamet River and the bay, all silver in the four o'clock light—the waterway winding in between the sands and the marshes."

The cemetery reminded Wilson of the seafaring nature of the community and how he and Dos Passos had at first tried more or less, to dissociate themselves from it: "But we had been living there, dining together, struggling with the native tradesmen and work-men . . . how much, in spite of all that was frivolous and 'escapist,' childish and futile in our lives, we had derived something from it and belonged to it—and Katy's death for the moment had given the whole thing dignity." Two days later, he was writing in his journal about courting Edna St. Vincent Millay in Truro "that first summer I had ever come to the Cape."

. . .

Edmund Wilson fell in love with Edna St. Vincent Millay in 1920 and proposed to her at her summer rental on Higgins Hollow Road. "She did not reject my proposal," he wrote, "but said that she would think about it." Millay never did agree to marry the twenty-five-year-old Wilson, although she was his first lover and inspired his first visit to the Outer Cape.

Millay, whose work Wilson admired extravagantly, would be-come the first woman to win a Pulitzer prize for poetry. Her poem about Truro was read at the funeral of Jacqueline Kennedy Onassis. It is called "Memory of Cape Cod."

The wind in the ash-tree sounds like surf on the shore at Truro.
I will shut my eyes . . . hush, be still with your silly bleating,
    sheep on Shillingstone Hill . . .

They said: Come along! They said: Leave your pebbles on the sand
    and come along, it's long after sunset!
The mosquitos will be thick in the pine-woods along by Long Nook,
    the wind's died down!
They said: Leave your pebbles on the sand, and your shells, too,
    and come along, we'll find you another beach like the beach at
    Truro.

Let me listen to wind in the ash . . . it sounds like surf on the
    shore.

Wilson rented a house in Truro Center in the winter of 1939 while finishing one of his most important books, *To the Finland Station.* Throughout the 1930s, he had stayed at the summer homes of various friends, including O'Neill, Millay, Glaspell and Dos Passos. Then he and his young wife, Mary McCarthy, rented a house for the off-season from Polly Boyden, an aspiring novelist. Leon Edel, who edited Wilson's journals, observed that "in this life of monotonous regularity, Wilson not only rounded out his largest book but wrote his famous essay on Dickens." In Wilson's journal chapter, "Chicago and Truro Center, 1939-40," he reflected on the wind and silence of Truro, and on death: "April 1940. Here at the top of the house I lie alone–glad to hear only the wind in the window frame–or silence, silence–of the dullness of neighbors who do not know one another–of friends who have slid away . . . of death, of a person who never again can reach one, that one never again can reach."

The couple worked, pushed their baby in his carriage up and down the hills of Truro, and drank in the evenings. When summer came, Wilson bought the farmhouse in Wellfleet that would be one of his two country homes for the rest of his life. McCarthy was a woman of strong opinions, and her marriage to Wilson (his third of four) broke up in 1945. That summer she returned to the Truro house alone with their son. She called it a "wonderful, strange, bittersweet" time, and a crossroads in her writing life.

Other writers had gravitated to Truro. The critic Dwight Macdonald lived in what McCarthy called "the fish house" in North Truro; the Italian novelist Niccolo Tucci was in one of the Long Nook bungalows; other novelists in town included Charles Jackson and James T. Farrell. McCarthy relished the many wonderful beach conversations. In her biography, *Mary McCarthy: A Life*, Carol W. Gelderman says, "They read Shakespeare aloud in groups, feasted on picnics in the moonlight, had talks at night by the fire, and went swimming in the phosphorescent water."

McCarthy's strength was the acerbic wit she brought to social commentary. She went on to dissect modern life in stories for *The*

New Yorker and in novels such as *The Groves of Academe, The Group* and *A Charmed Life*. The last is a satire of "rusting freelancers" and their dissolute, destructive lives in a town thought to resemble Wellfleet and Truro. She wrote much of it while living in a house in Wellfleet just over the line from South Truro.

Wilson, a writer for *The New Yorker* and esteemed by many as America's outstanding man of letters, left five volumes of journals that are sprinkled with observations and anecdotes about Truro artists and writers. Among the writers are Phyllis Duganne, a year-rounder who wrote short stories for national magazines and the booklet about the South Truro Meetinghouse for the Truro Neighborhood Association; and Joan Colebrook, a transplanted Australian and contributor to *The New Yorker*, who wrote novels, travel books and a memoir. Colebrook bought the Dos Passos house in South Truro.

. . .

Dwight Macdonald, a *New Yorker* staff writer and critic of politics, literature and culture, stayed in summer cottages in North Truro, Truro Center and South Truro. On his first visit, he found that the hills were "full of writers and radicals." Among his extended-stay guests for several summers in the 1940s was the poet John Berryman, whose *Dream Songs* won a Pulitzer prize. Later in Macdonald's career, one of his books of poems was illustrated by Ben Shahn, also a summer resident of Truro.

Macdonald and his wife were summer socializers, and his biographer, Michael Wreszin, says Macdonald "had begun to be a leader for this community of writers, artists and assorted bohemians, always arranging picnics, clam digs and get-togethers of one kind or another." Not to mention nude bathing on the ocean beaches, which at least once drew the attention of the Truro police. Macdonald and his friends were probably the first, but would not be the last, to bring group nudity to Truro beaches.

Robert Nathan, a novelist who achieved popular if not critical success for several decades, sometimes used Truro as a setting for his novels. Pamet Harbor is the setting for the climax of his most famous novel, *Portrait of Jenny* (1940), which was made into a movie. The title character was based on a Truro painter, Helen Sawyer. *Mia* (1970) takes place in the Pamet valley, much of it in "the parsonage," Nathan's summer home on North Pamet Road, and uses real Truro people, including Phat Francis. "We passed Phat Francis on his way home," wrote Nathan. "He was walking, and dressed, as always, in a rusty suit too small for him—it was the only suit he had—and a battered top hat which he wore on public occasions. One of his dogs, a sorry scurfy bitch, followed at his heels."

During his long career, Nathan published more than fifty slim books of fiction and poetry. He was a skilled storyteller of what his publisher called "satiric fantasy," but some critics thought he lapsed into sentimentality. Apparently, he steered clear of the literary crowd in Truro; Edmund Wilson never mentions him in his journals.

Gilbert Seldes, media and cultural critic, spent summers in Truro in the 1950s and 1960s and was famous in town for his Fourth of July parties. His daughter told Michael Kammen, his biographer, that it seemed as though the entire literary population of the town attended. Seldes did not send out invitations, but hundreds of freeloaders showed up. He also conducted literary seminars. Starting in 1965, according to Kammen, Seldes "took a number of young people under his wing and provided them with a kind of group tutorial each Sunday on American literature and culture, primarily from the 1920s and '30s." Seldes was the first major critic to analyze the effects of mass communications on society. His best-known book, *The Seven Lively Arts*, was published in 1942 when he was thirty-one years old. Seldes, Nathan and Dos Passos all went to Harvard and were on the staff of the *Harvard Monthly* at the same time.

Norman Mailer wrote the first draft of his career-launching novel, *The Naked and the Dead*, in Truro, although he later made Provincetown his base of operations for the next half-century. He and his first wife rented a bayshore cottage on Beach Point in North Truro for the summer of 1946, after he was discharged from the army. The book was the first and most famous of the World War II novels. Mailer won Pulitzer prizes for two later books. Another novel, *Tough Guys Don't Dance*, set in Provincetown and Truro, was based on the murder of four women whose bodies were found in the woods of Truro. He also wrote the screenplay and directed the movie of the same name. Some of the scenes were shot in Truro.

. . .

The New Yorker's most prolific writer and its *de facto* Truro correspondent, E.J. ("Jack") Kahn, Jr., was the author of twenty-seven books. Two of them, *About the New Yorker & Me* (1979) and *Year of Change: More About the News Yorker and Me* (1988), contain almost as much about his family and social life in Truro as about his social and writing life in New York City. Kahn spent almost every summer in Truro from 1950 until his death in 1994. Three articles about Truro and the Outer Cape appeared in *A Reporter Here and There* (1961). "Truro," he wrote, "is a small and unimposing town, but we love it. In 1954 we bought a house there, on a knoll in the Pamet River valley, after we had come to realize how fond we were of Truro, with its solid, plain old homes, its astonishingly smooth white beaches, its rolling dunes and moors, and its genial inhabitants–both the year-rounders and the 'foreign element,' as the native Cape Codders sometimes refer to us summer people."

Kahn contributed an estimated three million words to *The New Yorker*, more than any other contributor. He was a war correspondent in World War II and the Korean War, and he roamed the world looking for stories and profiles. He astonished colleagues with his range and versatility. His reporting ranged from Idi Amin to David Rockefeller, from Micronesia to South Africa, from Coca-Cola to the 1970 census.

Sebastian Junger wrote much of *The Perfect Storm*, the 1997 runaway best-seller, at his parents' summer home in Truro. He told a newspaper interviewer, "I was sitting in an under-heated house in the woods, writing this thing on a piece of plywood nailed to two sawhorses in my bedroom." Junger says a surfing experience at Ballston Beach inspired part of his book. A big wave drove him to the bottom, and the near-drowning sensation helped him imagine the deaths of the crew of a fishing boat that sank in the North Atlantic during the devastating storm of October 1991.

The same storm sent waves crashing over the coastal dune at Ballston Beach and into the upper Pamet River. As it happens, the U.S. Coast Guard officer in Boston who was in charge of daring rescue operations that saved the crews of other boats during the storm was Captain Roland ("Bud") Breault, who retired from the Coast Guard and in 1996 became the town administrator. *The Perfect Storm* was made into a movie, Junger bought a house in Truro and published a second best-seller, *Fire*, a collection of articles from his work as a reporter and foreign correspondent.

Other novelists who have put Truro into their works include Elinor Lipman, who evokes winter in Truro in *Isabel's Bed*, a novel set largely in an ultramodern mansion on the bayshore; Maria Flook, author of two novels, who used a Beach Point cottage colony as the model for a cottage colony in *Open Water*; and Robin Lippincott, who sets his novel, *Our Arcadia*, in Truro of the 1920s. Poet and novelist Toby Olson used Truro and its golf course as part of the setting for *Seaview*, which won a PEN/Faulkner award. Annie Dillard wrote *The Living*, set in the Pacific Northwest; her next novel will be set in Truro and Provincetown in the 1950s and 1960s.

Waldo Frank was widely renowned during the height of a career from the 1920s through the 1940s for his dozen novels and social criticism and as editor of literary reviews. Anne Bernays has written eight novels; and with her husband, Justin Kaplan, she wrote *The Language of Names*. R.V. Cassill, who wrote *Clem Anderson*, was also the editor of the *Norton Anthology of Short Fiction*. Other novelists include Paul Brodeur, Joseph Finder, Margaret Erhart, Jane Johnston, Sylvia Rothschild and James Halperin.

· · ·

Alan Dugan is Truro's prize poet. Winner of two National Book Awards, a Pulitzer Prize and the Prix de Rome, he has directed a poetry workshop at the Truro Center for the Arts at Castle Hill for many years. He has published nine books of poetry. Robert Pinsky, the nation's poet laureate from 1997 to 1999 and member of the American Academy of Arts and Letters, has published eleven books, including a translation of Dante's *Inferno*. Toby Olson has published eighteen books of poetry. John Skoyles, who has two booklets of poetry, tells in his book of essays how he and his son fish at Head-of-the-Meadow Beach. Other published poets include Rebecca Wolff, Keith Althouse, Rosalind Pace, Gray Burr, Naomi Chase, Leila Coburn, Ruth O'Reilly, Patric Pepper, Frank Dickerson and Mary Ann Larkin.

· · ·

In sheer number of volumes, no one equals Catherine Woolley, who also wrote under the pseudonym Jane Thayer. The doyenne of Truro's writers, Woolley has written eighty-six children's books plus a book on how to write for children. Her most famous title, published in 1959 and still in print, is *The Puppy Who Wanted a Boy*. Two hundred of her closest friends celebrated her ninetieth birthday in 1994 with a party in the front yard of Pilgrim Library. The town's new library has a children's reading room dedicated to Woolley, who has lived in Truro for more than forty years.

Another successful author of children's books is Nancy Dingman ("Ding") Watson, who published twenty-five books. One of them, *Tommy's Mommy's Fish,* was inspired in 1971 by the fishing adventures of her young son Tommy at Ballston Beach. Twenty-five years later, she reissued the book with new illustrations by her grown son, Thomas Aldrin Dingman Watson, who also lives in Truro. Three of her daughters, Wendy, Clyde and Cameron, have also

294 RICHARD F. WHALEN

written children's books. A couple who wrote a children's book were Laura and Jack Johnson. He also wrote three small books of tales and anecdotes about Cape Cod, and in 1946 he founded the *Cape Codder* newspaper.

In the theater world, Jig Cook was Truro's first playwright. William Gibson achieved lasting fame with two of his plays, *Two for the Seesaw* and *The Miracle Worker*. He has also written a book on Shakespeare's dramaturgy. Joseph Anthony wrote plays for the stage and television but is best known as the director of many Broadway hits in the 1950s and 1960s. Lee Falk, internationally syndicated cartoonist, also was a playwright, produced more than three hundred plays and directed another hundred in his long career in the theater world. His wife, Elizabeth Moxley Falk, a theater and opera director, wrote *The Words and the Music* for the Players Club in New York City.

Lee Falk is best known as the creator of *The Phantom* and *Mandrake the Magician*, among the most popular and long-running comic strips in the world. A movie was based on his crime-fighting hero, the phantom. Truro's other celebrity cartoonist is Howie Schneider, creator of the nationally syndicated *Eek & Meek* comic strip, editorial cartoonist for the *Provincetown Banner*, and author of ten illustrated books.

Justin Kaplan won a Pulitzer prize and National Book Award for *Mr. Clemens and Mark Twain* and another National Book Award for *Walt Whitman: A Life*. He was also the general editor of the sixteenth edition of *Bartlett's Familiar Quotations*. Peter Manso wrote *Mailer: His Life and Times* and *Brando: The Biography*. Rosemarie Redlich Scherman wrote *Literary America*, illustrated by her husband, the photographer David Scherman.

In *Steve Nelson, American Radical*, Nelson tells of his years as a Communist party official until 1956. Arrested for sedition during the McCarthy era of witch hunts, he was jailed but his conviction was reversed in a case that went to the U.S. Supreme Court. Nicholas Pillegi has written books about Mafia figures that were made into movies. A biography of Eleanor of Aquitaine was published by Amy R. Kelly. Wendy Veevers-Carter wrote *Island Home* about her life on an island in the Indian Ocean.

. . .

Gary Becker, a Nobel prize winner, is one of several economists who have lived or summered in Truro. A professor at the University of Chicago, he has done much of his writing at his Truro summer home. Robert B. Reich, a university professor and contributor to *The New Yorker*, has written books on politics and social/economic policy, including *Locked in the Cabinet*, a wry account of his experience as secretary of labor in President Clinton's first administration. Albert Z. Carr, a noted historian and economist, wrote many books on politics and government. Barry Bluestone is the author of books on labor unions, management and the national economy.

Dexter Keezer, president of Reed College before World War II and vice president and chief economist at McGraw-Hill Publications after the war, wrote several books on economics and one on being a college president, *The Light That Flickers*. Keezer was active in Truro civic affairs as president of the Truro Neighborhood Association and often wrote letters to local newspaper editors. He left a small endowment fund to help Truro's poor at Christmas time.

William J. Miller, a reporter and editor for *Newsweek, Time, Life* and *Fortune*, published a book on communism and a biography of Henry Cabot Lodge. Paul Brodeur has written *New Yorker* articles and several books on the dangers of asbestos, tobacco, depletion of the ozone layer, radiation from electric power lines and radar–and what he sees as a government-industry cover-up. In articles, he has been critical of the radiation hazard of radar domes at Otis Air Force Base on Cape Cod and at the old North Truro Air Force Station, which he can see from his house. Katherine T. Kinkead, also a *New Yorker* writer, along with her husband, Eugene, published a book on how Yale admits its freshman class.

Stephen Kinzer, a *New York Times* correspondent, is the author of *Crescent and Star: Turkey Between Two* Worlds and co-author of a book on U.S.-Guatemala relations. Michael J. Berlin, also a journalist, wrote a book about the media coverage of the Tiananmen Square demonstration in Beijing and co-authored a study of Henry Kissinger. Liam Mahony wrote about the work of Peace Brigades International. Joan Lebold Cohen wrote books about China and the Far East, including one with her husband, Jerome Alan. Seth Rolbein, a TV and print journalist, has written several books, including two on pollution at the Massachusetts Military Reservation at the other end of Cape Cod. He was editor of a group of six Cape Cod newspapers in 1998-9.

Vice President Al Gore spent less than a month in Truro during the summer of 1996, but he is the author of *Earth in the Balance* on global warming and the environment, a subject close to the hearts of many in Truro. He and his family stayed out of sight behind Secret Service patrols, but if they return they will qualify as legitimate Truro summer people.

. . .

Truro's professors have published. L. Thomas Hopkins, a Truro native, was a professor at Columbia and other universities and the author of more than ten books on education. He was also a moderator of Truro town meetings. Maurice Charney, an English professor at Rutgers University, is the author or editor of more than twenty books, including *All of Shakespeare*. Harry C. Bredemeier, also at Rutgers, was a professor of sociology for fifty-one years and the author of five books. Robert L. Jackson taught Russian literature at Yale University and published more than twenty books. Lewis Paul Todd wrote history texts, including *The Rise of the American Nation*. Richard H. Powers, who taught at the University of Massachusetts at Amherst, was the author of several history books. Brown University Professor Philip Benedict is the author of *Rouen During the Wars of Religion*. The poet

Wallace Stevens is the subject of a book by William Burney, who taught at Central Connecticut State University. The four-volume *World of Mathematics* was compiled and edited not by a university professor but by a lawyer, James R. Newman, who was also on the board of editors of *Scientific American*. Robert Riley, a fashion expert exhibit curator at the Fashion Institute of Technology, co-authored *The Fashion Makers*.

Although not numerous, nature writers are well represented by Howard S. Irwin, William Longgood and Annie Dillard, who won a Pulitzer Prize for her first book, *Pilgrim at Tinker Creek*. Irwin, former president of the New York Botanical Garden and the author of several books, is the general editor of a thousand-page, revised edition of *America's Garden Book*, originally written by Louise and James Bush-Brown. He also served as chair of the Truro Conservation Commission. Longgood described the joys and trials of raising bees and growing vegetables in Truro in two books, *The Queen Must Die* and *Voices from the Earth*. The author of several non-fiction books, he won a Pulitzer Prize as a New York City newspaper reporter.

Dr. Charles S. Davidson, best known in Truro for his leadership in efforts to protect the town's natural resources and preserve open space, was a physician who published numerous papers and a book on liver diseases and nutrition. He was associated for many years with the medical units of both Harvard and M.I.T Frederick A. Washburn, wrote a history of Massachusetts General Hospital and a book about a World War II hospital. He was the first president of the Truro Neighborhood Association.

Letters between a physician in a M.A.S.H. field hospital in Korea in the 1950s and his young wife back home were published in *We Will Not Be Strangers*, edited by Dorothy Horwitz. Her husband, Dr. Melvin Horwitz, was a surgeon in the M.A.S.H. unit during the Korean War. Ernest Hartmann has written four books on sleep and dreams. Penelope Russianoff, a clinical therapist, wrote books on psychology. Barrie R. Cassileth is the author of a reference work on alternative medicine.

In the world of broadcasting, Palmer Williams was a CBS news executive and producer of award-winning TV documentary films and news programs, including *CBS Reports* and *60 Minutes*. Adrian Murphy was president of the CBS radio division. He also worked with Gilbert Seldes on one of the first television interview programs. Henry Morgan, who had a long career as a radio comedian, was one of the regulars at the Ballston Beach Cottages until he bought a house in Truro. Tony Kahn (no relation to E.J. Kahn, Jr.) has received a dozen New England Emmy awards for his programs and scripts for National Public Radio and PBS. He has also published translations from the Russian. Alice Furland has written radio essays for the BBC and for National Public Radio for two decades.

In the how-to category, Michael Snell, a literary agent and book packager, is co-author of *From Book Idea to Best Seller;* and Naomi Palmer published *How to Speak Better Bridge*. Homeowners in Truro who hire house cleaners may learn something from Louise Rafkin's book, *Other People's Dirt: The Curious Adventures of a Housecleaner*. In it, she also comments favorably on Truro's dump and swap shack.

In the world of art criticism, Eleanor Munro, wife of the late E.J. Kahn, Jr., has written *Memoir of a Modernist's Daughter* and *Originals: American Women Artists*. Hayden Herrara has written books on Matisse and other artists, and George Biddle published *Artist at War*.

· · ·

The painters, sculptors and photographers of Truro, although less written about than their colleagues in the word trade, have been no less important in the history of the town. Three of them—Edward Hopper, Ben Shahn and Walker Evans—achieved significant renown for their work.

One of America's most important artists, Edward Hopper, owned a studio-cottage in Truro, and many of his paintings are of scenes in the town. In 1934, he and his wife, Josephine ("Jo") Nivison, also a painter, built their live-in summer studio on a knoll overlooking Cape Cod Bay and worked there almost every summer for thirty years. Until the 1950s, when both were in their seventies, they had neither electricity nor a telephone.

Before building their own cottage, they had rented for a few years in South Truro, and in 1930 Hopper began painting the first of his many Truro scenes, giving the paintings titles such as *Corn Hill, South Truro Church, South Truro Post Office* and *Shacks at Pamet Head*. He painted scenes along the railroad, including the stations and the cold storage plant; and in 1930 he painted that inspiration for scores of painters, Highland Light A painting he considered "one of the very best" of his watercolors was *House on Pamet River*. His well-known painting of a Mobil gas station entitled *Gas*, now at the Museum of Modern Art, was allegedly inspired in part by Jack's Discount Gas in Truro.

Gas stations, railroad stations, barns and shacks were typical subjects for Hopper, who was classed as a realist at a time when abstract painting was coming into vogue. Major museums acquired Hopper paintings, including the Metropolitan Museum of Art and the Whitney Museum of American Art, as well as the Museum of Modern Art. In 1956, he was elected to the American Academy of Arts and Letters. A television documentary on Hopper and his paintings was made in 1994 by an Austrian filmmaker, Wolfgang Hostert, who later moved to Truro. The "docudrama," which showed Truro scenes that Hopper painted, featured townsfolk who remembered Hopper and Nivison. Hopper's works–many of them spare, somber pictures of lonely, silent men and women–have been widely exhibited and reproduced and have entered into the American imagination.

Nivison, also an accomplished artist, was overshadowed by her husband. In *Edward Hopper: An Intimate Biography*, actually a dual biography, Gail Levin describes how the two were as much rivals as partners. Nivison had been painting for years before she married Hopper, and she continued to paint, often alongside him.

Some of her paintings were exhibited at the Metropolitan and the Whitney. After her death, however, nearly all her works were lost, according to Levin. Two that survived hang in the Truro Historical Society's collection.

Ben Shahn, who bought a summer cottage in Truro in 1924, was an illustrator, painter, muralist and photographer who won popular and critical recognition for his politically controversial works. In 1947, he was ranked fifth by art critics, curators and museum directors who were asked to name the ten best painters in America. Shahn placed just ahead of Hopper. A versatile artist who saw no distinction between commercial art and fine art for an artist of integrity, he was renowned for his murals and posters that were protests against injustices. He painted illustrations for *Fortune, Time, Harper's* and other magazines and made a number of propaganda posters during World War II.

His daughter, Judith Shahn, contributed more than 350 drawings to *The New Yorker*. A painter, printmaker and graphic artist, her work has appeared in other national magazines and been acquired for a numerous public and private collections. She and her husband, the poet Alan Dugan, live in the house her father bought.

Jerry Farnsworth and his wife, Helen Sawyer, started the Farnsworth School of Art in North Truro in 1933. Farnsworth was best known for his portraits and figures. His works are in the Metropolitan, the Whitney and other major museums. He also produced nine covers for *Time* magazine and twenty-two portraits for *Fortune*, painted President Truman's portrait, and wrote three books on how to paint.

Helen Sawyer came to Truro with her parents early in the century and stayed at Mort Small's Highland House. She studied with Charles Hawthorne in Provincetown, where she met her future husband. She was primarily a landscape painter. The Whitney acquired several of her paintings. In 1941, the couple opened an art school in Sarasota, Florida.

William and Lucy L'Engle were another couple who painted. Unlike the reclusive Hoppers, however, they were at the center of the Truro-Provincetown summer social circles. The L'Engles bought the Shebnah Rich house in 1924, used it as their summer home into the 1960s and often threw parties there. The two had met while studying in Paris. They spent their first summers on Cape Cod in Provincetown, where Lucy studied with Charles Hawthorne, and then moved to Truro. In 1997, their grandson, Daniel L'Engle Davis, found a dozen paintings in the attic of the house, and the historical museum at Highland House mounted a retrospective exhibit of their work.

Just as many novelists began their careers as journalists, many painters began as commercial illustrators. Edward Hopper made a living as a commercial illustrator for the first fifteen years of his career. Farnsworth and others combined commercial work with their art. Edward A. Wilson was a leading illustrator for dozens of novels early in the twentieth century during what's been called "the gilded age of American illustration." His illustrations were in editions of *Robinson Crusoe, Treasure Island, The Last of the Mohicans* and other popular classics. He also drew covers for *Fortune* magazine. His lithographs include *Hogback Meeting House*, whose subject was the South Truro Meetinghouse, and *Time Marches On*, one of several he made of his neighborhood in Truro. He was one of the founders of the Truro Historical Society, and a number of his works are in display at in the museum. Several of his paintings are at the Metropolitan Museum of Art.

Courtney Allen enjoyed a successful career as an illustrator in New York City before moving to Truro. He, too, had studied with Charles Hawthorne in Provincetown early in the century. In his North Truro studio, he produced magazine illustrations, carvings of waterfowl and ship models, as well as a dioramas of the Sandwich Glass Works, the signing of the Mayflower Compact and the Wharf Theater in Provincetown, where O'Neill's plays were first staged. He was one of the founders of the Truro Historical Society, and its museum displays some of his works in a room named for him.

Three painters made major contributions to the World War I effort. Hopper's early fame was based largely on his patriotic post-

302   RICHARD F. WHALEN

ers, including *Smash the Hun*. C. Arnold Slade was living in Paris when the war broke out, and his sketches of war scenes and a painting, *Letter from the Front*, were widely reproduced. In his Truro home, the former church, he painted Truro landscapes and portraits of U.S. senators, generals, admirals and a U.S. vice-president. Gerrit Beneker's contribution to the war effort was a poster of a workman in overalls, *Sure! We'll Finish the Job*. Millions were posted across the nation to promote Liberty Loans.

George Biddle, painter, muralist and sculptor, was the leader of forty-two artists commissioned in 1943 by General George C. Marshall to obtain an historical record of World War II in the form of drawings, paintings and other graphic materials. Biddle toured North Africa and Italy and published his impressions in his journal. The Metropolitan Museum and the Museum of Modern Art acquired several of his works.

Other notable illustrators and painters were Cleveland Landon Woodward, who drew illustrations for an edition of the Bible; Thomas Blakeman, who was president of the Provincetown Art Association; Eben Given, who also ran the grocery store in Truro Center; and Arthur Musgrave.

Truro's sculptors include Sidney Simon, Douglas Huebler, Budd Hopkins, Delores Filardi and Joyce Johnson. Simon and Henry Varnum Poor founded the Skowhegan School of Painting and Sculpture in Maine in 1947. Poor also painted watercolors of the Pamet marshes and a mural at the department of the interior in Washington D.C. Simon's works are in the Whitney and other major museums, and he was elected a member of the American Academy of Arts and Letters. Douglas Huebler, a leading conceptual artist, was a dean of the California Institute of the Arts. His works are in the Museum of Modern Art and the Guggenheim Museum, among others.

Budd Hopkins is a sculptor, painter and investigator of Unidentified Flying Objects. His sculptures are in collections of the Guggenheim and the Whitney. He has also written three books on reported sightings of UFOs and UFO abductions. For a time in the 1960s and 1970s, Truro was a center of UFO sightings. Hopkins reported seeing one in 1964 while driving to Provincetown. Two years later, an airman at the North Truro Air Force Station claimed that he had been abducted into a UFO from a telephone booth in front of Dutra's Market. A decade later, Hopkins reported that several people in Truro had seen strange lights over Cape Cod Bay.

Joyce Johnson, sculptor and for many years the Truro correspondent for *The Cape Codder* newspaper, founded the Truro Center for the Arts at Castle Hill in 1971. One of her sculptures is in Truro's namesake town in Cornwall, England. She was the first president and director of Castle Hill, when classes were held in a stable on Castle Road (which probably started out as "Cassill" Road after the Cassill family.) Castle Hill has offered a wide range of artistic training, from painting and poetry to jewelry and papermaking. The initial faculty included Sidney Simon and Harry Hollander, an artist in plastics, who was among the first to see the potential for an art school in Truro. Over the years, the faculty has included many of Truro's noted artists and writers. Among the guest lecturers have been Derek Walcott and Saul Bellow, Nobel prize winners in literature.

Among the many notable artists of Truro in the second half of the twentieth century who have exhibited in the Northeast are Paul Resika, with works in the Metropolitan Museum of Art collection; Serge Chermayeff, artist and professor of design and architecture at Harvard and Yale; Jim Peters, a former navy officer with a degree in nuclear engineering, who has paintings in the Guggenheim; watercolorist George Yater, director of the Provincetown Art Association for several years, and his wife Shirley Yater; Malcolm Preston, town meeting moderator; and Bernard and Winita G. ("Nene") Vibber Schardt. She also created sets and puppets for television programs. Also Milton Wright, Marston Hodgin, Morris Kantor, Nancy Ellen Craig, Leslie Jackson, Anna Poor, Elsa Johnson Tarantal, Wallace Bassford, William Evaul, Hal MacIntosh, Edmund Duffy, Ellen LeBow, Carmen Cicero, Adrian

Murphy, John E. Wallace, Kim Kettler, Joan Pereira, Nancy Berlin, Charles Sovek, Mary Fassett, Michelle Weinberg, Oren Sherman, Martha Malicoat Dunigan, and Louis C. "Woody" English.

• • •

Truro is not an art gallery town, but it does have two of the more unusual show places on Cape Cod. The Susan Baker Memorial Museum—which is neither a museum nor a memorial—is her closed-in front porch, where she displays her bold, blunt, witty paintings and sculptures, often bawdy, sometimes outrageous. In her other persona, she is a serious landscape painter and has published a book of paintings of scenes from the life of Marcel Proust. Down the road from Baker's "museum" is the front-yard folk art of Albert ("Abbie") Tinkham, whose elaborate roadside displays celebrate all the major holidays with large groupings of statues, illuminated figurines, artificial flowers, wind chimes, flags, and other typical yard decorations, all carefully lighted for nighttime viewing.

Until the dump was closed and became a transfer station, Richard ("Dickie") Steele, the dumpmaster, created an evolving folk-art construction. His shack blossomed with a montage of signs, abandoned furniture and toys and other miscellaneous but colorful debris—all carefully arranged for maximum effect. His folk-art construction was captured in a painting by Truro artist Peter Hooven that was hung in Town Hall.

• • •

Walker Evans, considered the preeminent American photographer of his generation, spent the summers of 1930 and 1931 with Ben Shahn and his family at their summer cottage in Truro. During his second visit, he and Shahn mounted a joint exhibit in a barn loaned by Shahn's neighbors, the DeLuze family. In what was probably the first exhibit of his career, Evans showed his photographs of the

DeLuze family and their home. The photographs were in the same documentary style that would characterize his career, most notably in his book with the writer James Agee, *Let Us Now Praise Famous Men*. The Metropolitan Museum of Art acquired many of Evans's negatives and papers and mounted a major exhibition of his works.

For the two-day backyard exhibit, Shahn painted portraits of the heroes and villains of the notorious Dreyfus case, a scandal that involved accusations of anti-Semitism in France in the 1890s. The audience for the challenging images exhibited by the two artists was a mix of locals, summer visitors and artist friends, including Edward Hopper.

Later in the century, photographers of note included David E. Scherman and Claire Flanders. Scherman was a photojournalist with *Life*, became a senior editor of the magazine and edited several books of photographs. Flanders's photographs of gardens and interiors have been shown in several galleries and published in architectural magazines. Carlotta Junger, Sebastian's sister, wrote the Insight guide to Cape Cod and has had photographs in several travel guides. Natasha Babaian has also written for Insight guides and contributed photographs.

. . .

The most distinguished of composers with Truro connections is Elliott Carter, who summered in Truro in the 1940s. The world premiere of his *Symphony of Three Orchestras* was performed by the New York Philharmonic Orchestra in 1977, and two of his string quartets won Pulitzer prizes. In 1985, President Reagan awarded him a National Medal of Arts. Arthur Berger, composer, music critic and professor, built a summer cottage in Truro in the early 1970s, after staying as a guest of Gardner Jencks, a composer of works for the piano. In the 1940s and 1950s, Berger was music critic for the *New York Sun* and then the *New York Herald-Tribune*. The three occasionally got together for musicales at Jencks's house on the Pamet River. William Flanders, husband of photographer Claire Flanders, is a song-writer who has performed across the country and made a number of records and CDs.

The number of authors, artists, photographers and composers who picked Truro for summer homes, second-career homes or retirement homes is striking, especially given the size of the town. Its year-round population ranged from about 500 to 1,800 during the years it was most popular with people in the arts. Literature, visual art and music have been cottage industries in Truro, a somewhat invisible industry but important nevertheless to the economy and ambience of the town. By the end of the twentieth century, however, property values and rents had soared, and only those who had achieved material success could afford to make Truro a place for their creative endeavors.

CHAPTER 19:
NATIONAL DEFENSE AND
A NATIONAL PARK

When the United States entered World War II, the people of Truro once again had reason to fear that the enemy would reach their shores. Many remembered that during World War I a German submarine had lobbed a few shells onto Cape Cod at Orleans. The threat of landing parties of saboteurs was real, for Nazi saboteurs were captured after they came ashore from submarines off Florida, Long Island and Maine.

Truro was on the alert, and rumors circulated through town. The *Barnstable Patriot* reported in January 22, 1942, that mysterious gunfire was heard offshore and fishermen were warned not to go to sea: "Enemy submarines outside!" The Nazi submarine offensive off Cape Cod had begun ten days earlier. Submarines sank freighters and tankers for more than a year. Debris from torpedoed ships littered the Cape Cod shoreline. Coast Guardsmen with police dogs patrolled the beaches.

Katy Dos Passos wrote to her husband that it was rumored that a German submarine had been sunk off Highland Light: "It must be true because dozens of planes appeared and dropped depth charges. We heard shooting somewhere on the back shore this morning, and there is considerable excitement among the population . . . Convoys passing the back shore are in danger of shelling . . . That is why Highland Light goes out at night every now and then. The threat of a shell or two through the town is what people seem to be considering."

Robert Nathan and Edward Hopper also described the wartime atmosphere in Truro. Nathan's 1943 book, *Journal for Josephine,* contrasts "ordinary observations of wartime summer on the Cape" with the fear of hostilities. Nathan served as an airplane spotter, but saw only U.S. Navy and Coast Guard planes. His book opens with a thunderstorm that he describes as sounding like cannons. "I thought of submarines off the coast;" says Nathan, "it would be so easy for them to put a landing party ashore on one of the beaches . . . My guns are oiled and ready, but I am not; I would have to be very much excited to shoot at someone." He heard rumors that a submarine had been seen less than a mile away in the Atlantic and that one had been sunk in Cape Cod Bay near the canal.

Hopper, who continued to summer in Truro during the war, served as an air raid warden on Thursday mornings from four to eight o'clock and hoped he would not "fall asleep on duty and bring disgrace on my family and friends." In letters to a friend, he said that survivors of a ship torpedoed off Cape Cod were brought to Provincetown and that: "We are quite close to the war at sea here."

In her book about Provincetown, Mary Heaton Vorse mentioned destroyers, submarines and a submarine tender in the harbor. "The iron wall of naval vessels out in the harbor was no dream," she wrote. Dive bombers "with their incredible noise" practiced bombing runs. Windows rattled with the sound of naval target practice. Sailors on shore leave strolled the streets. Everybody, she said, drank too much.

As happens during wartime, rumors ran through the town. One of them had Nazi saboteurs landing at Ballston Beach. Years later, E. J. Kahn, Jr., noted in a journal entry for October 13, 1986 that a neighbor told him that in 1942 "some Germans, presumably off a submarine, came ashore at our own Ballston Beach and were spirited off by the FBI and the Coast Guard. Five of the intruders were shot along our very own Pamet River . . . and nary a word about it was ever made public."

Reports of a suspected landing were also recalled by Truro native Elizabeth ("Betty") Groom, who was about ten years old at the time. She heard that the National Guard had searched houses after discovering a raft on the beach south of Highland Light and footprints leading inland. The rumors of Nazi landings in Truro may have sprung from reports, confirmed after the war, of the three Nazi landings elsewhere on the East Coast that led to the execution of six Nazis after secret military tribunals. Coast Guard histories mention no enemy landings on Cape Cod.

Truro sent sixty-five citizens off to war, including four women. For those remaining at home, it would have been small comfort, if any, when the army brought in several anti-aircraft guns and dug emplacements for them on top of the cliff overlooking the Atlantic Ocean. The emplacements and barracks were the beginning of Truro's military base just south of Highland Light.

· · ·

Shortly after World War II, people in Truro were again on the alert for enemy incursions. This time they were radar specialists and they were watching visual display screens at two installations on the bluffs overlooking the Atlantic Ocean. One radar installation was at the North Truro Air Force Station; the other was an experimental radar in South Truro that had been designed by M.I.T. scientists and engineers. Both radars scanned the skies during the Cold War, when Americans feared that Soviet bombers might drop bombs on the nation's cities. .

North Truro was the site of one of the first operational radars in the nation's automated air defense system, which eventually had several hundred such radars. The U.S. Air Force had taken over the World War II artillery site in 1948 and bought additional acreage for what would be the North Truro Air Force Station. Using advanced radar and communications equipment, the station tracked aircraft approaching Cape Cod and the Northeast over the Atlantic Ocean from 1951 to 1984. Its six radar domes, visible for miles around, were among the first radars in what would become the SAGE system (Semi-Automatic Ground Environment), the nation's first early-warning air defense system. As a sideline, the radars also tracked flights of migratory birds for the U.S. department of the interior.

The station became a small town within a small town, with about two hundred air force personnel, many of them highly trained technicians. The station had almost a hundred structures, including twenty-seven homes for officers and senior enlisted men with families. Others rented homes and apartments in Truro and neighboring towns. The station had its own generating plant, wells for water, sewage disposal system, commissary, gymnasium, softball field, movie theater, bowling alley, recreation building, library and hobby shop. Sentries with guard dogs patrolled the perimeter of the top secret installation.

By all accounts, the military base and the small town enjoyed amicable relations. Some of the personnel joined churches, the rescue squad and the volunteer fire department. They helped raise money for local charities. Their softball team joined the local league, and night games were played on their lighted field. Their children went to the Truro elementary school. Initially there was some classroom overcrowding, but the Air Force paid tuition for children of the air force personnel.

Meanwhile, in 1951, the same year the North Truro radars began tracking approaching aircraft, M.I.T. scientists were building an experimental radar installation in the woods of South Truro that would be an even more advanced air defense system. When word of it reached town officials, wrote Robert Buderi in *The Invention that Changed the World*, "Anxious congressmen and town fathers . . . worried that the scheme might make their home turf the target of a Soviet nuclear attack."

South Truro's radar was the most powerful in a network that grew from twelve to thirty radars from Maine to Long Island. Called the Cape Cod System, the network, which was controlled by one of the world's earliest computers, was the prototype for the SAGE system. The DEW-line (for Distant Early Warning radars) was later added across northern Canada and Alaska. With the experimental Cape Cod System, MIT's Lincoln Laboratory demonstrated for the defense department that great quantities of radar data could be transmitted over telephone lines and processed by a computer for instant analysis. By 1954, says Buderi, "some five hundred sorties [by U.S. military aircraft] had been flown against the network." In his view, today's computer networks and the Internet owe "a tremendous debt" to the computerized Cape Cod network of radars that was anchored by the radar in South Truro.

The radar installation, its radio antenna towers, buildings and surrounding hundred acres comprised the most valuable property in Truro. In 1956, Tom Kane wrote in his newspaper column: "Biggest tax on the list, Massachusetts Institute of Technology, for their South Truro installation, $2,297.86. Phew." This compared with an average tax of about $115 for the typical homeowner, according to Kane, who was also the town assessor.

With the SAGE system fully operational in 1958, M.I.T. shifted the South Truro radar installation to a newly formed MITRE Corporation (for M.I.T. REsearch). One of MITRE's projects was a SAGE back-up system installed at the North Truro Air Force Station in 1965. After South Truro's experimental radar had served its purpose, the radar dome was torn down and the Cape Cod National Seashore acquired the property, now known as the "old MITRE site."

When the Cold War ended, the air force deactivated the North Truro Air Force Station. Its radar operations became semi-automatic in the 1970s and were shut down in 1985. Most of the 125-acre station, including all the buildings, went into the Cape

Cod National Seashore, which had been formed in 1961. The Federal Aviation Administration took over the radar installation as part of its air traffic control system and also kept watch for unscheduled, incoming aircraft for the defense department. In 1995, a single radar was constructed to replace the older radars. Standing almost a hundred feet tall, the long-range radar scanned the skies for 250 miles out to sea and up to 100,000 feet.

What to do with the abandoned military base became an issue for the national seashore and the Town of Truro. One suggestion was to adapt some of it for low-income housing. Also mentioned was razing it all and returning the land to nature. At the end of the century, national seashore and town officials and volunteers were working to create a center for the arts and the environment by lining up art studios, environmental laboratories, educational institutions and other partners. Two projects were already making partial use of the site. The national seashore renovated the commissary into a laboratory for its biologists, and town meeting in 1998 voted to support a nursery to test the viability of indigenous plants and trees and grow them for use in the town. Volunteers did the work in the three-acre nursery next to the biology laboratory.

. . .

When prosperity returned after the Depression of the 1930s and the austerity measures of World War II, Cape Cod became a vacation destination attractive to millions living in the Northeast. And retirees began to arrive in significant numbers. Route 6, the mid-Cape highway, completed in 1952, gave motorists quick access to resorts and beaches the full length of Cape Cod. Over the next four decades, the population of Cape Cod would quadruple, by far the fastest growth in Massachusetts.

Truro's growth was much slower. As it had been with the railroad, Truro and Provincetown were the last towns reached by the new, broad, straight highway, which bypassed the villages of Truro

Center and North Truro. Truro business saw little gain, as most of the cars kept going to Provincetown and its many tourist attractions.

Slowly, residential and commercial construction began to accelerate for the first time in more than a century. The town's rural character and its waterfront and waterview lots attracted people with money and a desire for seaside vacation homes. For most of Truro's history, the idea had been to build in the shelter of hollows inland from the windy beach bluffs and close to the water table for wells. Now, newcomers wanted to buy building lots as close to the beaches, river banks and ponds as they could afford. Elisha Cobb's farm in South Truro and property on Corn Hill and all along the bayshore were north to High Head were sold for summer homes overlooking Cape Cod Bay. Truro began to change in mid-century from a small, country town–almost a backwater–to a summer-home and retirement town whose growth could threaten the open landscape and seascape vistas that attracted people to Truro in the first place.

In 1955, the specter of over-development on Cape Cod inspired far-sighted initiatives for land-use controls not only by the town but also by the federal government. In Truro, after several failed attempts over more than two decades, town meeting created a planning board to recommend residential and commercial zones. The residents, however, debated five years before passing the first zoning bylaw in 1960. During succeeding decades, the bylaw was often amended, although not without controversy. From the beginning, the debate was over the short-term financial gains of property sales and real estate development versus the longer-range benefits and esthetic values of controlled growth and preservation of open space. Meanwhile, on the national scene in 1955, the federal government unveiled a parks proposal that would have the greatest impact on Truro of any event in its history.

. . .

Cape Cod's sand beaches stretching the full length of its Atlantic Ocean coast were a priority for conservationists as early as 1892, when a Massachusetts conservation group recommended setting aside land in Orleans for recreation "where thousands of inland people might bathe and walk by the sea." The National Park Service published the first formal study 1939. It recommended a seashore park from one end of Cape Cod to the other and even extending off-Cape to Duxbury, but World War II interrupted any action on the plan.

In 1954, the National Park Service embarked on a comprehensive, eighteen-month study of beaches and shorelines on the East and Gulf coasts. Its report, *The National Park Service Seashore Recreation Survey*, recommended sixteen seashore areas for recreation parks. At the top of the list was the Atlantic Ocean shore on the Outer Cape. For the general public, the park service published an attractive brochure, *Our Vanishing Shoreline*. No one on Cape Cod paid much attention to the federal initiative until State Senator Edward C. Stone of Osterville, a conservation-minded legislator, urged the *Cape Codder* newspaper to give careful consideration to the proposal. The newspaper followed up with a lengthy article calling attention to plans for a park from Provincetown to Chatham.

In 1959, the National Park Service published a detailed plan, *Cape Cod, a Proposed National Seashore Investigation Report*. The report recommended a park of twenty-nine thousand acres, much more than a narrow strip along the Atlantic Ocean beach. Several Massachusetts members of the House of Representatives introduced bills based on the plan. Cape Cod newspapers took varying positions. The park service held informational meetings in Eastham and Chatham, and town officials offered their opinions.

Francis P. Burling, an Orleans town official and managing editor of the *Cape Codder* when it first published the park service proposal, described the various positions of the towns in his 1977 booklet, *The Birth of the Cape Cod National Seashore*. The proposal called for Truro and Wellfleet to provide the most land, about eight thousand and ten thousand acres respectively. Truro's selectmen said in their annual report that the impact "was like a bomb burst."

Burling wrote that Wellfleet, which had an outspoken opponent in the chairman of the board of selectmen, probably showed the greatest opposition. Eastham's citizens responded favorably in an opinion survey. In Provincetown, the federal government proposed to take over the Province Lands, which were already owned by the Commonwealth of Massachusetts, so there was no opposition except by those who hoped the town could secure a hundred acres or so for expansion. The commissioners of Barnstable County, which encompasses all Cape Cod, favored the proposal, although they "felt that the proposed area should be reduced in size.".

The first of more than a dozen public meetings and Congressional hearings was held in Eastham on March 23, 1959. Conrad Wirth, director of the National Park Service outlined his plans and took questions. Among the five hundred in attendance was E.J. Kahn, Jr., who was writing an article for *The New Yorker* magazine on the plans for a national seashore. He had been summering in Truro for five years, and his own house would be within the park. He summarized the drift of the questions and answers:

> When would the park come into being? Probably not for ten years or fifteen years after Congress passed a suitable appropriations bill. What would happen to the homes in the park area? People could give them to the government as a tax-deductible contribution, or they could sell them to the government at a price to be fixed by negotiation, and after selling they could, if they wished, have life tenancies. But wouldn't the Park Service have the right of eminent domain? Yes, but the agency hardly ever exercised it. What would keep the parts of the towns not within the park from being overrun by commercial development? Local zoning. How would the towns be compensated for the loss of tax

revenues from the property usurped by the government?
Well, Congress might vote a special grant . . . and in any
event the towns might well boom, since within the park
itself no food or lodging would be provided for visitors.

Despite Wirth's reassurance at the Eastham meeting and another
at Chatham, many on the Outer Cape were wary of the federal
government's intentions. They worried about arbitrary confiscation of their property; Burling termed it "tremendous opposition
from the homeowner." Others foresaw land removed from the tax
rolls and from legitimate development; they had their own vision
of their town's future. As Burling put it: "Visions of sub-divisions
danced in their heads." Some were also disturbed by the prospect
of the federal government taking the Outer Cape from the natives
and opening it up to hordes of visitors who would jam the roads
and set up tents in campgrounds, as campers were doing in the
parks out West. With fifty million people living within a day's
drive of the Outer Cape, they worried about busloads of day-trippers, who would arrive, as the saying went, with a clean shirt and
a $10 bill and leave without changing either one of them.

The Provincetown *Advocate* took an editorial position opposed
to the park, but its salty Truro columnist, Tom Kane, had no problem with a park around his house on South Pamet Road. As quoted
by Kahn, he told how he would greet the visitors: "We'll dress the
kids in tattered clothes, wrap our child bride in a moth-eaten blan-
ket, shove a short-stemmed clay pipe in her mouth, decorate her
hair with seagull feathers, and have her sit out on the front lawn,
staring in stony silence at the passing tourists. Around her we'll
display all her hooked and braided rugs, and perhaps some of our
wood carvings."

Most of the Cape Cod newspapers, including the *Cape Codder*,
were in favor of a park, and they probably reflected the thinking of
most of their readers. Supporters and opponents wrote letters to
the editors that ranged from the closely reasoned to the purely
outraged. Kahn wrote that in Truro "some of the opponents of the

park are not on speaking terms with lifelong friends who have become its proponents."

> On the evening of June 24, 1959, Truro voters met in a special town meeting to discuss the proposed park, which would encompass more than two-thirds of the land in Truro. The selectmen had mailed an opinion survey to Truro property owners, both year-rounders and summer people. Rarely did the selectmen schedule a town meeting during the summer, but this was a special occasion; and about two hundred people filled the Truro Central School gymnasium. About half were summer people. They could ask town meeting's permission to speak but could not vote unless their voting residence was in the town.

The oratory at Truro's special town meeting was less impassioned than Kahn had expected. Selectmen John Worthington began by reporting the results of the postcard survey: 403 were for the idea of a national park and 277 against. He also noted, however, that only 138 of those in favor were for the kind of park officially proposed in bills before Congress. Then came a voice from the floor. As Kahn reported it: "The town's foremost real-estate man, Antone Duarte, Jr., took another view, saying that inasmuch as only twenty percent of the postcards favored the one kind of park that had been officially proposed, eighty percent of the community could be said to be against a park." After an hour's debate, Duarte offered a resolution opposing the park as described in bills before Congress. His resolution passed 50-30.

Of Truro's selectmen, Worthington was the most outspoken. He told Kahn, "If we don't have a park, sooner or later some real-estate operators are going to cut the Lower Cape all to pieces with their bulldozers. That's what the Cape can't bear." Burling quotes Selectman John R. Dyer, Jr., as saying diplomatically that the selectmen "were not entirely opposed to the idea of a national park. We more or less tried to calm the community down." Dyer would

RICHARD F. WHALEN

later be appointed Truro's first representative to the Cape Cod National Seashore Advisory Commission.

The concept of a national seashore park on the Outer Cape had bi-partisan support from the two U.S. senators from Massachusetts, Democrat John F. Kennedy, who had a home in Hyannis Port, and Republican Leverett Saltonstall. Three months after Truro's special town meeting, they introduced a bill that located boundaries and spelled out many of the provisions eventually enacted into law. Their constituents statewide would see advantages to a national seashore park on Cape Cod that they could visit, and their colleagues in the Senate were generally conservation-minded.

Truro voters at the annual town meeting in February 1961 again expressed their opposition, this time with a decisive 80-13 vote. In Washington, however, the proponents were lining up the votes. The Senate unanimously approved legislation in July, and ten days later the House passed a similar bill, 278-82. A conference committee reconciled the few differences, and the measure went to President Kennedy for his signature. One of the last changes was to delete the word park from the legislation so that it became the Cape Cod National Seashore. This was done to allow hunting and fishing, activities not normally allowed in national parks. President Kennedy signed *Public Law 87-126* on August 7, 1961, almost five years after State Senator Stone had visited the offices of the *Cape Codder* to alert the newspaper to federal government's plans. Then it was up to the National Park Service to acquire the land.

It would take more than twenty years to assemble Cape Cod National Seashore from approximately 4,200 lots, homesites, estates, businesses, abandoned land and land owned by various town and state entities. Privately owned properties in Truro ranged in size from tiny building lots to Ossie Ball's thousand-acre tract. In many cases, lot boundaries or titles were obscure. Every parcel had to be researched and negotiated with the owner. In addition, the large number of homes and cottages that would be within the national seashore boundary presented problems requiring novel

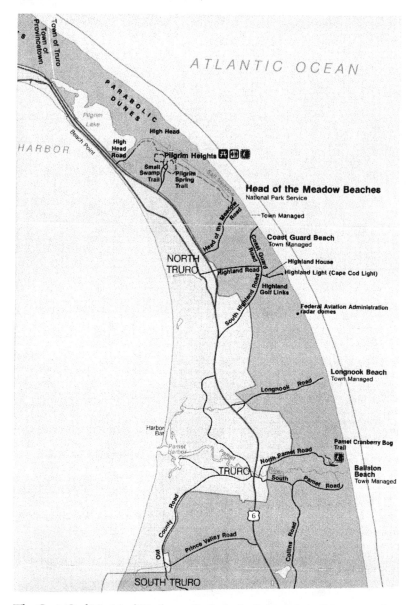

The Cape Cod National Seashore, the dark-shaded portion of the map, takes up 70 percent of Truro's area. (Detail of map courtesy of the National Park Service.)

solutions. In his testimony at the final hearing on March 6, 1961, Stewart L. Udall, secretary of the interior, had referred to the "unusual provisions in national park legislation," which he described as "pioneering."

The acquisition procedure was straightforward for owners of undeveloped land. They had three options: They could sell their land to the government at fair market value as determined by appraisers; they could donate it and take a tax deduction; or they could go to court in eminent domain proceedings that would determine fair market value.

Several of the unusual provisions were designed for the more than six hundred owners of improved properties within the national seashore boundary. These owners could continue to own their homes and cottages on up to six acres of land, as long as their town adopted a zoning bylaw that set a three-acre lot size and restricted any change in the use of the land and buildings. In that case, the federal government would suspend its power of eminent domain. For their land in excess of six acres, owners of improved property had the same options as owners of unimproved property. The provision regarding improved properties meant that more than six hundred homes and cottages built in what would become the national seashore before a cut-off date of September 1, 1959, could remain private property on up to six acres. The first town to adopt the bylaw was Truro, where more than two hundred homes and summer cottages could be kept by their owners.

Another provision solved a problem created by the time needed by the federal government to acquire unimproved land. Some landowners in the 1960s took a chance and built homes or cottages on their land after the cut-off date and before the government could get around to acquiring it. They were gambling that at worst they would get fair market value for their improved property. For this situation, the legislation provided that although they would have to sell their improved property to the government, they could choose to take reduced, annual payments and stay in their homes or summer cottages for up to twenty-five years or for their lifetime.

They could even sell this right, if they wished. The amount of the reduced payment would be one percent of the purchase price per year for twenty-five years or for a period of years based on actuarial tables for the life span of the owner, whichever was less.

This seemed to be a win-win solution for a difficult transition period between 1959 when legislation for the seashore was pending and the time a land owner signed an agreement. The owners would not be evicted, and the government would spend less for their properties. When these leaseholds began to expire, there were protests from people who had to leave. A few of the expiration dates extended into the twenty-first century.

Another unique provision in the legislation provided initial funding. For the first time, the federal government would acquire land for a park that was almost all privately owned and that included 660 dwellings. Other national parks had been created mostly from wilderness already owned by the federal government, or from land donated to the government, or from land that was unoccupied or only sparsely populated. So, for the first time, legislation creating a park included an appropriation to buy the land. The appropriation was sixteen million dollars; the final cost after twenty years would be nearly forty-three million dollars.

The legislation also provided payments for five years to the six towns to replace in part lost tax revenues, and it created a 10-member Cape Cod National Seashore Advisory Commission to give the towns a voice in the management of their new neighbor. Each of the six Outer Cape towns are represented. Massachusetts has two seats, Barnstable County one, and the Department of the Interior one. Although the commission was created as an advisory body, the national seashore administration was required to seek the advice of the commission on policies related to land acquisition, commercial development and recreational activities.

By the mid-1980s, the government had essentially completed acquisition of 26,670 acres of land on the Outer Cape within boundaries almost identical with those originally proposed. The 70 percent of Truro in the Cape Cod National Seashore included all the Atlantic Ocean coastline in the town, Pilgrim Lake and the sand dunes north of it, most of High Head and Pilgrim Heights, and then a wide, irregular swath between Route 6 and the ocean to about half a mile south of Truro Center. From there, it expanded west to include all the land between the ocean and Old County Road, and at the Wellfleet boundary, it stretched from the ocean to Cape Cod Bay. Nearly all the bay beach–from Beach Point to the Wellfleet boundary–remained private.

. . .

The two most significant issues before the Cape Cod National Seashore Advisory Commission were nude sunbathing on an ocean beach in Truro and how to regulate off-road vehicles (ORVs) on the national seashore beaches.

Nude sunbathing and swimming had been a tradition for years at Brush Hollow Beach south of Ballston Beach. Until the 1970s, nude bathers were few and discreet. By 1973, however, several hundred nudists were using Brush Hollow Beach, which is not on any road and is a half-mile from the Ballston Beach parking lot. Visiting nudists were filling the parking lot and tramping over the dunes and through the woods. Vacationers and neighbors complained. The advisory commission recommended controls, and the park service issued a regulation prohibiting public nude bathing in the national seashore. The American Civil Liberties Union sued to overthrow the regulation. A federal judge, after a survey trip from Boston to view the crowds and the nudity firsthand, upheld the national seashore regulation.

On August 23, 1975, demonstrators arrived to oppose, in the name of free speech, any regulation of bathing costumes. Almost four thousand nude bathers, supporters and on-lookers clogged the road to Ballston Beach and the woods around Brush Hollow Beach. Television news cameras recorded the event, and nude bathing in Truro was in the national news for a day or two. The ban on nudity continued in force, but the national seashore tempered strict enforcement by issuing warnings and taking names for first violations.

Whether and under what conditions ORVs should be allowed on the ocean beach was one of "the most intractable of management problems," according to Charles H. W. Foster, the first chairman of the advisory commission and author of *The Cape Cod National Seashore: A Landmark Alliance* (1985). The commission became the public forum for the debate. ORV owners wanted to continue to have reasonably free access to the beaches, primarily for fishing. Conservationists contended that ORVs were damaging environmental and aesthetic aspects of a public beach. They wanted ORVs banned or limited to a few areas at specified times. Seashore administrators were concerned not only about equity but also about the challenge of enforcing complex regulations on remote beaches. They launched a "negotiated rule-making process" in the 1990s and eventually reached a solution for ORV use that everyone could accept.

Despite the anxiety and mistrust in 1959 about its establishment, most of the Outer Cape inhabitants came to feel quite positive about the Cape Cod National Seashore in their backyard. A survey conducted for the National Park Service by the University of Vermont in 1992-93 concluded that residents of the six towns were "generally positive about how Cape Cod National Seashore affected them and their communities." A large majority thought it was doing a good job preserving natural and historic resources and found its employees to be friendly and helpful.

Increased traffic was the only problem of any significance. The survey respondents also expressed concern about visitor behavior and some recreational activities. Not appropriate, in their view, were hunting, jet skiing and nude sunbathing. They supported restrictions on ORVs, nude sunbathing, and bicycles and dogs on nature trails. Some complained of inadequate parking at beaches and limited access for boating and fishing.

At the end of the century, Truro residents in general seemed quite happy to have the national seashore as a neighbor, although it was not without its critics. The complexity and rigor of federal regulations and the sometime conflicting goals of the national seashore and the town generated heated discussion at times. Town officials dealing with the federal government about moving the lighthouse or managing the golf course concession found themselves caught up in a maze of federal regulations and time-consuming negotiations.

CHAPTER 20:
PRESERVING OPEN SPACE
WHILE SHORELINES ERODE

With the Cape Cod National Seashore acquiring 70 percent of Truro's land, conservationists realized that the demand for waterfront building lots would increase significantly, and in 1962 they persuaded the town to create a conservation commission. In the following year, the Commonwealth of Massachusetts enacted a wetlands protection law to be administered by local conservation commissions. Despite the new law, much of Truro Center–the post office and the retail building behind it–was built on filled wetland next to the Pamet River.

With rapid growth came town planners. The planning board hired a Boston consultant to develop a master plan for the town, the first of four land-use plans. The consultant's main recommendation was to move Truro Center to Pamet Harbor and create a large marina there. This was considered too radical and nothing came of it. The master plan would be followed by an open space plan, a plan for management of the Pamet River Greenway and a local comprehensive plan.

Open space, essential to the rural character prized by many residents and summer-home owners, was rapidly disappearing.

Town meeting proved reluctant to take donated, buildable lots off the tax rolls for conservation, and in 1981 Dr. Charles Davidson, attorney Ansel Chaplin and several other environmentally minded citizens founded the Truro Conservation Trust to acquire land for open space through tax-deductible donations of land, cash or securities. By the end of 2000, the non-profit trust would hold more than sixty parcels totaling 250 acres, including fifty acres at High Head overlooking Provincetown Harbor, thirty acres of wetland at the mouth of the Pamet River, sixteen acres that would have been part of a twenty-two-house subdivision and one and a half acres at the heart of Truro Center.

The town government's first open space plan was put together by its conservation commission in 1984. Its mission statement set the tone for the rest of the century: "The great natural beauty and rural atmosphere of Truro are among its priceless qualities. Future land use and change must take cognizance of this so that as much as possible of the scenic beauty and quiet ambiance are retained for future generations—and also to maintain property values (and the tax base) now as well as for the future." The report recommended writing a management plan for the Pamet River and its harbor, opening the river to tidal flow for its full length, acquiring wetlands, adopting zoning regulations to protect coastal dunes and limiting commercial development along Route 6.

The Pamet River valley was the subject of a study commissioned by the Truro Conservation Trust and published in 1987. The 145-page *Pamet River Greenway Management Plan* offered more than eighty recommendations to protect the water quality, preserve scenic views and improve recreational use. The two reports called attention to the issues raised by those who wanted to preserve the town's natural resources and scenic features. Except for the acquisition of open space, however, little was done with the recommendations.

. . .

For all the efforts to preserve the natural environment, the saltwater environment that surrounds Cape Cod will ultimately drown it. Truro and all of Cape Cod will disappear under the ocean in about five thousand years, perhaps even sooner, according to studies of erosion rates and the effect of global warming. Ocean water will erode the shorelines, fill the valleys and eventually wash away the last of Truro's landscape. Truro and the rest of sandy Cape Cod will become underwater banks, like Georges and Stellwagen and the Grand banks.

Cape Cod is a newborn infant in geologic time and just as fragile. If one year is taken to represent the earth's age, Cape Cod did not exist until about two minutes ago. The sand, gravel and pockets of clay that make up Cape Cod were left by a retreating glacier of the last Ice Age, some twelve thousand to sixteen thousand years ago. The glacier had expanded out from central Canada when the world's climate was much colder. It covered all of New England, and in some places was more than a mile thick. As the climate warmed, the retreating glacier left behind millions of tons of sandy, rocky debris scraped from the mountains of Canada and New England. One of the highest piles of sandy glacial debris became Cape Cod.

When the glacier started its retreat, sea level was about three hundred feet lower than it is today. The missing water was locked up as snow and ice in the world's enormous glaciers. The Atlantic Ocean shoreline off the Outer Cape was about four miles farther east. Georges Bank, Stellwagen Bank and the Grand Banks were dryland. The remains of saber-toothed tigers and woolly mammoths have been discovered on Georges Bank. The prehistoric animals no doubt also roamed the higher terrain now known as Cape Cod.

As the climate warmed, the glaciers melted and the sea level rose. The rising ocean waters flooded a low spot that became Cape Cod Bay. Cape Cod itself began to take shape as a sandy peninsula. At that time, High Head was the end of the peninsula formed by the glacial deposits. Beach Point and the sandy hook of Provincetown began to extend from High Head only six thousand years ago, after the Indians arrived. The end of the Cape was formed primarily by sand washed there from Truro's beaches, a process that continues today. Cape Cod geologist Robert Oldale estimated that when the first Indians arrived the rising sea level was still at least fifty feet lower and the ocean shoreline at least a mile farther east.

The fragile, eroding land that is Truro is bounded by salt water not only on the east and the west but underneath as well. The glacial deposit that forms Cape Cod extends hundreds of feet down to bedrock. Above the bedrock, salt water from the ocean and bay permeates the glacial deposit the full width of the town. Drilling deep enough anywhere in Truro will reach salt water. Above the salt water "floats" a lens of rain-supplied fresh water, because fresh water is less dense. Geologists call the freshwater lens a "sole source aquifer" because Truro is totally dependent for water on the rain that falls on Truro and seeps into the aquifer. Pond surfaces are the top of the lens, or watertable. Truro can thus be imagined as floating on its freshwater lens, which in turn is floating on salt water above the bedrock.

For centuries, Atlantic Ocean waves have been eroding the Outer Cape shoreline at an average of two to three feet a year. Truro has been somewhat more vulnerable because it is hit head-on by the prevailing northeasterly storm winds in the winter. Waves hitting the beach not only pull sand out to sea but wash it away both north and south in alongshore currents. Sand moving north continues to form the end of Cape Cod and supply the Peaked Hill sand bars. The storm waves then undermine the base of the coastal bank, which retreats as more sand slides down onto the beach. These sand slides can be dangerous. In 1973 an eleven-year-old boy died when he was buried by a sand slide at Long Nook Beach.

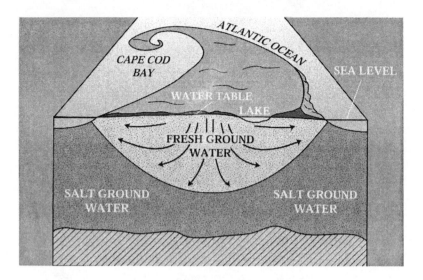

Truro and its fresh water "float" on salt water, which lies above the bedrock.(Illustration by the U.S. Geologic Survey courtesy of the National Park Service.)

Geologists note that paradoxically it is the very erosion of Cape Cod's shoreline that prevents quick destruction and prolongs its life. Sand eroded from the beaches is pulled into the water, where it forms shoals and sandbars offshore that absorb most of the force of storm waves. If big storm waves could break continually on its sandy shoreline, Cape Cod would quickly be washed away. It is between sandbars that shoreline erosion is greater; that's where the waves can break closer to shore or sometimes directly on the beach to pull more sand farther off shore with their undertow.

The offshore sandbars and shoals have been the best protection for waterfront properties. Bulkheads, seawalls, jetties and groins have rarely been successful in stopping the erosion, and sometimes they have accelerated it or simply shifted it to neighboring property. "Coastal erosion, accretion and shoreline retreat are vital to Cape Cod," says Oldale. "Tampering with these processes may eventually destroy the very Cape Cod that towns and individual property owners are trying to save."

If the geologists and oceanographers are right, many dwellings that crowd close to the bay and ocean shorelines will not long survive on their present foundations. The few cottages that are within a hundred feet of the ocean beach bluffs will probably have to be moved or demolished within fifty years. The Ballston Beach Cottage colony, built close to the ocean beach at the turn of the century, succumbed to ocean erosion. Debris from foundations has turned upon the beach almost every year. In the 1990s, a cottage near the Wellfleet boundary was demolished before it fell to the beach below. An ocean-front cottage near Ballston Beach has been moved back from the eroding cliffs, and another has been raised on pilings to let the retreating dune move back underneath it. The ocean will undermine the pilings, probably before mid-century; and it, too, will have to be moved or demolished.

Truro has two low spots on the Atlantic Ocean shore where storm waves have crashed over the beach dune and sent sea water cascading into Truro. The most recent breaches were in at Ballston Beach at the head of the Pamet River, but the overwashes at the head of East Harbor's creek in the nineteenth century generated the most concern. They were a major factor leading to construction of the two dikes at East Harbor (now Pilgrim Lake).

At Ballston Beach, ocean waves have broken through the beach dune at least seven times in recorded history. The earliest mention was by Alexander Young in 1841 in his edition of *Mourt's Relation*. He refers to "a narrow beach and embankment, which the water has been known to break over." Overwashes also occurred in 1896, 1937, 1973, 1978, 1991 and 1992. The low sand dune at Ballston Beach, which separates the ocean from the head of the Pamet River valley is nothing more than "a plug of beach and dune sand" in the words of geologist Stephen Leatherman. Ocean waves and winds have built the plug and maintained it for many centuries. As the coastline has retreated inland, the plug has migrated with it into the Pamet River valley.

In 1980, the town stopped bulldozing the drifted sand from the loop road at the washover point and from the nearby beach parking lot, closing the loop connecting North Pamet and South Pamet roads and allowing storms winds and waves to push the dune west. The national seashore installed snow fencing to hold the blowing sand and allow the dune to re-build.

What was probably the largest overwash in Truro's recorded history occurred in 1991 when ocean waves in the "Halloween Nor'easter" tore a hundred-foot wide breach in the plug. Tons of sea water poured into the upper half of the Pamet River, a fresh water marsh for more than a century. The salty flood water slowly drained through small culverts at Truro Center into the lower, tidal half of the Pamet River. Just a year later, another storm crashed through the same breach, taking out the snow fencing that had been put across the opening. For several months, sea water continued to flow through the gap at the highest of the high tides. The snow fencing was replaced, and at the end of the 1990s the barrier dune plug was higher by two levels of fencing. No one believed, however, that it would stop the next big storm.

On the bay side, erosion of the high banks is generally much slower and more irregular. Oceanographer Graham Giese, a Truro resident, estimates the annual average rate of erosion at up to six inches a year but with periods of stability and even accretion between episodes of erosion. The erosion is thus pushing the house-topped shoreline inland by about forty or fifty feet per century. In the 1990s, erosion at one point on Cape Cod Bay threatened to undermine a house, which was moved back from the crumbling cliff edge by the same company that moved the lighthouse. The smooth curve of the bayshore in Truro, however, suggests that over the centuries the erosion, with one exception, has been quite uniform from end to end.

Powerful waves in northeast storms in 1991 and 1992 broke through the
coastal bank at Ballston Beach near the head of the Pamet River. Tons of ocean
water poured into the upper Pamet and its marshes, long a fresh-water environment. After the first breakthrough, shown above, the Cape Cod National
Seashore put up snow fencing to catch blowing sand and help the coastal bank
re-build, but the overwash a year later swept right through. (Photo by Joyce
Johnson.)

The exception is at low-lying Beach Point, with its concentration of motels, cottage colonies and summer homes. At the north end, where the inlet to East Harbor used to be, the beach is growing rapidly. Alongshore currents from the south bring the sand and deposit it there. Some of the sand is coming from the south end of Beach Point. As a result, about a third of Beach Point is growing, a third is shrinking and the middle third is relatively stable. As Giese put it in 1979: "To the glee of the property owners to the north, their shoreline is building out at the rate of six to ten feet per year, while to the distress of their brethren to the south the beaches are disappearing and cottages and motels are threatened." Periodically, when a storm with strong west winds coincides with the highest of high tides, waves crash at the thresholds of several cottage colonies and motels; and salt-spray blasts the buildings and spills over their tops.

Truro is getting narrower every year, and the rising sea level caused by global warming may be speeding up the process. The warming trend that began after the last Ice Age accelerated in the twentieth century. Glaciers around the world have been shrinking; in thirty years they will be gone from Glacier National Park. The sea level at Truro's shorelines has risen at least a foot since 1900, and coastal geologists note that even a seemingly small rise in the sea level can greatly increase erosion of shorelines.

. . .

The 1990s proved to be the hottest decade on record, and scientists became increasingly concerned about the effects of global warming on agriculture and sea levels. They blamed what they called a greenhouse effect caused by the doubling of carbon dioxide emissions since pre-industrial times. Carbon dioxide, a harmless gas, results from burning coal, oil and natural gas. It rises into the atmosphere where it slows the escape of heat from the earth and accelerates global warming.

"I think beach erosion has met its match in Harry Lancaster."

(Cartoon from the Howie Schneider Unshucked feature in the *Provincetown Banner*.)

Some scientists predicted a dramatic increase in global warming of two to six degrees over the twenty-first century, much higher than the one-degree rise in the twentieth. This projected increase for a single century would approach the total increase of five to nine degrees over the past 140 centuries. If they prove to be correct (and few scientists demur), polar glaciers will melt even more rapidly, a warmer ocean will expand, sea level will rise several feet, and Truro's shore front properties and uplands will be much more vulnerable to storm waves. What to do about the increase in global warming caused by man-made greenhouse gases became a political issue. Vice President Al Gore, who spent a few summer weeks in a Truro ocean-front home, published a book about global warming and the greenhouse effect. Adding to the impact on Truro was confirmation by Harvard scientists that New England is sinking, perhaps as much as an inch every twenty-five years.

Skeptics among the climatologists, however, pointed to sudden changes in the earth's temperature in the past and suggested that global warming could end suddenly, even within a few decades. Deep-sea currents in the North Atlantic seemed to be an important factor. Others questioned whether the computer models really proved that man-made emissions of carbon dioxide could have the dire greenhouse effect. Still, if the majority of scientists prevail, erosion of Truro's shorelines could be much more rapid in the next century and Cape Cod could be submerged long before the year 7000.

· · ·

Eroding shorelines and silting sand threatened the town's two most prominent features in the late twentieth century–Highland Light on the edge of the ocean coastal bank and Pamet Harbor on the shifting sands of the bayshore. The lighthouse site had been secure for two centuries, but by the mid-1980s storm waves had worn away the coastal bank to within 120 feet of the lighthouse. Half the original ten-acre plot of land was gone. At least a hunded feet would be needed between the lighthouse and the top of the cliff to support the heavy equipment. Time was running out for Highland Light.

Built in 1857 and the most prominent landmark in Truro, the lighthouse became one of the most powerful in North America in 1932 when a thousand-watt bulb replaced the kerosene lamp, an electric motor powered the revolving light, and a new lens boosted the light to four million candlepower. The lens replaced an optical apparatus of 1901 that floated on liquid mercury and was rated at about 192,000 candlepower, less than five per cent of today's light. The foghorn of vibrating reeds was also converted to electricity, but by 1977 it was no longer needed and its booming wail was silenced.

The threat to the lighthouse next door to its headquarters spurred the Truro Historical Society into action. Its president, Gordon Russell, and its treasurer, Robert Firminger, both retired businessmen, led a brigade of volunteers to mobilize local support. Their strategy included raising funds to demonstrate the commitment of the town to save the lighthouse. They could not hope to raise the full amount needed—an estimated $1,500,000—but they could try to raise 10 percent and they did. They also collected about 150,000 signatures of visitors from around the world on a petition to save the lighthouse. Their campaign in turn won the support of the Commonwealth of Massachusetts, the National Park Service, the U.S. Coast Guard, the U.S. Army Corps of Engineers and the U.S. Congress. It took a full decade to energize all the government agencies, coordinate reports required for various government approvals, arrive at a joint agreement on a new site for the lighthouse, and finally secure federal funding.

On a misty day in May 1996, a ground-breaking ceremony drew federal and state legislators and about two hundred spectators. In June, the contractors, who were specialists in moving houses, industrial chimneys and lighthouses, dug slots in the lighthouse foundation, inserted steel beams under the 430-ton building, and laid steel rails on which to slide the lighthouse and the keeper's house to the new foundation. To the amazement of all, they used Ivory soap to grease the skids. Huge rams driven by compressed air pushed the lighthouse about thirty feet a day. In nineteen days, the lighthouse reached its new site, and on a windy Sunday evening in November all the dignitaries reconvened to turn on the light at its new location—almost six hundred feet from the edge of the still-eroding cliff. Highland Light would be safe for perhaps two centuries. When it has to be moved again, the move will be much easier. The new foundation was built so that steel beams and power jacks can be slipped underneath it with little effort. Highland Light had become a portable lighthouse.

· · ·

A bold and dramatic move saved the lighthouse, at least for a few centuries. Keeping Pamet Harbor open at low tides proved more perplexing. Ten-foot tides in Cape Cod Bay flood into the lower Pamet valley twice a day. At high tide, there is plenty of water for boat traffic but not at low tide. Silting has been a constant problem. For a century after the Civil War, Pamet Harbor was almost deserted. In its profile of Truro in 1897, a state report opened with the observation that "Truro differs much from Provincetown, as it has neither harbor nor fishing vessels."

The most ambitious attempt to improve navigation in Pamet Harbor and the most radical change in its configuration came in 1919 when the Commonwealth of Massachusetts cut a new channel through the barrier beach dune nearly half a mile south of the river's naturally occurring wide mouth at Corn Hill. The narrow channel was directly in line with the straight stretch of river bed under the railroad bridge. Presumably, this was done so the tidal current could ebb and flow strongly in a straight line and scour the channel rather than meandering north to Corn Hill. The state also dredged an anchorage, but it much of it silted in within a few years.

Mort Small ridiculed the project. In one of his local history booklets, published in 1926, he wrote:

Thousands of dollars were spent there, but instead of dredging the old harbor a ditch was dug straight out through the beach near the Truro railway station. This of course caused a dead water head with no current and soon the narrow mouth of the ditch began to fill with sand, and at the present time hardly a small dory can get in and out. If there was ever, anywhere, a more shameful waste of money, then we have not heard of it, a case of monumental folly.

In 1932, Arthur Tarbell wrote in *Cape Cod Ahoy!* that the mouth of the Pamet River "is now closed by silting." Mellen Hatch wrote in 1939 that "Pamet Harbor, a hundred years ago the scene of such wholesome activity, is now deserted."

Interest in making the tidal inlet into a navigable harbor revived in the early 1950s. Rock jetties were built out from both sides of the inlet, and for a time they appeared to stop the silting. The Pamet Harbor committee told town meeting that tons of sand from the beach were prevented from entering the harbor mouth. Within a few years, however, silting resumed and the town was again debating whether to fund more dredging.

In the mid-1960s, the town obtained state aid for major dredging that made the channel four feet deep at low tide. The abandoned railroad bridge, a public hazard and impediment to navigation up river, was removed. Again, however, the channel and boat basin, which was used almost exclusively by pleasure boats, began to silt up. That was the last dredging for thirty years. In 1996, dredging began yet again, but the work was considered incomplete and more was done two years later. At the end of the century, the consensus was that periodic dredging would be required every few years if the town wanted to maintain a harbor that could be used at low tide.

The entire Pamet River Valley, with the entrance to the harbor from Cape Cod
Bay at the bottom and the Atlantic Ocean at the top. Ten-foot tides surge
through the harbor channel twice a day, but shoaling sand still makes navigation difficult despite the stone jetties. Much of the sand comes from the south,
carried by an alongshore current. The old harbor channel came in from the
left. The railroad trestle, now gone, crossed the river at the triangular parking
lot. The Pilgrims walked along the north shore, on the left, about two thirds of
the way to the Atlantic. (Photo by Kelsey-Kennard.)

Meanwhile, wind, wave and tidal flow continue to shape and re-shape the contours and depths of the Pamet River mouth and the beaches to the north and south. Already, storm waves on Cape Cod Bay occasionally break through the low barrier beach dune about half way between the new man-made inlet with its rock jetties and the site of the old, wider river mouth nearly half a mile north. During these storms, water from the bay spills into the old riverbed. Coastal geologist Graham Giese has said that a new, natural inlet may form there within a few years. What this will mean for the future of Pamet Harbor remains to be seen.

· · ·

As if the issues of rapid growth, diminishing open space and eroding shorelines were not enough, all the town's public buildings were scheduled to be replaced at the end of the century. For about a decade, voters considered priorities and costs for an ever-shifting mix of construction projects to be financed by bond issues. They included a new and/or renovated town hall, a new elementary school, a new police-fire station, a new library, a four-classroom addition to the new school and a state-mandated capping of the landfill by 2000.

Dumping at the landfill ended in 1990, and trash that was not recycled was compacted and transferred by truck to an off-Cape electric power generating plant. Capping with a membrane prevented rainwater from leaching contaminants into the water table. Shortly after the transfer station was equipped with a compactor, Truro almost had a million-dollar deal to take Provincetown's trash. Provincetown saw a bargain for both towns and approved the deal in 1992.

Truro opinion, however, was divided. As the town's annual report described it: "Should Truro share its beloved 'dump' with its neighbor, big, bad Provincetown? Why? For money! Not on your life, it was finally decided by a bristling town meeting after weeks of see-saw battle that created its own roster of heroes and anti-heroes." Voters initially approved the deal with Provincetown, but six weeks later a second special town meeting withdrew the approval. Despite the prospect of extra revenue equal to 10 to 20 percent of the town's operating budget, opponents expressed concern about increased truck traffic, especially in the summer, and the unknowns of being responsible for another town's trash,

Another burning issue in 1992 was whether to adopt a town charter that would raise the number of selectmen from three to five, create the position of town administrator and spell out how the town would be managed. For as long as anyone could remember, three selectmen had run the town without professional help, but the complexities brought on by economic growth, ever more complex budgets and increasing state regulations added to the burden of administration. "Controversy boiled around the activities of the charter commission," noted the annual report. The charter passed by only six votes out of six hundred.

The most difficult issue during the 1990s was what to do about Town Hall, an historic, 150-year-old building badly in need of repair or replacement. For more than a decade, the town debated an ever-shifting array of options: Restore the building as an historic treasure and add an annex; replace it with a replica; build a new town hall next to the old one, next to the new library or next to the new police-fire station, and save the old one and refurbish it for some other use. Meanwhile, the new school opened in 1991, the police-fire station in 1993, and the library in 1999; but an addition to the elementary school was put on hold, and Town Hall continued to deteriorate.

Although the town's operating budget moved steadily higher, its tax rate remained the lowest on Cape Cod and one of the lowest in the state. The budget reached $6,600,000 in fiscal 1999, which seemed to many like a lot of money for a small town of about 1,800 year-round inhabitants. But the tax rate of $7.60 per $1,000 of assessed valuation for fiscal 1999 was the lowest on Cape Cod because the town's real estate valuations were the highest. Its land and buildings were valued at almost $600 million, or about

$300,000 per year-round resident. Since Truro had no industry, tax revenues from residential and commercial property financed the town. The biggest taxpayers included the owners of expensive waterfront and waterview houses and the motels, cottage colonies and condominiums along Beach Point.

Other cross-border issues with Provincetown involved school-children and, once again, fresh water. Provincetown decided in 1905 that it had to improve its drinking water. It bought two tracts of land in North Truro for well fields and began to install water mains. Later, it would also pump water from the old North Truro Air Force Station. Reasonably enough, Provincetown agreed to provide Truro water to Beach Point and to nearby parts of North Truro and ultimately as far south as the school and the police-fire station. This cross-border arrangement, the only way for Provincetown to get acceptable drinking water directly from the ground, inevitably led to disputes over water rights.

At the end of the century, water issues between the two towns were manifold—how much Provincetown could safely take from Truro's water table, whether Provincetown was losing too much water through leaks, how far the water mains could be extended in Truro, and who could hook up to them. While all of Provincetown got its water from Truro, most of Truro's homes got their water from wells. The irony was not lost on Truro townsfolk wary of relations with neighboring towns, especially those aware that Provincetown itself was built on sand that ocean currents washed there from Truro.

Schooling became an issue with Provincetown when the Truro school committee proposed a four-classroom addition. With class-room space to spare, Provincetown saw an opportunity to improve its financial situation by taking Truro's sixth grade for tuition pay-ments; then Truro would not have to build an addition. The Truro school committee argued that it was not that simple or cost-effec-tive, but Truro voters twice turned down the proposed addition. The complexities of pupil demographics and cross-border finan-cial arrangements were quite a contrast to simpler days when

Samuel Spear moved from house to house to teach groups of neighborhood children of all ages in a kitchen/living room.

At the end of the century, the town's population growth and pace of residential construction accelerated dramatically. Its population grew three times faster in the 1990s than in the 1980s—17.2 percent versus 5.9 percent. Home construction grew even faster. Building permits for 1997 through 1999 were 50 percent higher than the four-decade average of thirty-seven new homes per year. Waterfront and waterview lots sold at a premium, some for more than half a million dollars. Ridge tops and bayshore bluffs sprouted expensive, architect-designed houses, almost all of them second homes. By the end of the century, more than two-thirds of all the residences in Truro were vacation homes. Although the planning board wanted to slow the pace of new construction, town meeting rejected a cap of forty-two building permits a year for new homes.

At the same time, preservation of open space accelerated. The voters agreed in 1998 to pay a 3 percent surcharge on their property taxes to purchase open space under the Cape Cod open space land acquisition program, with the state providing a 50 percent match for three years. The first purchase was a four-acre parcel near Truro Center for $225,000. The selectmen agreed to accept the town's first conservation restriction, which lowered the taxes on a lot fronting on Cape Cod Bay in return for deeded restrictions on development. And the non-profit conservation trust made its major acquisition of sixteen acres that would have been part of a twenty-two-house subdivision off Depot Road.

Growth management became a by-word if not a bylaw. Town meeting adopted a local comprehensive plan that had a central goal of maintaining Truro's rural character. The Cape Cod Commission, which has the power to review certain development projects, certified the plan. A committee of town officials monitored whether Truro adhered to the plan and organized workshops to gather opinions and keep growth management issues before resident voters and non-resident taxpayers.

At the turn of the millennium, Truro was still Cape Cod's least developed town. It still retained something of its rural, seaside character despite a proliferation of vacation homes and its growth to nearly two thousand year-round residents, a figure not reached since the 1850s. In the future, the challenge will be to manage the growth of a town that continues to attract retirees and vacation homeowners whose very numbers threaten the rural, seaside qualities that draw them to the town. If the town achieves an effective balance between human and environmental needs, Truro will continue to be one of the most desirable places to live and work on Cape Cod, especially for those who appreciate a tiny town with a tremendous history.

APPENDIX A

Captain Martin Pring's Narrative of His 1603 Voyage

The text of Martin Pring's narrative was first printed in 1625 in *Purchas His Pilgrims,* a collection of narratives of voyages of discovery. An annotated transcript and an introduction are provided by David B. Quinn and Alison M. Quinn in *The English New England Voyages 1602-1608.*

Over the centuries, historians have differed on the location of Pring's anchorage. Edgartown on Martha's Vineyard was suggested in Jeremy Belknap's *American Biography* (1794 and 1798). B.F. De Costa argued for Plymouth Harbor in his 1878 article, "Gosnold and Pring, 1602-1603", in the *New England Historical and Genealogical Register.* In the mid-twentieth century, David B. Quinn, a British academic historian, and the Reverend Warner F. Gookin a retired clergyman of Martha's Vineyard, suggested Truro. Gookin had left an unpublished paper when he died in 1952, and Quinn published it, with his own commentary, in 1967 in the *New England Quarterly* as "Martin Pring at Provincetown, 1603?".

Gookin argued that Pring's description of his anchorage fit Cape Cod, not Plymouth Harbor, and that the river he saw was most likely the Pamet in Truro. Quinn added that Pring's "small baricado" could be the "old fort or palisado" found by the Pilgrims. H. Roger King agreed with their interpretation in his *Cape Cod and Plymouth Colony in the Seventeenth Century* (1994).(See my article, "Where did Captain Martin Pring Anchor in New England?" in the summer 1998 issue of the *Historical Journal of Massachusetts*.)

There is no byline for the Pring narrative in *Purchas His Pilgrims*, and the text is somewhat ambiguous about its authorship. The long title concludes "Under the command of me Martin Pring," indicating that he was the author. Later in the account, however, Pring is referred to twice in the third person, once as "our captain." Quinn and Quinn conclude that the narrative is "undoubtedly based on" Pring's journal or the ship's log, whether he personally penned it or not.

Comments on excerpts from Pring's text are in [square brackets]. Orthography and some grammar have been modernized.

[Title]

A voyage set out from the city of Bristol at the charge of the chiefest merchants and inhabitants of the said city with a small ship and a bark for the discovery of the north part of Virginia [i.e. New England] *in the year 1603, under the command of me Martin Pring:*

[The narrative opens with a short account of Sir Walter Raleigh's granting permission for the voyage, based on a patent from Queen Elizabeth.] . . . Leave being obtained of him under his hand and seal, they speedily prepared a small ship called the *Speedwell* in burden of about fifty tons, manning the same with some thirty men and boys, wherein went for master and chief commander in the voyage one Martin Pring, a man very sufficient for his place, and Edmund Jones his mate, and Robert Saltern . . . , as their chief agent, with a bark called the *Discoverer*, of six and twenty tons or thereabouts, wherein went Master William Browne and Samuel Kirkland his mate, both good and skillful mariners, being thirteen men and a boy in all in that bark. The aforesaid ship and bark were plentifully victualled for eight months, and furnished with slight merchandises thought fit to trade with the people of the country, as hats of divers colors, green, blue and yellow, apparel of coarse kersey and canvas ready-made, stockings and shoes, saws, pickaxes, spades and shovels, axes, hatchets, hooks, knives, scissors, hammers, nails, chisels, fishhooks, bells, beads, bugles [beads], looking glasses, thimbles, pins, needles, thread, and such like. They set sail from Kingrode [at Bristol] the twentieth day of March.

We set sail from Milford Haven [in Wales, west of Bristol], where the winds had stayed us a fortnight, in which space we heard of Queen Elizabeth's death, the tenth of April 1603. . . . [Pring describes his course to the Azores and the coast of Maine, where he landed briefly to look for sassafras, then continued southwest.] . . . Departing hence we bore into that great gulf, which Captain Gosnold overshot the year before, coasting and finding people on the north side thereof. Not yet satisfied in our expectation, we left them and sailed over, and came to anchor on the south side in the latitude of 41 degrees [Truro's latitude] and odd minutes, where we went on land in a certain bay, which we called Whitson Bay, the name of the worshipful master John Whitson, then mayor of the city of Bristol, and one of the chief adventurers, and finding a pleasant hill thereunto adjoining, we called it Mount Aldworth, for Master Robert Aldworth's sake, a chief furtherer of the voyage, as well with his purse as with his travel. Here we had sufficient quantity of sassafras.

At our going on shore, upon view of the people and sight of the place, we though it convenient to make a small baricado to keep diligent watch and ward in, for the advertisement and succor of our men, while they should work in the woods. During our abode on shore, the people of the country came to our men sometimes ten, twenty, forty or threescore, and at one time one hundred and twenty at once. We used them kindly and gave them

RICHARD F. WHALEN

divers sorts of our meanest merchandise. They did eat peas and beans with our men. Their own victuals were mostly of fish.

We had a youth in our company that could play upon the gitterne [cithern], in whose homely music they took great delight, and would give him many things, as tobacco, tobacco pipes, snake skins six foot long, which they use for girdles, fawn skins, and such like, and danced twenty in a ring, and the gitterne in the midst of them, using many savage gestures, singing Io. Ia, Io, Ia, Ia, Io; him that first broke the ring, the rest would knock and cry out upon. Some few of them had plates of brass a foot long, and a half a foot broad, before their breasts. [They probably obtained the brass ornaments from Indian tribes to the north who had acquired them from European fishermen working off Nova Scotia.] Their weapons were bows of five or six feet long of witch-hazel, painted black and yellow, the string of three twists of sinews, bigger than our bowstrings. Their arrows are of a yard and handful long, not made of reeds, but of a fine light wood very smooth and round with three long and deep black feathers of some eagle, vulture or kite, as closely fastened with some binding matter as any fletcher of ours can glue them on. Their quivers are full a yard long, made of long dried rushes wrought about two handfuls broad above, and one handful beneath, with pretty works and compartments. Diamant wise of red and others colors [diamond-shaped designs].

We carried with us from Bristol two excellent mastiffs of whom the Indians were more afraid than of twenty of our men. One of these mastiffs would carry a half-pike in his mouth. And one Master Thomas Bridges, a gentleman of our company, accompanied only by one of these dogs, passed six miles alone in the country having lost his fellows and returned safely. And when we would be rid of the savages' company we would let loose the mastiffs, and suddenly with outcries they would flee away. These people in color are inclined to swart, tawny or chestnut color, not by nature but accidentally [with dyes or paint], and do wear their hair braided in four parts, and trussed up about their heads with a small knot behind, in which hair of theirs they stick many feathers and toys for bravery and pleasure. They cover their privates only with a piece of leather drawn betwixt their twists [thighs] and fastened to their girdles behind and before, whereunto they hang their bags of tobacco. They seem to be somewhat jealous of their women, for we saw not past two of them, who wear aprons of leather skins before them down to the knees, and a bear's skin, like an Irish mantle, over one shoulder. The men are of stature somewhat taller than our ordinary people, strong, swift, well-proportioned, and given to treachery, as in the end we perceived.

Their boats, whereof we brought one to Bristol, were in proportion like a wherry of the River Thames, seventeen feet long and four-foot broad, made of the bark of the birch tree, far exceeding in bigness those of England; it was sewed together with strong and tough osiers or twigs, and the seams covered over with rosin or turpentine little inferior in sweetness to frankincense, as we made trial by burning a little thereof on the coals at sundry times after our coming home; it was also open like a wherry and sharp at both ends, saving that the beak was a little bending roundly upward. And though it carried nine men standing upright, yet it weighed not at the most above sixty pounds in weight, a thing almost incredible in regard of the largeness and capacity thereof. Their oars were flat at the end like an oven peele, made of ash or maple, very light and strong, about two yards long, wherewith they row very swiftly. Passing up a river, we saw certain cottages together, abandoned by the savages and not far off we beheld their gardens and one among the rest of an acre of ground and in the same was sown tobacco, pompions [squash], cucumbers and such like; and some of the people had maize or Indian wheat among them. In the fields we found wild peas, strawberries very fair and big, gooseberries, raspices [raspberries], hurst [blueberries] and other wild fruits.

Having spent three weeks upon the coast before we came to this place where we meant to stay and take in our lading according to our instructions given us in charge before our setting forth, we pared [prepared) and dug up the earth with shovels and sowed wheat, barley, oats, peas and sundry sorts of garden seeds, which for the time of our abode there, being about seven weeks, although they were late sown, came up very well, giving certain testimony of the goodness of the climate and of the soil. And it seemth that the woad [dyers weed], hemp, flax, rape-seed and such like which require a rich and fat ground would prosper excellently in these parts. For in divers places here we found grass about knee deep.

As for trees the country yieldeth sassafras, a plant of sovereign virtue for the French pox, and some of late have learnedly written good against the plague and many other maladies, vines, cedars, oak, ash, beech, birch trees, cherry trees, bearing fruit whereof we did eat, hazel, witch-hazel, the best wood of all other to make soap-ashes withall, walnut trees, maples, holy to make bird-lime with, and a kind of tree bearing a fruit like a small red pear-plum with a crown or knob on top (a plant whereof carefully wrapped up in earth, Master Robert Saltern brought to Bristol).

The beasts here are stags, fallow deer in abundance, bears, wolves, foxes, lusernes [lynx] and (some say) tigers [pumas], porcupines and dogs with sharp and long noses, with many other sorts of wild beasts, whose cases [skins] and furs being hereafter purchased by exchange may yield no small gain to us, since we are certainly informed the Frenchmen brought from Canada the value of thirty thousand crowns in the year 1604 [a remark probably added by the publisher] almost in beaver and otter skins only. The most usual fowls are eagles, vultures, hawks, cranes, herons, crows, gulls, and great store of other river and sea fowl. And as the land is full of God's good blessings, so is the sea replenished with great abundance of excellent fish, as cod sufficient to load many ships, which we found upon the coast in the month of June, seals to make oil withall, mullets, turbots, mackerels, herrings, crabs, lobsters, creises [crayfish?] and mussels with ragged pearls in them.

By the end of July we had loaded our small bark called *Discoverer* with as much sassafras as we thought sufficient and sent her home to England before, to give some speedy contentment to the adventurers; who arrived safely in Kingrode about a fortnight before us. After their departure we so bestirred ourselves that our ship had gotten in her lading, during which time there fell out this accident. On a day about noon tide while our men which used to cut down sassafras in the woods were asleep, as they used to do for two hours in the heat of the day, there came down about seven score savages armed with their bows and arrows, and environed our house or barricado, wherein were four of our men alone with their muskets to keep sentinel, whom they sought to have come down unto them, which they utterly refused, and stood upon their guard. Our Master likewise being very careful and circumspect, having not past two with him in the ship put the same in the best defense he could, lest they should have invaded the same, and caused a piece of great ordnance to be shot off, to give terror to the Indians, and warning to our men which were fast asleep in the woods; at the noise of which piece they were a little awakened and began to call for Fool and Gallant, their great and fearful mastiffs, and full quietly laid themselves down again, but being quickened up eftsoones again with a second shot they roused up themselves, betook them to their weapons and with the mastiffs, great Fool with a half-pike in his mouth, drew down to their ship; whom when the Indians beheld afar off, with the mastiffs which they most feared, in dissembling manner they turned all to a jest and sport and departed in a friendly manner. Yet not long after, even the day before our departure, they set fire to the woods where we wrought [worked], which we did behold to burn for a mile space, and the very same day that we weighed anchor, they came down to the shore in greater number, to wit, very near two hundred by our estimation, and some of them came in their boats to our ship, and would have had us come in again, but we sent them back and would none of their entertainment.

About the eighth or ninth of August we left this excellent haven at the entrance whereof we found twenty fathoms water, and rode at our ease in seven fathoms being landlocked, the haven winding in compass like the shell of a snail, and it is in latitude of one and forty degrees and five and twenty minutes . . . We came at length into Kingrode, the second of October 1603. The *Discover* was out five months and and half. The *Speedwell* was out six months upon the voyage.

APPENDIX B

Mourt's Relation

One of the most important historical documents on the European colonizing of America, *Mourt's Relation* includes the first detailed description of what would become the town of Truro. The somewhat mysterious title was a nickname given to it by an historian in 1636. The long title of the seventy-eight-page book is given below. Whoever he was, Mourt did not write the "relation." No author's name is given. "G. Mourt" is the name at the end of a short, introductory note that refers to "these relations coming to my hand from both known and faithful friends, on whose writings I do much rely." Mourt thus claims to have arranged publication, but nothing is known about him unless he was George Morton, a merchant who arrived in Plymouth in 1623. (Dexter, xx; Heath, xv; Willison, 447) But that would mean Morton's name was spelled quite differently in the book he says he brought to publication. That seems unlikely.

On the basis of internal evidence, historians generally consider that the authors to have been William Bradford and Edward Winslow. (Dexter, xvi; Willison, 196; B. Smith, 108; Heath, x-xv) They are the only two Pilgrims who are known to have been writ-

354 Richard F. Whalen

ers. The immediacy and specificity of the narrative suggest that it was written soon after the events described, perhaps from notes in a journal. Bradford was probably the author of the Truro sections since Winslow is not listed among those who explored Truro. (Young, 126) The original manuscript text was almost certainly heavily edited and shaped by the publisher before he printed it.

In the excerpts that follow, orthography and some minor points of grammar have been modernized for easier reading. Commentary is shown in [square brackets].

[The title]

A relation or journal of the beginning and proceedings of the English Plantation settled at Plymouth in New England by certain English adventurers both merchants and others. With their difficult passage, their safe arrival, their joyful building of, and comfortable planting themselves in, the now well defended town of New Plymouth.

Printed for John Bellamie, and are to be sold at his shop at the Two Greyhounds in Cornhill near the Royal Exchange. 1622.

[Excerpt]

Wednesday, the 15th of November [1620], they [sixteen men] were set ashore [at Provincetown]; and when they had ordered themselves in the order of a single file and marched about the space of a mile by the sea, they spied five or six people with a dog coming towards them, who were savages; who, when they saw them, ran into the wood and whistled the dog after them. First they supposed them to be Master Jones, the master [of the Mayflower] and some of his men, for they were ashore and knew of their coming; but after they knew them to be Indians, they marched after them into the woods, lest other of the Indians should lie in ambush. But when the Indians saw our men following them, they ran away with might and main; and our men turned out of the wood after them, for it was [the way] they intended to go, but they could not come near them. They followed them that night about ten miles [probably five or seven] by the trace of their footings and saw how they had come the same way they went, and at a turning point perceived how they ran up a hill, to see whether they followed them. At length night came upon them and they were constrained to take up their lodging. So they set forth three sentinels, and the rest, some kindled a fire, and others fetched wood, and there held our rendezvous [camp] that night [at the north end of Pilgrim Lake].

In the morning, so soon as we could see the trace [of the Indians] we proceeded on our journey and had the track until we compassed the head of a long creek [at the upper end of East Harbor, now Pilgrim Lake]; and there they took into another wood, and we after them, supposing to find some of their dwellings. But we marched through boughs and bushes, and under hills and valleys, which tore our very armor in pieces, and yet could meet with none of them, nor their houses, nor find any fresh water, which we greatly desired and stood in need of, for we brought neither beer nor water with us, and our victuals were only biscuit and Holland cheese, and a little bottle of aquavitae, so as we were sore athirst. About ten o'clock we came into a deep valley full of brush, woodgaile [myrtle? bayberry?] and long grass, through which we found little paths or tracks, and there we saw a deer and found springs of fresh water, of which we were heartily glad, and sat us down and drunk our first New England water, with as much delight as ever we drunk drink in all our lives.

When we had refreshed ourselves, we directed our course full south that we might come to the shore, which within a short while after we did, and there made a fire that they in the ship might see where we were, as we had direction; and so marched on towards this supposed river [Pamet River]. And as we went, in another valley we found a fine, clear pond of fresh water, being about a musket shot broad and twice as long [the pond at Pond Village]. There grew also many small vines, and fowl and deer haunted [roamed] there. There grew much sassafras. From thence we went on and found much plain ground, about fifty acres, fit for the plough, and some signs where the Indians formerly planted their corn. After this, some thought it best, for nearness of the river, to go down and travel on the sea sands, by which means some of our men were tired, and lagged behind. So we stayed and gathered them up and struck into the land again [probably at Great Hollow], where we found a little path to certain heaps of sand, one whereof was covered with old mats and had a wooden thing like a mortar whelmed [upsidedown] on the top of it, and an earthen pot laid in a little hole at the end thereof. We, musing what it might be, digged and found a bow, and, as we thought, arrows, but they were rotten. We supposed there were many other things, but because we deemed them graves, we put in the bow again and made it up as it was and left the rest untouched because we thought it would be odious unto them to ransack their sepulchres.

We went further and found new stubble, of which they had gotten corn this year and many walnut trees full of nuts and a great store of strawberries and some vines. Passing thus a field or two, which were not great, we came to another, which had also been new gotten, and there we found where a house had been and four or five planks laid together. Also we found a great kettle, which had been some ship's kettle and brought out of Europe. There was also a heap of sand made like the former, but it was newly done, we might see how they had paddled it with their hands, which we digged up, and in it we found a little old basket full of fair Indian corn, and digged farther and found a fine great new basket full of very fair corn of this year with some six and thirty goodly ears of corn, some yellow and some red and others mixed with blue, which was a very goodly sight. The basket was round and narrow at the top. It held about three or four bushels, which was as much as two of us could lift up from the ground, and was very handsomely and cunningly made. But whilst we were busy about these things, we set our men sentinel in a round ring, all but two or three which digged up the corn. We were in suspense what to do with it and the kettle, and at length, after much consultation, we concluded to take the kettle and as much of the corn as we could carry away with us; and when our shallop came, if we could find any of the people and come to parley with them, we would give them the kettle again and satisfy them for their corn. So we took all the ears and put a good deal of the loose corn in the kettle for two men to bring away on a staff. Besides, they that could put any into their pockets, filled the same. The rest we buried again, for we were so laden with armor that we could carry no more.

Not far from this place we found the remainder of an old fort or palisado, which as we conceived, had been made by some Christians. This was also hard by that place which we thought had been a river, unto which we went and found it so to be, dividing itself into two arms by a high bank [Tom's Hill], standing right by the cut or mouth, which came from the sea. That which was next unto us was the less [the Little Pamet]. The other arm was more than twice as big and not unlike to be a harbor for ships, but whether it be a fresh river or only an indraught of the sea we had not time to discover, for we had a commandment to be out but two days. Here also we saw two canoes, the one on the one side, the other on the other side. We could not believe it was a canoe till we came near it. So we returned, leaving the further discovery hereof to our shallop and came that night back again to the fresh water pond [at Pond Village], and there we made our rendezvous that night, making a great fire, and barricade to windward of us, and kept good watch with three sentinels all night, every one standing when his turn came, while five or six inches of match was burning [for their guns]. It proved a very rainy night.

In the morning we took our kettle and sunk it in the pond and trimmed our muskets, for few of them would go off because of the wet, and so coasted the wood again to come home, in which we were shrewdly puzzled and lost our way. As we wandered we came to a tree where a young spritt [a sapling] was bowed down over a bow, and some acorns strewed underneath. Stephen Hopkins said it had been made to catch some deer. So as we were looking at it, William Bradford, being in the rear, when he came looked upon it, and as he went about, it gave a sudden jerk up and he was immediately caught by the leg. It was a very pretty device, made with a rope of their own making and having a noose as artificially made as any roper in England can make, and as like ours as can be, which we brought away with us. In the end we got out of the wood and were fallen about a mile too high above the creek [at the upper end of Pilgrim Lake] where we saw three bucks, but we had rather have had one of them. We also did spring up three couple partridges, and as we came along by the creek we saw great flocks of geese and ducks, but they were very fearful of us. So we marched some while in the woods, some while on the sands, and other while in the water up to the knees till at length we came near the ship, and then we shot off our pieces and the long boat came to fetch us. Master Jones and Master Carver being on the shore, with many of our people, came to meet us. And thus we came both weary and welcome home and delivered in our corn into the store to be kept for seed, for we knew not how to come by any and therefore were very glad, purposing, so soon as we could meet with any of the inhabitants of that place to make them large satisfaction. This was our first discovery . . . [The Pilgrims then returned to the Mayflower for ten days.]

When we were set forth [on their "second discovery"], it proved rough weather and cross winds; so as we were constrained, some in the shallop, and others in the long boat, to row to the nearest shore the wind would suffer them to go unto, and then to wade out above the knees. The wind was so strong as the shallop could not keep the water, but was forced to harbor there that night [East Harbor/Pilgrim Lake]. But we marched six or seven miles further [to around Great Hollow], and appointed the shallop to come to us as soon as they could. It blowed and did snow all that day and night, and froze withal. Some of our people that are dead took the original of their death here.

The next day [December 8] about eleven o'clock our shallop came to us and we shipped ourselves; and the wind being good, we sailed to the river we formerly discovered, which we named

Cold Harbor [Pamet Harbor]; to which when we came, we found it not navigable for ship; yet we thought it might be a good harbor for boats, for it flows there twelve feet at high water. We landed our men between the two creeks [on Tom's Hill] and marched some four or five miles by the greater of them, and the shallop followed us [up the Pamet River]. At length night grew on, and our men were tired with marching up and down the steep hills and deep valleys, which lay half a foot thick with snow. Master Jones, wearied with marching, was desirous we should take up our lodging, though some of us would have marched further. So we made there our rendezvous for that night under a few pine trees; and as it fell out, we got three fat geese and six ducks to our supper, which we ate with soldiers' stomachs, for we had eaten little all that day. Our resolution was next morning to go up to the head of this river, for we supposed it would prove fresh water.

But in the morning our resolution held not, because many liked not the hilliness of the soil and badness of the harbor. So we turned towards the other creek [the Little Pamet] that we might go over and look for the rest of the corn that we left behind when we were here before. When we came to the creek, we saw the canoe lie on the dry ground, and a flock of geese in the river, at which one made a shot and killed a couple of them; and when we had done, she [the canoe] carried us over by seven or eight at once. This done, we marched to the place where we had the corn formerly, which place we called Cornhill, and digged and found the rest, of which we were very glad. We also digged in a place a little further off and found a bottle of oil. We went to another place, which we had seen before, and digged and found more corn, viz. two or three baskets full of Indian wheat [i.e. corn] and a bag of beans, with a good many of fair wheat ears. Whilst some of us were digging up this, some others found another heap of corn, which they digged up also; so as we had in all about ten bushels, which will serve us sufficiently for seed. And sure it was God's good providence that we found this corn, for else we know not how we should have done; for we knew not how we should find or meet with any of the Indians, except it be to do us a mischief. Also, we had never in all likelihood seen a grain of it if we had not made our first journey; for the ground was now covered with snow and so hard frozen that we were fain with our curtlaxes and short swords to hew and carve the ground a foot deep and then wrest it up with levers, for we had forgot to bring other tools. Whilst we were in this employment, foul weather being towards, Master Jones was earnest to go abroad; but sundry of us desired to make further discovery and to find out the Indians habitations. So we sent home with him our weakest people and some that were sick and all the corn; and eighteen of us stayed still and lodged there that night, and desired that the shallop might return to us the next day and bring us some mattocks and spades with them.

The next morning we followed certain beaten paths and tracks of the Indians into the woods, supposing they would have led us into some town or houses. After we had gone a while, we light upon a very broad beaten path well nigh two feet broad. Then we lighted all our matches [for the guns] and prepared ourselves, concluding that we were near their dwellings. But in the end we found it to be only a path made to drive deer in, when the Indians hunt, as we supposed.

When we had marched five or six miles into the woods and could find no signs of any people, we returned again another way; and as we came into the plain ground we found a place like a grave, but it was much bigger and longer than any we had yet seen. It was also covered with boards, so as we mused what it should be and resolved to dig it up; where we found first a mat and under that a fair bow and then another mat and under that a board about three quarters [of a yard] long, finely carved and painted, with three tines or broaches on the top, like a crown. Also between the mats we found bowls, trays, dishes and such like trinkets. At length we came to a fair new mat and under that two bundles, the one bigger, the other less. We opened the greater and found in it a great quantity of fine and perfect red powder and in it the bones and skull of a man. The skull had fine yellow hair still on it and some of the flesh unconsumed. There was bound up with it a knife, a packneedle and two or three old iron things. It was bound up in a sailor's canvass cassock and a pair of cloth breeches. The red powder was a kind of embalment and yielded a strong but no offensive smell. We opened the less bundle likewise and found of the same power in it and the bones and head of a little child. About the legs and other parts of it was bound strings and bracelets of fine white beads. There was also by it a little bow, about three quarters [of a yard] long and some other odd knacks. We brought sundry of the prettiest things away with us and covered the corpse up again. After this we digged in sundry like places but found no more corn nor any thing else but graves.

There was a variety of opinions amongst us about the embalmed person. Some thought it was an Indian lord and king. Others said the Indians have all black hair and never any was seen with brown or yellow hair. Some thought it was a Christian of some special note, which had died amongst them, and they thus buried him to honor him. Others thought they had killed him and did it in triumph over him.

Whilst we were thus ranging and searching, two of the sailors, which were newly come on shore, by chance espied two houses, which had been lately dwelt in, but the people were gone. They, having their pieces [guns] and hearing nobody, entered the houses and took out some things and durst not stay but came again and told us. So some seven or eight of us went with them and found how we had gone within a flight shot of them before [i.e. near them recently]. The houses were made with long young sapling trees bended and both ends stuck into the ground. They were made round like unto an arbor and covered down to the ground with thick and well wrought mats; and the door was not over a yard high, made of a mat to open. The chimney was a wide open hole in the top, for which they had a mat to cover it close when they pleased. One might stand and go upright in them. In the midst of them were four little trunches [stakes] knocked into the ground and small sticks laid over on which they hung their pots and what they had to seethe [cook]. Round about the fire they lay on mats, which are their beds. The houses were double matted, for as they were matted without, so were they within, with newer and fairer mats. In the houses we found wooden bowls, trays and dishes, earthen pots, handbaskets made of crabshells wrought together; also an English pail or bucket; it wanted a bail but it had two iron ears. There was also baskets of sundry sorts, bigger and lesser, finer and some coarser. Some were curiously wrought with black and white in pretty works, and sundry other of their household stuff. We found also two or three deer's heads, one whereof had been newly killed, for it was still fresh. There was also a company of deer's feet stuck up in the houses, harts' horns and eagles' claws and sundry such like things there was; also two or three baskets full of parched acorns, pieces of fish and a piece of broiled herring. We found also a little silk grass and a little tobacco seed, with some other seeds which we knew not. Without was sundry bundles of flags [reeds] and sedge, bulrushes and other stuff to make mats. There was thrust into a hollow tree two or three pieces of venison, but we thought it fitter for the dogs than for us. Some of the best things we took away with us and left the houses standing still as they were.

So it growing towards night and the tide almost spent we hasted with our things down to the shallop and got aboard [the Mayflower] that night, intending to have brought some beads and other things to have left in the houses in sign of peace and that we meant to truck [trade] with them; but it was not done by means of [because of] our hasty coming away from Cape Cod. But so soon as we can meet conveniently with them we will give them full satisfaction. Thus much our second discovery.

APPENDIX C

Thomas Paine's 1706 Letter to the Boston Legislature

In this letter, the only surviving letter by Paine that has been found, he protests on behalf of the Pamet settlers that the General Court in Boston has imposed a condition for township status that the settlement cannot accept, namely, that they must share with Indians land held in common, which they had purchased from the Indians. Paine does not name the addressee.

Pamett: April 15, 1706

Honored

Sir, I received the copy which you sent me and have communicated the matter to the inhabitants of this place. But upon mature consideration they are not willing to have a township upon such terms as are therein proposed, for the lands which we are now possessed of here at Pamett have been by our predecessors and ourselves fairly bought of the Indians and as honestly paid for. Now if we must take these Indians in to be fellow commoners with ourselves in those lands which we have so honestly bought of them, it will be very unlikely for us to perform that article in the conditions (namely) to have forty families settled within [one word torn off, probably "three"] years; but instead thereof many of those which are already settled will be forced to pluck up stakes and be gone, and then how can any rational man think we shall be able to settle and maintain a minister. Sir, the people of this place have (considering their smallness both in number and estate) been at great charges in building a meetinghouse and procuring a minister and have gone through the same with great cheerfulness, and it hath pleased God so to bless our endeavors that we have had a hopeful young man (a son of the college) to preach the word of God unto us for above two years last past, under whose ministry we have sat with great delight, whose settlement hath been deferred for above a year only for want of power to act as a town in that matter. Sir, we have all along persuaded ourselves that the general assembly would strengthen our hands in this good work, but this unexpected disappointment hath put us to a very great nonplus. What the issue of it will be God only knoweth. But how ever, this we humbly pray that if the general court don't see cause to strengthen our weak hands, they would not make us weaker, for we had rather continue as we have hitherto been (though under difficult circumstances) than to be put into a far worse condition.

By order of the Inhabitants of Pamett
Tho. Paine, Clerk

Sir, it is the desire of the inhabitants of Pamett that thou would be pleased to inform the general court of their minds in this matter.

APPENDIX D

The Act of 1709 Creating the Town of Truro

The act giving Pamet township status as "Truroe" was passed July 16, 1709 in Boston. The original is at the Massachusetts Archives; a photocopy hangs in town hall. The act is often called the "act of incorporation," but the word incorporation does not appear in the act; and the word did not come into common use until much later. After being read three times in the House of Representatives and three times in the Council (the upper chamber), the act was signed by the speaker of the House, the secretary of the Council and Governor Joseph Dudley.

· · ·

AN ACT for Making Pawmet a District of Eastham, Within the County of Barnstable, a Township, to be Called Truroe.

WHEREAS there is a certain tract of land known by the name of Pawmet, at present a district of Eastham and under the constablerick of that town, consisting of about forty families, and daily increasing, the said land extending about fourteen miles in length from the Province Lands at the extremity of Cape Cod, reserved for the fishery, and the lands of Eastham on the south, and running, northerly, as far as the land called the purchasers' lands, extends over the harbor named the Eastern Harbor, according to the known, stated boundaries thereof; the breadth thereof running from sea to sea across the neck of land commonly called Cape Cod; and whereas the inhabitants of the said district, by their humble petition, have set forth that they have built a convenient house to meet in for the public worship of God, and have, for some time, had a minister among 'em, humbly praying that they may be made a township, and have such necessary officers within themselves whereby they may be enabled to manage and carry on their civil and religious concerns, and enjoy the like powers and privileges as other towns within this province have and do by law enjoy,

BE IT THEREFORE ENACTED by His Excellency the Governor, Council and Representatives in General Court assembled, and by the authority of the same that the tract of land called Pawmett, described and bounded as above expressed, be and hereby is erected into a township, and made a distinct and separate town, and shall be called by the name of Truroe; and that the inhabitants thereof have, use, exercise and enjoy all the powers and privileges by law granted to townships within this province.

And the constable of the said place, for the time being, is hereby empowered and required to warn the inhabitants to assemble and meet together to choose selectmen and other town officials, to manage and carry on their prudential affairs until the next anniversary time for election of town officers. And the said inhabitants are enjoined to assemble and attend the said work, accordingly;

Provided that the inhabitants of the said town do procure and settle a learned orthodox minister to dispense the Word of God to them, within the space of three years next after the passing of this act or sooner.

Provided also that they pay their proportion to the present

province tax, as it is apportioned among them, respectively, by the selectmen or assessors of Eastham.

APPENDIX E

Town Meeting Pledges to Support Boston Revolutionaries

After the wreck of the *William* with its cargo of tea, town meeting excused Truro men who bought "noxious tea" from salvagers and pledged solidarity with the Boston revolutionaries in this report to the committee of correspondence in Boston.

. . .

At a meeting of the freeholder and other inhabitants of the Town of Truro legally assemble[d] on Monday February 28th, 1774, several persons appeared in the meeting of whom it [had] been reported that they had purchased some small quantities of the East India Company baneful tea lately cast ashore at Province Town; and in examining those persons it appeared to the meeting that their buying this noxious tea was through ignorance and inadvertence, and that they were induced thereunto by the base and villainous example of artful persuasions of some noted pretended friends to Government from the neighboring towns; and therefore this meeting thinks them excusable with an acknowledgment.

Then the town made choice of Capt. Joshua Atkins, Mr. Josiah Atkins, deacon Joshua Freeman, Doctor Samuel Adams, Messrs. Ephraim Hardding, Thatcher Rich, Nehemiah Hardding, Benjamin Atkins and Hezebiah Hardding to be a committee to prepare a proper resolve to be entered into by this town respecting the introduction of tea from Great Britain subject to a duty payable in America, who agreeable to desire retired about half an hour and then reported as followeth.

We, the inhabitants of the town of Truro, although by our remote situation from the center of public news deprived of opportunities of gaining so thorough knowledge of the unhappy disputes that exist between us and parent State as we could wish, yet, as our love of liberty and dread of slavery is not inferior perhaps to that of our brethren in any part of the province, think it our indispensable duty to contribute our mite in the glorious cause of liberty and our country by declaring in this public manner our union in sentiment with our much respected brethren of Boston manifested in their patriotic resolve enclosed in the late letter of their committee of correspondence to this town and our readiness to afford in our contracted sphere our best assistance in every prudent measure in defense of, or for the recovery of, our rights and privileges, and to avoid being brought into the deplorable state of wretched slavery with which we are threatened by the unconstitutional measures, persisted in by the administration, and in particular by their late dangerous and detestable scheme of sending teas to the colonies by means of the East India Co., subject to the unrighteous American duty, a scheme, as we apprehend, designed to take in the unwary and to continue and establish the tribute so unjustly forced from us, a tribute attended with the aggravation of being applied to maintain in idleness and luxury a set of worthless policemen and pensioners and their creatures who are continually aiming at the subversion of our happy Constitution, and whose examples tend to debauch the morals of the people in our seaports which swarm with them. And as we think the most likely method that we can take to aid in frustrating these inhuman designs of the administration is a disuse of that baneful dutied article, tea, therefore resolved, that we will not by any way or means knowingly promote or encourage the sale or consumption of any tea whatever while subject to an American duty, but all persons, whoever they may be, that shall be concerned in a transaction so dangerous to the well-being of this country shall be treated by us as the meanest and basest of enemies to their country's defense; and though we have the mortification to own that some few persons among us have been weak enough to be led astray by an old rescinder from all good resolutions, yet we cannot in justice to ourselves omit making public the fact that not any person in this town could be prevailed upon to accept of the infamous employment of transporting the tea saved out of the Messrs. Clarke's brigantine from Cape Cod to the Castle [Island in Boston Harbor], but the repeated solicitations of the owners were refused notwithstanding liberal promises of a large reward and though we had several vessels here unemployed; it affords us great pleasure and satisfaction that our highly esteemed brethren of the town of Boston have made so brave a stand in defense of American liberty; and that wisdom, prudence and fortitude accompanies all their proceedings. We return them our sincere and hearty thanks for the intelligence they have from time to time afforded us and hope they will continue in their opposition to every measure tending to enslave us, and wish their manly fortitude may be increasing under the great public grievances to which by their situation they are more particularly exposed to.

[Signed] Joshua Atkins, Sam. Adams, Josiah Atkins, Ehraim Harding, Joshua Freeman, Thatcher Rich, Nehemiah Harding, Benj. Atkins, Hezebiah Harding. Committee

The foregoing after being several times read was voted . . . to be expressive of the sentiments of the town, and that it be recorded on the town book, and a fair copy attested by the town clerk be transmitted to the committee of Correspondence of the Town of Boston.

Noted that the foregoing committee be a standing committee of correspondence for this town.

A true copy attest. Daniel Paine town clerk.

ANNOTATED BIBLIOGRAPHY

Manuscripts

Avery, the Reverend John. His will (1754). Barnstable Registry of Probate.

"Book of records of the Truro Lyceum, formed on the twenty-first day of Jan. 1853." At the Truro Historical Museum.

"Constitution of the South Truro Social Aid Society" (1862). At the Truro Historical Museum.

Cooper, William, for the Boston committee of correspondence. Letter to the Plymouth committee of correspondence, 17 December 1773. At the Massachusetts Historical Society.

"First Records of the Town of Eastham." Vol. 10 (1648-1772). Copied from the original by May Wilson, 1863. At Eastham Town Hall.

Freeman, Nathaniel, et al. Letter to the committee of correspondence in Sandwich MA, 13 Dec. 1773. At the Massachusetts Historical Society.

Greenough, John. Letters to Richard Clarke Esq. & Sons. Wellfleet MA, 26 March 1774; and 2 June 1774. At the Massachusetts Historical Society.

Pamet Proprietor Records, 1689-1838. At Truro Town Hall.

Prence/Paine land transactions, 1670, 1673 and 1690. At Plymouth County Commissioners office.

Massachusetts State Archives: 30: 246 (the "Sampson Indenture") and 30:438 (Indians vs. French); 51:147; 113:388, 389, 390, 528, 529, 530, 531, 696; 117: 282, 284. Microfilm.

Paine, Thomas. His will (1720). Barnstable County Registry of Probate.

[Rich, Maria]. Letter to "cousin Walter." 15 March 1863. At the Truro Historical Museum.

Snow, Nicholas. His will (1676). Barnstable County Registry of Probate.

Truro Town Records, 1709-1869. At Truro Town Hall.

Upham, Caleb. Letters to Dr. Samuel Adams, 5 August 1775 to 10 November 1781. At the Massachusetts Historical Society.

Webster, Daniel. Letter to the selectmen of Truro. Washington: 19 November 1841.

Young, Evelyn Wakefield. Letter to B.J. Allen, 6 February 1988. At the Truro Historical Museum.

Maps

"Beach Point, Provincetown (sic) Mass., showing U.S. jetties at the close of the year 1872." U.S. Engineer Office, Portland, ME [George Thomas?], 1872. The map shows jetties on Truro's Beach Point, which borders on Provincetown Harbor. At the Cape Cod National Seashore headquarters.

"Bounds of the Province Lands of the Commonwealth of Massachusetts, as fixed and marked by the Board of Harbor and Land Commissioners." Dated November 1893.
Includes bounds with Truro.

"Cape Cod from Highland to Nausett Light . . . made during part of July, August, September, October 1848. By Samuel A. Gilbert." U.S. Coast Guard.

"Counties of Barnstable, Dukes and Nantucket, Massachusetts" surveyed under the direction of Henry F. Walling, 1858. Names residences and other buildings and includes a detail of Truro Village on the Pamet River.

"The Extremity of Cape Cod, Including the Townships of Provincetown & Truro, with a Chart of Their Sea Coast and Cape Cod Harbour." By Major J.D. Graham, U.S. Bureau of Topographical Engineers. 1833, '34, '35. The first detailed chart of Provincetown Harbor waters and shoreline.

Maps of Early Massachusetts. Compiled and edited by Lincoln A. Dexter. Wilbraham MA: N.p.,1979.

"Plan of the Town of Truro in the County of Barnstable, survey'd in 1831 by John G. Hales." The earliest map by a professional cartographer.

Provincetown, map of. Bureau of Topographic Engineers. Washington: Hood, 1836. The map shows the boundary with Truro a mile farther northwest, probably the original boundary, which was later moved to the end of East Harbor.

"Provincetown Harbor, Massachusetts, 1857 . . . by H.L. Whiting . . . topography in 1848, hydrography in 1854, '55, '56." U.S. Coast Survey. Shows the extensive, shoaling flats along the Truro shore.

Truro sketch map by Benjamin (Dyer?), dated 1795. The earliest known map of Truro. At Massachusetts Archives.

"Velasco Map" of New England, so-named because it was enclosed with a letter from Alonzo de Velasco to Philip III of Spain in 1611. Its origin is unknown. (See Quinn and Quinn.) It gives the name "Milford Haven" to Provincetown Harbor and "Whitsuns Hed" to the tip of Cape Cod. .

Newspapers

Advocate (Provincetown MA): 23 July 1873, 25 August 1875, 24 August 1978, 21 August 1997, 2 October 1997, 20 October 1997, 29 January 1998.

Barnstable Patriot: 4 December 1855 (for Marjory Daw), 8 September 1863 (for the summer season), 17 October 1865, 7 November 1865, 29 July 1873, 29 August 1898 (for golf links), 14 September 1903, 30 August 1906, 24 March 1919, 6 September 1920 (for the pageant), 22 January 1942.

Boston Evening Transcript, 26 November 1935. Reprint, *The Cape Codder.* 29 March 1996.

Boston Weekly News-Letter. No. 1513, 25 January 1733. For Captain Henry Atkins voyages.

Cape Cod Times: 11 December 1991, 24 December, 1991, 13 December 1992.

Cape Codder: 10 February 1978, 1 November 1991, 8 November 1991, 15 December 1992, 9 March 1993, 9 November 1993, 22 August 1997, 22 September 1998.

Harvard University Gazette. 18 January 1996.

New York Sun: 30 September 1939

New York Times: 20 December 1994, 8 September 1997, 18 November 1997, 9 January 1998, 27 January 1998, 17 March 1998, 17 October 1999.

Provincetown Banner: 5 October 1995, 1 February 1996, April 3, 1997, 22 May 1997, 12 February 1998, 2 December 1999.

Yarmouth Register: 9 December 1841, 10 February 1842, 16 June 1854, 14 December 1855, 8 December 1893.

Zion's Herald and Wesleyan Journal. N.d. Reprint (n.d., n.p.). Letters by Lozien Peirce dated 21 and 28 September 1844, 15 October 1844.

Books and Articles

"Account of the Coast of Labrador." In *Collections of the Massachusetts Historical Society.* Vol. 1 first series (1792). For the voyage of Captain Henry Atkins.

Agaki, Roy H. *The Town Proprietors of the New England Colonies.* Philadelphia:
University of Pennsylvania Press,1924. Reprint. Gloucester MA, Peter Smith, 1963. Essential for an understanding of proprietorships.

All About Truro. League of Women Voters. N.d.

Applebaum, Stephen J. and Benno M. Brenninkmeyer. *Physical and Chemical Limnology of Pilgrim Lake, Cape Cod, Massachusetts: Final Report to the U.S. Department of Interior, National Park Service.* Chestnut Hill MA: Boston College, 1988.

Atkins, Captain Henry. Narratives of his whaling voyages. See Bernard, Francis.

Atlas of Barnstable County. Boston: Walker, 1907(?). Inset shows Beach Point in detail.

Avery, Samuel P. *The Avery, Fairchild and Park Families.* Hartford: 1919.

Baker, Florence W. *Yesterday's Tide.* South Yarmouth MA, 1941.

Barber, John Warner. *Historical Collections, Being a General Collection of Interesting Facts, Traditions, Biographical Sketches, Anecdotes, etc., Relating to the History and Antiquities of Every Town in Massachusetts, with Geographical Descriptions.* Worcester: Warren Lazell, 1839 and 1844.

Belknap, Jeremy. *American Biography.* Boston: Thomas and Andrews, 1794 and 1798. For Martin Pring's voyage.

Benson, Thomas Avery. *The Ancestral Lines of Herbert Spaulding Avery 1883-1968.* Bountiful UT: Family History Publishers, 1992.

Berger, Josef. See Digges, Jeremiah.

Berlin, Ira. *Many Thousands Gone: The First Two Centuries of Sla-*

very in North America. Cambridge MA: Harvard University Press, 1998.

Bernard, Francis. "Account of the Coast of Labrador." In *Massachusetts Historical Society Collections*, 1st series, vol. 1, 1792. A report of voyages by Captain Henry Atkins, found in the papers of Bernard, governor of the Province of Massachusetts Bay.

Beston, Henry. *The Outermost House: A Year of Life on the Great Beach of Cape Cod*. New York: Rinehart & Co., 1928.

Bird, Francis W. *Look Before You Leap into Another Great Bore*. Boston: Wright and Potter, State Printers: 1868. On his opposition to the dike at East Harbor.

Bonner, Nigel. *Whales of the World*. New York: Facts on File, 1989.

Bradford, William. *Of Plymouth Plantation, 1620-1647*. Boston: the General Court, 1898. Reprint with introduction by Francis Murphy, New York: Random House, 1981. A classic of colonial American history, it retells briefly the Pilgrims' exploration of Truro.

[Bradford, William, and Edward Winslow]. *A Relation or Journal of the Beginning and Proceedings of the English Plantation settled at Plymouth in New England. . . .* London: John Bellamie, 1622. No author's name is given. The narrative was later given the shorter, if misleading, title *Mourt's Relation*. Most historians conclude that Bradford and Winslow were the authors, with Bradford alone writing the section about Truro. See appendix B for details and excerpts. Miles Standish is better known than Bradford mainly because of Longfellow's fanciful, very popular and somewhat inaccurate poem, "The Courtship of Miles Standish" (1858).

Bradley, James W., Survey Director, et al. *Historic and Archaeological Resources of Cape Cod and the Islands*. Boston: Massachusetts Historical Commission, 1987.

Bradley, James W., Thomas F. Mahlstedt and Michael Gibbons. "European Contact and the Continuity of Mortuary Ceremonialism on Cape Cod: An Update from the Corn Hill Site, Truro, MA." *Archaeology of Eastern North America*, vol. 26 (1998).

Brigham, Albert Perry. *Cape Cod and the Old Colony*. New York:Grosset & Dunlop, 1920.

Brightman, Carol. *Writing Dangerously: Mary McCarthy and Her World*. New York: Clarkson N. Potter, 1992. .

Brown, Alexander Crosby. *Women and Children Last: The Loss of the Steamship Arctic*. New York: G.P. Putnam's Sons, 1961. For Captain John Collins of Truro.

Buderi, Robert. *The Invention that Changed the World*. New York: Simon and Schuster, 1996. With comments about Truro's radar installations.

Burke, Edmund. *Speeches on the American War*. Introduction and notes by A. J. George.
Boston: D.C. Heath & Co., 1898. Gives his comments about the range of Truro whalers.

Burling, Francis P. *The Birth of the Cape Cod National Seashore*. Plymouth MA: Leyden Press, 1977.

Calvin, William H. "The Great Climate Flip-Flop." *Atlantic Monthly*, January 1998.

Cape Cod Commission. *Outer Cape Capacity Study*, prepared in cooperation with
Whiteman and Taintor, planning consultants. [Barnstable MA]: 1996.

—. *Cape Trends: Demographic and Economic Characteristics and Trends, Barnstable County, Cape Cod*. Barnstable MA: 1998. Partially updated to 2000 on www.capecod commission.org

Carr, Virginia Spencer. *Dos Passos: A Life*. Garden City NY: Doubleday & Company, 1984.

Carter, Jane G. (Avery) and Susie P. Holmes. *Genealogical Record of the Dedham Branch of the Avery Family in America*. Plymouth MA: Winslow W. Avery, 1893. Despite its title, much of the book is on the Truro branch.

Chamberlain, Barbara Blau. *These Fragile Outposts: a Geologic Look at Cape Cod, Marthas Vineyard and Nantucket*. Yarmouth Port, MA: Parnassus Imprints, 1981.

Chesler, Ellen. *Woman of Valor: Margaret Sanger and the Birth Control Movement in America*. New York: Simon & Schuster, 1992.

Clark, Admont G. *Lighthouses of Cape Cod, Martha's Vineyard, Nantucket: Their History and Lore*. East Orleans MA: Parnassus, 1992. Valuable for his research on Pamet Harbor Light.

Coggins, Jack. *Ships and Seamen of the American Revolution*. Harrisburg PA: Stackpole, 1969.

Corbino, Marcia. *Helen Sawyer: Memories of a Morning Star*. Sarasota FL: Corbino Galleries, 1995.

Crosby, Katharine. *Blue-Water Men and Other Cape Codders*. New York: The Macmillan Company, 1947.

Dalton, J.W. *The Life-Savers of Cape Cod*. Sandwich MA, 1902. Reprint. Parnassus Imprints, Orleans MA, 1991.

Damon, the Reverend Jude. *Deaths in Truro, Cape Cod, 1786-1826*. Transcribed from his diary by John Harvey Treat. Salem MA Press, 1891. Damon was minister of the Truro church.

Damore, Leo. *In His Garden: The Anatomy of a Murder*. New York: Dell, 1981. An account of the murder of four young women whose bodies were found in Truro.

Davis, William Morris. "The Outline of Cape Cod." In *The Proceedings of the American Academy of Arts and Sciences* 31 (1896).

Davis, William T. *History of the Town of Plymouth*. Philadelphia: J .W. Lewis & Co., 1885. For Captain Martin Pring's voyage and disputed anchorage.

Dean, Cornelia. *Against the Tide: The Battle for America's Beaches*. New York: Columbia University Press, 1999.

De Champlain, Samuel. *Voyages of Samuel de Champlain 1604-1618*. Edited by W.L. Grant. New York: Barnes & Noble, 1907.

De Costa, Benjamin Franklin. "Gosnold and Pring, 1602-1603." In *The New-England Historical and Genealogical Register* 32 (1878).

____ . "Plymouth Before the Pilgrims." In *The Magazine of American History*. (December 1882.)

Dermer, Capt. Thomas. Letter to Samuel Purchas, 27 December 1619. Transcribed in *Sailors Narratives*. Edited by George Parker Winship. New York: Burt Franklin, 1905. On the wreck of a French ship on the Outer Cape.

Dewey, David R. "Economic and Commercial Conditions." In *The Commonwealth History of Massachusetts*, edited by Albert Bushnell Hart. Vol. 3 chap.12. New York: States History, 1929.

Dexter, Henry Martyn, ed. *Mourt's Relation or Journal of the Plantation at Plymouth*. Boston: Wiggin, 1865. A "literal reprint" with notes and commentary by Dexter.

Dexter, Lincoln, ed. *The Gosnold Discoveries in the North Part of Virginia, 1602, now Cape Cod and the Islands, Massachusetts: According to the Relations by Gabriel Archer and John Brereton, Arranged in Parallel for Convenient Comparison*. Sturbridge MA: 1982.

Deyo, Simeon L., ed. *History of Barnstable County, Massachusetts: 1620-1890*. New York: H.W. Blake & Co., 1890. Fourteen of the twenty-eight chapters are signed by "special contributors," but the chapter on Truro is one of those that is not. See the chapter on Provincetown for the East Harbor bridge and dike.

Dictionary of American Biography. For the Reverend James Freeman and Benjamin F. De Costa.

Dictionary of Surnames. Edited by Patrick Hanks and Flavia Hodges. New York: Oxford University Press, 1988. The entry reads: "Dangerfield: English (Norman): Habitation name, with fused preposition 'de,' from any of the various places in Normandy called Angerville, from the ON personal name Asgeirr (from as god + geirr speare) + OF ville, settlement, village. The English surname is now found chiefly in the W. Midlands."

Digges, Jeremiah [Josef Berger].) *Cape Cod Pilot*. New York: Viking Press, 1937. Reprint. MIT Press, 1969.

Driver, Clive. "John Reed and Louise Bryant." In the *Provincetown Advocate*, 21 September 1995.

Dudley, Paul. "An Essay on the Natural History of Whales, with a Particular Account of the Ambergris Found in the Sperma Ceti Whale." (1725) In *The Philosophical Transactions of the Royal Society of London* 7. London: C. and R. Baldwin, 1809. Captain Henry Atkins of Truro contributed to the paper.

Dudley, William S., ed. *The Naval War of 1812: A Documentary History*. Vol. 2. Washington DC: Department of the Navy, 1992.

Duganne, Phyllis. *The South Truro Meeting House*. Truro Neighborhood Association, 1938.

Dunford, Fred, and Greg O'Brien. *Secrets in the Sand: The Archaeology of Cape Cod*. Hyannis MA: Parnassus Imprints, 1997.

Dwight, Timothy. *Travels in New England and New York*. Vol. 3. New Haven: Timothy Dwight, 1822. Reprint with notes by Barbara Miller Solomon. Cambridge MA: Harvard University Press, 1969.

Dyer, John B. "Truro on Cape Cod: An Historical Address." In *Report of the Officers of the Town of Truro for the Year Ending Dec. 31, 1909*.

Dyer, John R., Jr. "The History of the Congregational meetinghouse in Truro." In the church program. N.d.

Echeverria, Durand. *A History of Billingsgate*. Wellfleet MA: The Wellfleet Historical Society, 1991. A history of Wellfleet to 1775. The town was know as Billingsgate for most of that time.

Edinberg, Joyce. "A Short History of the Truro Neighborhood Association." Truro MA: Truro Neighborhood Association, n.d (c. 1995).

Egan, Leona Rust. *Provincetown As a Stage*. Orleans MA: Parnassus Imprints, 1994.

Farnsworth, Jerry. *Portrait and Figure Painting*. New York: Watson-Guptill Publications, 1963.

Farson, Robert H. *Cape Cod Railroads*. Yarmouth Port MA: Cape Cod Historical Publications, 1990.

Fawsett, Marise. *Cape Cod Annals*. Bowie MD: Heritage, 1990. Essays on salt-marsh haying, Cape Cod fisheries and the wreck of the *Portland*.

Federal Writers' Project of the Works Progress Administration (WPA). Massachusetts: A Guide to Its Places and People. Boston: Houghton-Mifflin, 1937. Known as the "WPA Guide."

Felt, Joseph B. *Annals of Salem*. Vol. 2. Boston: 1849.

Ferris, George. "25th Annual Seascape, Cape Cod, Halloween Fly-In." In *Hang Gliding*, October 1999.

Finch, Robert. *A Place Apart: A Cape Cod Reader*. New York: W.W. Norton & Company, 1993.

Fish, John Perry. *Unfinished Voyages, a Chronology of Shipwrecks:*

Maritime Disasters in the Northeast United States from 1606 to 1956. Orleans MA: Lower Cape Publishing, 1989.

Forbes, R.B. "To the Naval and Military Committees." A broadside dated Barnstable Bay, 8 July 1861.Quoted in Henry C. Kittredge, *Cape Cod.*

Foster, Charles H.W. *The Cape Cod National Seashore: A Landmark Alliance.* Hanover NH and London: University Press of New England, 1985.

Franklin, John H., and Alfred A. Moss, Jr. *From Slavery to Freedom.* New York: Alfred A. Knopf, 1994.

Freeman, Eben. See Nye, Everett.

Freeman, Frederick. *The History of Cape Cod: the Annals of Barnstable County and of its Several Towns, including the district of Mashpee.* Boston, printed for the author, 1858 and 1862. Reprint. Yarmouth Port MA: Parnassus Imprints, 1965. He was the first historian to delve extensively into town records.

[Freeman, the Reverend James.] "A Description of Cape Cod." In *Massachusetts Magazine*, February/March, 1791. No author's name is given, but Freeman refers the reader to the article in his edition of *Mourt's Relation.*

___. *A Description of the Eastern Coast of the County of Barnstable from Cape Cod, or Race Point in Latitude 42^ 5' to Cape Malabarre of the Sandy Point of Chatham in Latitude 41^ 33' Pointing Out the Spots, on Which the Trustees of the Human Society Have Erected Huts, and Other Places Where Shipwrecked Seaman May Look for Shelter.* Boston: n.p. 1802. The author is given as "a member of the Humane Society." Underneath that on at least one copy someone has long ago written "James Freeman D.D."

—. Ed. "Mourt's Relation," in *Collections of the Massachusetts Historical Society* Vol. 8 series one. Boston (1802). No editor's name is given, but a long, introductory footnote identifies the editor as "r.s." and Freeman was recording secretary of the society. See also *Proceedings of the MHS*. Freeman's notes include observations about Truro in the late 1700s.

—. "A Topographical Description of Truro, in the County of Barnstable, 1794." In *Collections of the Massachusetts Historical Society*. Vol. 3, series one. Boston: (N.d.) Reprint. New York: Johnson Reprint Corporation, n.d. F.W.P. Greenwood identifies Freeman as the author of accounts of towns on Cape Cod.

Fulcher, L. Richard. "Stone Bowls on Cape Cod." In *The Bulletin of the Massachusetts Archaeological Society,* nos. 1 and 2, 1974.

Gelb, Arthur and Barbara. *O'Neill.* New York: Harper & Brothers, 1960.

Gelderman, Carol W. *Mary McCarthy: A Life.* New York: St. Martin's Press, 1988.

George, Diana Hume, and Malcolm A. Nelson. *Epitaph and Icon: A Field Guide to the Old Burying Grounds of Cape Cod, Martha's Vineyard and Nantucket.* Orleans MA: Parnassus Imprints, 1983.

Gibson, Marjorie Hubbell. *H.M.S. Somerset, 1746-1778: The Life and Times of an Eighteenth Century British Man-o-War and Her Impact on North America.* Cotuit MA: Abbey Gate House, 1992. The life history of the ship, a detailed account of the wreck, the salvage work, the fate of the survivors and several legends shown to be untrue.

Giese, Graham S. and Rachel B Giese. *The Eroding Shores of Outer Cape Cod*. Orleans MA: The Association for the Preservation of Cape Cod, 1974.

Giese, Graham S. et al. *Passive Retreat of Massachusetts Coastal Upland Due to Relative Sea-Level Rise*. Woods Hole (MA) Oceanographic Institution, 1987(?).

Glaspell, Susan. *The Road to the Temple*. New York: Frederick A. Stokes Company, 1927.

Gookin, Daniel. *Historical Collections of the Indians in New England*. Boston: Belknap and Hall, 1792. His reports were completed in 1674, per the *Dictionary of National Biography*.

Gookin, Warner F. "The Pilgrims as Archeologists." In *The Bulletin of the Massachusetts Archaeological Society* 11 (1950).

Gookin, Warner F. and Barbour, Philip L. *Bartholomew Gosnold*. Hamden CT, 1963. See also article by Quinn and Gookin.

Gosnold, Bartholomew. See Dexter, Lincoln A..

Graham, James D. *A Report Upon the Military and Hydrographical Chart of the Extremity of Cape Cod, Including the Townships of Provincetown and Truro, with Their Seacoast and Ship Harbour: Projected from Surveys Executed During Portions of the Years 1833, 1834 and 1835, Under the Direction of James D. Graham, Major, U.S. Corps of Topographical Engineers*. Washington: 1838. See also "The Extremity of Cape Cod" in Selected Maps, and U.S. House Committee on Commerce: *Harbors on the Sea and Lake Coasts*.

The Great Truro Mayflower Pilgrim Pageant at North Truro, August

25, 1920. N.p., n.d.

Greene, Lorenzo Johnston. *The Negro in Colonial New England, 1620-1776.* Port Washington, NY: Kennikat, 1942 and 1966.

Greenfeld, Howard. *Ben Shahn: An Artist's Life.* New York: Random House, 1998.

Greenwood, F.W.P. "Memoir of the Rev. James Freeman, D.D." In *Collections of the Massachusetts Historical Society.* Vol. 5 third series. Boston, 1836.

—. *A Sermon Preached in King's Chapel, November 22, 1835, the Sunday After the Funeral of the Rev. James Freeman, D.D.* Boston: Russell, Shattuck and Williams, 1835.

Grozier, E.A., *The Wreck of the "Somerset."* Provincetown: Advocate Press,1894. Reprint.*The New York World*, 16 May 1886. Marjorie Hubbell Gibson notes errors.

Hambourg, Maria Morris, et al. *Walker Evans.* New York: The Metropolitan Museum of Art in association with Princeton University Press, 2000.

Hannah, Samuel D. *The Proprietary Lands of Plymouth Colony and Cape Cod.* Hyannis MA: Patriot Press, 1980. Hannah (1867-1945), an advertising executive and then a real estate developer of New York and later Cape Cod, researched the legal history of proprietorships on Cape Cod. His papers, mostly about the Pamet Proprietors, were collected by his daughter, Julia M. Curtin, for publication. Hannah caused considerable controversy in the 1920s when he tried but failed to get the courts to recognize that some Cape Cod land, principally marshes, dunes and remote woodlands, was still owned by the long-dormant proprietary companies. Regarding the Pamet

Proprietors and their successors Hannah maintained that it was "very clear that this Propriety has never ceased to exist, although under different titles . . . what became of it? . . . who owns it and where is it?"

Harding, Walter. *The Days of Henry Thoreau.* New York: Alfred A. Knopf, 1965.

Hart, Albert Bushnell, ed. *Commonwealth History of Massachusetts.* Vol 3. New York: States History Company, 1929.

Hatch, Mellon C.M. *The Log of Provincetown and Truro on Cape Cod.* Boston: Fidelity Press, 1939.

Hawke, David Freeman. *Everyday Life in Early America.* NewYork: Harper & Row, 1988.

Hayward, John. *The New England Gazetteer Containing Descriptions of All the States, Counties and Towns in New England: Also Descriptions of the Principal Mountains, Rivers, Lakes, Capes, Bays, Harbors, Islands, and Fashionable Resorts Within that Territory.* Boston: Hayward, 1841; Parker, Elliot & Company, 1856.

Heath, Dwight B., ed. *Mourt's Relation: A Journal of the Pilgrims at Plymouth.* Bedford MA: Applewood Books, 1963.

Henderson, Helen. *Loiterer in New England.* New York: Doran,1919.

Hesse, Emily S. "The Private Domain of S. Osborne Ball." In *Yankee,* July 1966.

Higginson, Francis. *New Englands Plantation.* London: Michael Sparke, 1630.

Historic Cultural Land Use Study of Lower Cape Cod: A Study of the Historical Archaeology and History of the Cape Cod National Seashore and the Surrounding Region. Richard D. Holmes et al. A project of the University of Massachusetts Archaeological Services and the National Park Service. N.p., n.d. (Circa 1995) "The History of the Christian Union church of North Truro" in the church program, by "FWG," c. 1980s.

Hitchcock, Edward. *Report on the Geology, Mineralogy, Botany, and Zoology of Massachusetts.* Amherst MA: J.S. and C. Adams, 1833.

Hogan, Julia Rich. *Richard Rich of Piscataqua and Eastham: The Descendants of His Son, Richard Rich.* N.p, n.d. (Typescript)

Hopkins, Budd. *Missing Time: A Documented Study of UFO Abductions.* New York: Richard Marek Publishers, 1981.

Holmes, Richard D. See *Historic Cultural Land Use Study.*

Hornig, Dana, ed. *State of the Cape, 1994.* Orleans MA: Association for the Preservation of Cape Cod, 1993.

Howe, Henry F. *Prologue to New England.* Port Washington NY: Kennikat Press, 1969.

Huden, John C. *Indian Place Names of New England.* New York: Museum of the American Indian, 1962.

Hutchinson, Thomas (1711-1780). *The History of the Colony and Province of Massachusetts-Bay.* Cambridge MA: Harvard University Press, 1936.

Judith Shahn: Nineteen Forty Four—Nineteen Ninety Six:

Provincetown MA: Provincetown Art Association and Museum, 1996.

Kahn, E.J., Jr. *About the New Yorker and Me.* New York: G.P. Putnam Sons, 1979.

—. *A Reporter Here and There.* New York: Random House, 1961.

__. *Year of Change: More About The New Yorker and Me.* New York: Viking, 1988.

—. "Our Far-Flung Correspondents: An Irreplaceable Treasure." In *The New Yorker*, 19 September 1959.

—. "Stalking the Cape Cod Cougar." In *Boston Magazine*, July 1982.

Kammen, Michael. *The Lively Arts: Gilbert Seldes and the Transformation of Cultural Criticism in the United States.* New York: Oxford University Press, 1996.

Kane, Tom. *My Pamet: Cape Cod Chronicle.* Mount Kisco NY: Moyer Bell Limited, 1989. Life in Truro from the 1950s through the 1980s in selections from his newspaper columns.

Kendall, Edward Augustus. *Travels Through the Northern Parts of the United States in the Years 1807 and 1808.* New York: Riley, 1809.

King, H. Roger. *Cape Cod and Plymouth Colony in the Seventeenth Century.* New York: University Press of America, 1994.

Kittredge, Henry C. *Cape Cod: Its People and Their History.* Boston: Houghton Mifflin Company, 1930. Reprint with a post-epilogue by John Hay. Orleans MA: Parnassus Imprints, 1968. A few references to Truro, some quite significant, are scattered throughout. He relies mainly on Shebnah Rich.

—. *Mooncussers of Cape Cod*. Boston: Houghton Mifflin Company, 1937.

—. *Shipmasters of Cape Cod*. Boston: Houghton Mifflin Company, 1935.

Knowles, Joshua. See Rich for the October Gale of 1841.

Labaree, Benjamin Woods. *The Boston Tea Party*. New York: Oxford University Press, 1964.

Leatherman, Stephen P. *Cape Cod Field Trips: From Yesterday's Glaciers to Today's Beaches*. College Park MD: University of Maryland, 1988.

—.Ed. *Environmental Geologic Guide to Cape Cod National Seashore*. Amherst MA: University of Massachusetts, 1979.

Leatherman, Stephen P., Graham Giese and Patty O'Donnell. *Historical Cliff Erosion of the Outer Cape*. National Park Service, 1981.

Levin, Gail. *Edward Hopper: An Intimate Biography*. New York: Alfred A. Knopf, 1995.

Lombard, Asa Cobb Paine. *East of Cape Cod*. New Bedford MA: Reynolds-DeWalt Printing, 1976.

Loparto, Leonard W. "An Intensive Archaeological Survey of Parcel 96 on Corn Hill, Truro, Massachusetts." N.p., n.d (Typescript, c.1990s)

Lowenthal, Larry et al. *Highland Lighthouse and Keeper's Dwelling: Historic Structure Report.* Lowell MA: National Park Service, 1994. Lowenthal was the historian for the report. Lowenthal, historian of the National Park Service's North Atlantic Region, provides for the first time documented details about the second lighthouse.

Lowenthal, Larry and Regina Binder. *Highland House: Historic Structure Report.* Wellfleet MA: Cape Cod National Seashore, 1994.

Ludington, Townsend. *John Dos Passos: A Twentieth Century Odyssey.* New York: E.P. Dutton, 1980.

Macy, Obed. *The History of Nantucket, Being a Compendius Account of the First Settlement of the Island by the English, Together with the Rise and Progress of the Whale Fishery; and Other Historical Facts Relative to Said Island and its Inhabitants.* 2nd ed. Mansfield MA: Macy & Pratt, 1880.

Manning, Robert E. *Cape Cod National Seashore Visitor and Resident Study.* Boston: National Park Service, 1994. An opinion survey conducted by the University of Vermont.

Manso, Peter. *Mailer: His Life and Times.* New York: Simon and Schuster, 1985.

Mariani, Paul. *Dream Song: The Life of John Berryman.* New York: William Morrow and Company, 1990.

Marshall, Anthony L. *Truro, Cape Cod, As I Knew It.* Truro Historical Society, 1974.

Marvin, Winthrop L. *The American Merchant Marine: Its History and Romance from 1620 to 1902.* New York: Charles Scribner's Sons, 1919.

Massachusetts Bureau of Statistics of Labor. *Twenty-seventh Annual Report.* Boston: Wright and Potter, 1897. Includes a description of Truro in the 1890s and the Western Islanders. .

Massachusetts Department of Labor and Resources. *Population and Resources of Cape Cod.* Boston: Wright & Potter, 1922.

Massachusetts. "Historical Data Relating to Counties, Cities and Towns in Massachusetts." Prepared by Paul Guzzi. Boston:1975.

Massachusetts Historical Society. *Proceedings.* Boston: By the Society, 1879-1998.

Massachusetts, Acts and Resolves of. Boston: 1780-Present.

Massachusetts Bay, Acts and Resolves of. 21 vols. Boston: 1692-1780.

Massachusetts House Journals SCI/532. Boston 1722-1996.

Massachusetts Senate Unpassed Legislation (SCI231). Boston: 1783-1993.

McManamon, Francis P., and Christopher L. Borstel. *The Archaeology of the Cape Cod Seashore.* Washington: The National Park Service, 1982, rev. 1984.

Mellow, James R. *Walker Evans.* New York: Basic Books: 1999.

Meyers, Jeffrey. *Edmund Wilson: A Biography.* Boston: Houghton Mifflin Company, 1995.

Millay, Edna St. Vincent. *Collected Poems.* Edited by Norma Millay. New York: Harper & Row, 1956.

Mills, Hilary. *Mailer: A Biography*. New York: Empire Books, 1982.

MITRE Corporation. *MITRE, the First Twenty Years*. Bedford MA:1979.

Moffett, Ross. "The Hillside Site in Truro, Massachusetts." In *The Bulletin of the Massachusetts Archaeological Society* 11 (November 1949).

—. "Two Indian Sites Near Cornhill, Cape Cod." In the *Bulletin of the Massachusetts Archaeological Society* 4 (1953).

—. "A Review of Cape Cod Archeology." In *The Bulletin of the Massachusetts Archaeological Society* 19 (October 1957).

—. "An Unusual Indian Harpoon from Truro." In *The Bulletin of the Massachusetts Archaeological Society* 30 (1969).

Morison, Samuel Eliot. *The Maritime History of Massachusetts, 1783-1860*. Boston: Houghton Mifflin Company, 1921.

—. *The Oxford History of the American People*. New York: Penguin Books, 1994.

Mourt's Relation. See [Bradford, William and Edward Winslow]

Nason, the Reverend Elias. *A Gazetteer of the State of Massachusetts*. Boston: B.B. Russell, 1874.

Nathan, Robert. *Journal for Josephine*. New York: Alfred A. Knopf, 1943.

Naval Documents of the American Revolution, edited by William

James Morgan. 10 vols. Washington: Naval Historical Center, 1964-96. See vols 3, 4, 5, and 9.

New Plymouth in New England, Records of the Colony of. Vols 1-8 edited by Nathaniel B. Shurtleff, vols 9-12 by David Pulsifer. Boston: White, 1855-61. See 1650 *224 and *244 for Prence fishing rights, 1671 *47 for the Pamet Indian treaty.

Nickerson, W. Sears. *Land Ho!1620.* Edited by Delores Bird Carpenter. East Lansing MI: Michigan State University Press, 1997.

Noe, Marcia. *Susan Glaspell: Voice from the Heartland.* Macomb IL: Western Illinois University, 1983.

Noyes, Nicholas. *New-Englands Duty and Interest.* Boston: Massachusetts Bay Colony, 1698.

Nye, Everett I. *History of Wellfleet: From Earliest Days to Present Time.* N.p., 1920.

O'Brien, Greg, ed. *A Guide to Nature on Cape Cod and the Islands.* New York: Penguin Books, 1990. Revised edition. Hyannis, MA: Parnassus Imprints, 1990.

Oldale, Robert N. *Cape Cod and the Islands: the Geologic Story.* East Orleans: Parnassus Imprints, 1992.

—. "Giveth and Taketh Away: Coastal Erosion on Cape Cod." In *The Cape Naturalist* 23 (1995-6).

Paine, Josiah. "Extracts from the Diary of Moses Paine, of Truro, Mass." In *The New-England Historical and Genealogical Register* 44 (1900).

—.*Library of Cape Cod History and Genealogy.* Yarmouthport MA: C.W. Swift, 1916. Reprinted as *Cape Cod Library of Local His-*

tory and Genealogy: A Facsimile Edition of 108 Pamphlets Published in the Early 20th Century. Baltimore: Genealogical Publishing Co., 1992. For a short biography of Thomas Prence, sometimes spelled Prince.

—. *A History of Harwich.* Yarmouthport MA: Parnassus Imprints, 1971 reprint of 1937 edition.

Payne, H. Morse. *Payne/Paine Family.* Yarmouth Port MA: Historical Society of Old Yarmouth, 1978.

Peirce, Lozien. See *Zion's Herald.*

Perley, Sidney. *Historic Storms of New England.* Salem MA: Salem Press Publishing, 1891.

Perry, E.G. *A Trip Around Cape Cod.* 3d ed. Boston and Monument Beach MA: N.p., 1898.

Phillips, E.E. *Pilgrim Heights.* N.p., n.d. (c. 1911) A promotional brochure; at the Truro Historical Museum.

Plimoth Plantation. "Irreconcilable Differences," an exhibition on the interaction of colonists with the Indians. 1995.

Plymouth Colony Records. See New Plymouth.

Portnoy, John W. *Pilgrim Lake Management and Nuisance Midge Outbreaks: Review and Update, 4 April 1991.* Cape Cod National Seashore.

Pratt, the Reverend Enoch. *A Comprehensive History, Ecclesiastical and Civil, of Eastham, Wellfleet and Orleans, County of Barnstable, Mass. from 1644 to 1844.* Yarmouth MA: Fisher, 1844.

Pring, James H., M.D. *Captaine Martin Pringe, the Last of the Eliza-bethan Seamen.* London: Simpkin Marshall, 1888. See also the entry for Martin Pring in the *Dictionary of National Biography.*

Pring(e), Martin. "A Voyage Set Out from the Citie of Bristoll at the Charge of the Chiefest Merchants and Inhabitants of the Said Citie with a Small Ship and a Barke for the Discouerie of the North Part of Virginia in the year 1603. Under the Command of Me Martin Pringe." In *Purchas His Pilgrims.* Vol. 4. London: Stansby/Fetherstone, 1625. See Quinn and Quinn for an annotated edition.

Proceedings of the Massachusetts Historical Society 1 (1795-1835). Boston: 1879.

Provincetown Arts, an annual. 1987-1999.

Quarles, Hillary. *Cultural Landscape Inventory, Summary Report, North Truro Air Force Station.* Cape Cod National Seashore: 1995.

—.*Cultural Landscape Inventory, Summary Report, Pamet Cranberry Bog. A report for the Cape Cod National Seashore, 1995.*

Quinn, David B. *England and the Discovery of America.* New York: Knopf, 1974.

Quinn, David B. and Alison M. Quinn, eds. *The English New England Voyages 1602-1608.* London: The Hakluyt Society,1983. Includes an annotated edition of Pring's narrative with and introduction and extensive notes and commentary.

Quinn, David B., ed. with Allison M. Quinn and Susan Hillier.

North America, from Earliest Discoveries to First Settlements, vol. 3. New York: New American World, 1979.

Quinn, David B., and Warner F. Gookin. "Martin Pring at Provincetown in 1603?" In *The New England Quarterly* 40 (1967)..

Quinn, William P. *Shipwrecks Around Cape Cod*. Orleans MA: Lower Cape Publishing, 1973.

—. *The Saltworks of Historic Cape Cod*. Orleans MA: Parnassus Imprints, 1993.

—. *Cape Cod Maritime Disasters*. Orleans MA: Lower Cape Publishing, 1990.

Rathbone, Belinda. *Walker Evans: A Biography.* Boston: Houghton Mifflin Company, 1995.

Redfield, A.C. and K.O. Emery. *Report on a Survey of Pilgrim Lake, made for the scientific advisory committee of the Cape Cod National Seashore. August 16, 1969.* (Typescript).

Resident and Business Directory of Cape Cod. South Framingham MA: N.p. 1901.

Rich, Evelyn. "Richard Rich of Eastham on Cape Cod and Some of His Descendants." In *The New England Historical and Genealogical Register*. Boston: 1930. She was a daughter of Shebnah Rich.

Rich, Shebnah. *The Mackerel Fishery of North America: Its Perils and Its Rescue*. Boston: Massachusetts Fish and Game Association of Boston, 1879.

—. *Truro–Cape Cod or Land Marks and Sea Marks.* Boston: D. Lothrop & Company, 1883. Reprint, Rutland VT: Charles E. Tuttle Company, 1988.

Richardson, Robert D., Jr. *Henry Thoreau: A Life of the Mind.* Berkeley CA: University of California Press, 1986.

Robbins, Maurice. "A Brass Kettle Recovery at Corn Hill Cape Cod." In *The Bulletin of the Massachusetts Archaeological Society,* 3 and 4 (1968).

Robinson, Mark H., Project Manager. *Pamet River Greenway Management Plan.* North Truro MA: Truro Conservation Trust, 1987.

Rogers, Fred B. "The Lankenau Hospital Research Institute Marine Experimental Station on Cape Cod." In *Transactions & Studies of the College of Physicians and Surgeons of Philadelphia.* April 1975.

Ruckstuhl, Irma. *Old Provincetown in Early Photographs.* New York: Dover Publications, 1987. Includes many photographs of Truro by Louis Snow from around 1900.

Russell, Howard S. *Indian New England Before the Mayflower.* Hanover NH: University Press of New England,1980.

Salisbury, Neal. *Manitou and Providence: Indians, Europeans and the Making of New England 1500-1643.* New York: Oxford University Press, 1982.

Salwen, Bert. "Indians of Southern New England and Long Island: Early Period." In *Handbook of North American Indians: Northeast.* Edited by William C. Sturtevant. Vol. 15. Washington: Smithsonian Institution, 1978.

Sandelin, Clarence K. *Robert Nathan*. New York: Twayne Publishers, 1968.

Sanderson, Ivan T. *Follow the Whale*. New York: Bramhall House, 1956.

Sanger, Margaret. *An Autobiography*. New York: W.W. Norton & Company, 1938.

Seckler, Dorothy Gees. *Provincetown Painters: 1890s-1970s*. Edited by Ronald A. Kuchta. Syracuse NY: Everson Museum of Art, 1977.

Sewall, Samuel. *Diary 1674-1729*. Edited by M. Halsey Thomas. New York: Farrar Straus and Giroux, 1973. 1:890. A footnote to an 1883 edition issued by the Massachusetts Historical Society (vol. 7, fifth series) suggests that Sewall gave Avery a religious work by a Protestant theologian and Oxford professor named Peter Martyr (d. 1562). More likely the book was *De Orbe Novo* by the historian (d.1526) of the same anglicized name. Sewall was a merchant and jurist who wrote a "vindication of America" in *Phenomena* (1697), wherein he discusses Columbus's discovery of a "New World," suggests that it be named Columbina after Columbus and mentions Peter Martyr the historian.

Shipton, Clifford K. *Biographical Sketches of Those Who Attended Harvard College*. Vol. 5. General editor John L. Sibley. Boston: Massachusetts Historical Society, 1937 et seq. Generally known as *Sibley' Harvard Graduates*.

Shrand, Hyman Dr. Interviews February 1998 re the Jenny Lind tower.

Sibley's Harvard Graduates. See Shipton, Clifford K.

Small, Isaac Morton. *Highland Light: This Book Tells You All About It.* Provincetown MA: The Advocate Press, 1891. Unaccountably, Small nowhere recognizes that there were three lighthouses, even though his father was keeper of the second. Small conflates the first and second.

—. *Just a Little About the Lower Cape Personal and Otherwise.* Middleborough MA: Nemaskett Press, 1922.

—. *Just a Little About the Lower Cape from Provincetown to Brewster, and the Journey of the Mayflower Pilgrims.* North Truro: N.p., 1926. Much of the material appeared in the 1922 booklet with the similar title.

—. *Shipwrecks on Cape Cod.* Chatham MA: Chatham Press, 1928.

—. *True Stories of Cape Cod.* New Bedford MA: Reynolds, 1934.

Smith, Bradford. *Bradford of Plymouth.* Philadelphia and New York: Lippincott, 1951.

Smith, John. *A Description of New England.* London: H. Lownes for R. Clerke, 1616. Reprint. Boston: Veazie, 1865.

Smith, Leonard H., ed. *Cape Cod Library of Local History and Genealogy: A Facsimile Edition of 108 Pamphlets Published in the Early 20th Century.* Baltimore MD: Genealogical Publishing Co., 1992

Smith, William C. *A History of Chatham, Massachusetts.* Chatham Historical Society: 1971.

Snow, Edgar Rowe. *Famous Lighthouses of New England.* Boston:

Yankee,1945.

—. *A Pilgrim Returns to Cape Cod.* Boston: Yankee, 1946. Regarding the Jenny Lind tower, Snow states flatly that "later she sang from one of those towers to the many who could not get into the hall." Hyman Shrand, a physician, scanned the biographies of Jenny Lind and Boston newspaper accounts of her concerts October 11 and 12, 1850, at the auditorium above the Fitchburg railroad station in Boston. None mentions her singing from a tower of the building, even though her success in calming an unruly crowd is reported in detail. See Shrand.

—. *Great Storms and Famous Shipwrecks of the New England Coast.* Boston: Yankee, 1943.

Stackpole, Edouard A. *The Sea-Hunters: The New England Whalemen During Two Centuries, 1635-1835.* Philadelphia: Lippincott, 1953.

Starbuck, Alexander. *History of the American Whale Fishery.* Waltham MA: 1878. Reprint. Secaucus NJ: Castle Books,1989.

Sterling, Dorothy. *Our Cape Cod Salt Marshes.* Orleans MA: The Association for the Preservation of Cape Cod, 1976.

Stevens, William K. *The Change in the Weather.* New York: Delacorte Press, 1999.

Stiles, Ezra. *Extracts from the Itineraries and Other Miscellanies of Ezra Stiles, D.D., LL.D. 1755-1794 with a Selection from His Correspondence.* Edited by Franklin Bowditch Dexter. New Haven: Yale University Press, 1916.

Strahler, Arthur N. *A Geologist's View of Cape Cod.* New York:

Doubleday, 1966. Reprint. Parnassus Imprints, Orleans, MA, 1988.

Stratton, Eugene Aubrey. *Plymouth Colony: Its History & People, 1620-1691*. Salt Lake City: Ancestry, 1986.

Swift, Charles F. *Cape Cod*. Yarmouth: Register, 1897.

Tarbell, Arthur Wilson. *Cape Cod Ahoy!: A Travel Book for the Summer Visitor*. Boston: Richard G. Badger, 1932.

Temme, Virge Jenkins, et al. *Historical and Architectural Documentation Reports of North Truro Air Force Station*. Champaign IL: U.S. Air Force, 1995.

Thoreau, Henry David. *Cape Cod*. Boston: Ticknor and Fields, 1865. Reprint, with an introduction by Robert Finch. Hyannis MA: Parnassus Imprints, 1984.

—. *The Correspondence of Henry David Thoreau*. Edited by Walter Harding and Carl Bode. New York: New York University Press, 1958. Reprint. Westport CT: Greenwood Press, 1974.

—. *The Journal of Henry David Thoreau*. Edited by Bradford Torrey and Francis H. Allen. New York: Dover Publications, 1962.

Trayser, Donald G. and Alice Alberta Lowe. *Eastham, Massachusetts, 1651-1951*. The Eastham Tercentenary Committee, 1951.

Truro Conservation Commission. "Town of Truro Open Space Plan." 1984 (Typescript).

Truro Conservation Trust. Newsletters Nos. 15 (1997), 16 (1998), 17 (1999).

Truro, Report of the Officers of the Town for the Year Ending Dec. 31, 1909. Hyannis MA: Goss, 1910.

Truro Annual Reports, 1978-99.

U.S. Army Corps of Engineers. *Pamet River Investigation, Truro, Massachusetts.* Boston [?]: 1998.

U.S. Coast Guard. *The Coast Guard at War.* 30 vols (Typescript). 1944-54. See vols 17, 20. In telephone interviews February 1998, Coast Guard historians Robert Sheina and Robert Browning said they knew of three landings by Nazis on the East Coast but none on Cape Cod.

U.S. Congress. *Report on . . . the Extremity of Cape Cod, with a large scale detailed map.* By Major J.D. Graham. Exec. Doc. 121, vol. 5, 25th Cong., 2d sess. (1837-38).

U.S. House Committee on Commerce. Report on *Harbors on the Sea and Lake Coasts,* including a report by Colonel J.D. Graham, Corps of Engineers, on Provincetown Harbor and the need for a dike at East Harbor. Ex. Doc. 59, No. 10, 49th Congress, 1866; and an accompanying "Report of the Chief of Engineers" (1866).

U.S. House Committee on Harbors. Hearings 26 March to 3 April 1868 on Provincetown Harbor and East Harbor. House Doc. 241 (1868).

U.S. Life-Saving Service. Annual reports, 1873-1915. Includes detailed reports of many shipwrecks off Truro.

U.S. National Park Service. "Cape Cod National Seashore Zoning Standards" (1962). In *Code of Federal Regulations,* title 36, chap.1, part 27.

——. *Cape Cod: A Proposed National Seashore Field Investigative Report.* By E.C. Martinson and W.C. Applegate. "prompted by the Seashore Recreation Area Study Survey of the Atlantic and Gulf coasts, completed by the National Park Service in 1955." [Washington]: National Park Service, 1958.

——. *Forging a Collaborative Future: General Management Plan, Cape Cod National Seashore.*1998.

——. *Master Plan, Cape Cod National Seashore, Massachusetts,* 2nd ed. South Wellfleet MA: Cape Cod National Seashore, 1970.

U.S. Public Law 87-126, establishing Cape Cod National Seashore, 7 August 1961, with appendix B "Use Guidelines for Private Property." The text of the law can be found in Burling and in Foster. The guidelines are available at the national seashore headquarters.

U.S. Senate: Letter by H.G. Wright, Acting Chief of Engineers, 26 February 1879 on East Harbor dike. Sen. Exec. Doc. 4 (46-1) U.S. serial set.

Vital Records of Truro, Massachusetts, to the End of 1849. Transcribed by George Ernest Bowman. Boston: Massachusetts Society of Mayflower Descendants, 1933.

Vonnegut, Kurt. "There's a Maniac Out There" in *Wampeters, Foma & Granfallons.* New York: Delacorte, 1974.

Vorse, Mary Heaton. *Time and the Town: a Provincetown Chronicle.* New York: Dial, 1942. Reprint. Cape Cod Pilgrim Memorial Association, 1990.

Webb, the Reverend Benjamin. *The Present Scope and the Future Gain of the Christian Life*. Boston: 1733. His discourse in 1732 was "occasioned by the much lamented death of Mrs.Ruth Avery."

Weinstein-Farson, Laurie. *The Wampanoag*. New York: Chelsea House, 1989.

Wellfleet, Truro & Cape Cod Cemetery Inscriptions: Section 7. N.p.: Pine Grove Cemetery Association, 1983.

Wellfleet, Truro & Cape Cod Cemetery Inscriptions: Section 8. Compiled by Evelyn Spelman Dyer. N.p.: Rich Family Association, 1984.

Whalen, Richard F. "Where Did Captain Martin Pring Anchor in New England?" In *The Historical Journal of Massachusetts* 26 no. 2 (summer 1998).

Whelan, Harold A. *Catholicism on Cape Cod*. Center Rutland VT: Mercury, 1984.

Wieser, C. Robert. "The Cape Cod System." In *Annals of the History of Computing* 5, no. 4 (October 1983). On the radar installations in Truro.

Willison, George F. *Saints and Strangers*. New York: Reynal & Hitchcock, 1945. The most comprehensive book on the Pilgrims, which he calls a "group biography." The "saints were the Pilgrim Separatists, and the "strangers" were the others on the *Mayflower*.

Wilson, Edmund. *The Thirties*. New York: Farrar Straus & Giroux, 1980.

___.Journals in five vols by decade, *The Twenties* through *The Six-ties*. New York: Farrar Straus Giroux, 1975, 1980, 1983, 1986 and 1993.

—. "Epilogue, 1952, Edna St. Vincent Millay." In *The Shores of Light: A Literary Chronicle of the Twenties and Thirties*. New York: Farrar, Straus and Giroux, 1952.

Wood, William. *New England's Prospect*. London, 1634. Reprint. Amherst: University of Massachusetts Press, 1977.

Worthington, Diana. Interviews February 1998.

WPA Guide to Massachusetts. See Federal Writers Project.

Wreszin, Michael. *A Rebel in Defense of Tradition: The Life and Politics of Dwight Macdonald*. New York: Basic Books, 1968.

Wright, H.G. Letter on East Harbor dike. See U.S. Senate.

Young, Alexander, ed. *Chronicles of the Pilgrim Fathers from 1602 to 1625*. Boston: Little & Brown, 1841. Includes his annotated edition of *Mourt's Relation*.

Acknowledgments

Many individuals and institutions assisted on this history of Truro—many more than could be listed here—but I must note in particular the support of Gordon Russell and B.J. Allen of the Truro Historical Society, who read and commented on an early draft; also my wife, Carol Pearson Whalen, and Dr. Richard P. Keating, former selectman and library trustee, who both gave a later draft a close reading and most valuable critique. The late Clive Driver, local historian and newspaper columnist, was able to read through half the manuscript before his death and offer comments.

The book benefitted greatly from reviews of sections by specialists in their fields of knowledge: Frank Ackerman and Lauren McKean of the Cape Cod National Seashore; James Baker, Plimoth Plantation historian; James W. Bradley, director of the Peabody Museum of Archeology; oceanographer Graham Giese; former Truro Selectmen John Snow; Truro annalist Betty Groom; Joyce Johnson, artist and journalist; Larry Lowenthal, historian with the National Park Service; artist Judith Shahn; and Diana Worthington and Diane Shumway of the Truro Historical Museum. As always, however, any errors or misinterpretations that remain must be charged to the author's account.

Early primary sources were graciously made available by Cynthia Slade, Truro's town clerk; also by William T. Milhomme,

supervisor at the Massachusetts State Archives; Virginia Smith at
the Massachusetts Historical Society; Hope Morrill at the library
of the Cape Cod National Seashore and Linda Rasori at the Plymouth County Commissioners office. Michael J. Crawford of the
Naval Historical Center provided information on the Revolutionary War, and Frank Mastrovita of the MITRE Corp.on the MI-
TRE site.

Historical records for Truro and secondary sources are to be
found in a number of libraries. On Cape Cod, the most useful for
this book were Sturgis Library in Barnstable and the Nickerson
room at Cape Cod Community College, presided over by Mary
Sicchio. Other libraries consulted were the Widener at Harvard
University and the Boston Public Library; also libraries at Plimoth
Plantation, the New England Historic and Genealogical Society,
the American Antiquarian Society, and the Cape Cod National
Seashore; and the public libraries in Eastham, Orleans,
Provincetown, Truro and Wellfleet. My thanks to the staffs of all
the libraries for their assistance. Marilyn Fifield at the Cape Cod
Commission provided demographic data. Also of great value was
the work of newspaper reporters, who write the first rough drafts
of history, and historical columnists Laurel Guadazno, Noel Beyle
and "Ye Olde Scribe," Norman Pope.

Diana Worthington also contributed to the chapters on Truro's
artists and writers and on her parents, John and "Tiny"
Worthington. Nat Champlin helped on the location of the wreck
of the *Somerset*, and Marjorie Hubbell Gibson on the shipwreck
salvage records. Joseph Lowell scanned early Eastham records and
provided several transcriptions, and Joseph Tunney assisted on
deciphering the Sampson Indenture.

Others who provided assistance include both Barbara Bakers,
Bing Bingham, Anne and Ken Brock, Ellen Burr, Ansel Chaplin,
Michael Commeau, Lurana Cook, Charles Davidson, Fred
Dunford, Joyce Edinberg, John Perry Fish, Helen Gaspar, the Rev-
erend E. Bonnie Goodwin, Laurel Guadazno, Stephen W. Hannah,
Ruth Hollander, Howard Irwin, Hamilton Kahn, Kenneth Kinkor,

Helen Mourton, Theodore Postol, Nan Reed, Irma Ruckstuhl, Robert Scheina, Judith Shahn, Hyman and Hannah Shrand, Betsy Smith, Shirley Smith, Mary Stackhouse, Bert Stranger, Ding Watson, and Adele and Reuben Wisotzky. And special thanks to A.L. Morris and Lex Paradis for their encouragement and collaboration in the early stages.

I gratefully acknowledge receiving permission to use "Memory of Cape Cod" by Edna St. Vincent Millay, from *Collected Poems*, HarperCollins, copyright 1923, 1951 by Edna St. Vincent Millay and Norma Millay Ellis. All rights reserved. Reprinted by permission of Elizabeth Barnett, literary executor.

INDEX